Animation in Germany

This book provides a comprehensive account of German animation history, as well as an analysis of the current state of the industry in competition with American and cheaper international products in the face of dwindling budgets.

Covering film and TV, 2D and 3D animation, this book considers how Europe has lost its domestic territory of narratives to international competitors. A connection is made between film history and contemporary history: World War I, the Weimar Republic, National Socialism, World War II, the Federal Republic and German Democratic Republic, Reunification, the European Union, Digitalization and Globalization, and a turn of eras initiated by pandemic, war, and inflation.

This book will be of great interest to academics, students, and professionals working and researching in the field of animation.

About the Author

Rolf Giesen, PhD, is a German film historian, screenwriter, lecturer, and collector who specializes in VFX and animation. He has shared his knowledge through numerous university and public lectures, cinematheque exhibitions, and monographic, historiographic, and lexicographic books such as *Acting and Character Animation*. He received the Award for Outstanding Contribution to Animation Studies, 32nd World Festival of Animated Film – Animafest Zagreb 2022.

European Animation

European Animation explores the current state of animation production in various European countries derived from a social, historic, political, economic and artistic background. The series tells what made animated movies possible in Europe and is a prognosis foreseeing a change in future animation production.

Series Editor

Rolf Giesen is a German film historian, screenwriter, lecturer, and collector who specialized in VFX and animation, Germany.

Animation in Germany
Rolf Giesen

For more information about this series, please visit: http://www.routledge.com/ European-Animation/book-series/EUANIM

Animation in Germany

Rolf Giesen

CRC Press
Taylor & Francis Group
Boca Raton London New York

CRC Press is an imprint of the
Taylor & Francis Group, an **informa** business

Designed cover image: Animation film project *Angst* (c) brave new work GmbH/Red Parrot Studios

First edition published 2024
by CRC Press
2385 Executive Center Drive, Suite 320, Boca Raton, FL 33431

and by CRC Press
4 Park Square, Milton Park, Abingdon, Oxon, OX14 4RN

CRC Press is an imprint of Taylor & Francis Group, LLC

© 2024 Rolf Giesen

Library of Congress Cataloging-in-Publication Data
Names: Giesen, Rolf, author.
Title: Animation in Germany / Rolf Giesen.
Description: First edition. | Boca Raton : CRC Press, 2024. | Series:
European animation series | Includes bibliographical references and index.
Identifiers: LCCN 2023004571 (print) | LCCN 2023004572 (ebook) |
ISBN 9781032451336 (hbk) | ISBN 9781032451343 (pbk) | ISBN 9781003375548 (ebk)
Subjects: LCSH: Animated films–Germany–History. | Animation
(Cinematography-Germany–History. | Animated films–Political
aspects–Germany–History. | Animators–Germany.
Classification: LCC NC1766.G3 .G53 2024 (print) | LCC NC1766.G3 (ebook) |
DDC 791.43/340943–dc23/eng/20230215
LC record available at https://lccn.loc.gov/2023004571
LC ebook record available at https://lccn.loc.gov/2023004572

ISBN: 9781032451336 (hbk)
ISBN: 9781032451343 (pbk)
ISBN: 9781003375548 (ebk)

DOI: 10.1201/9781003375548

Typeset in Times
by codeMantra

Contents

Introduction

The first U.S. soldier to enter the Dachau Concentration Camp as liberator was Robert Bernard Sherman. Robert was born on December 19, 1925, to Russian Jewish immigrants in New York City. He was interested in violin, piano, painting, and poetry. On D-Day, he was among the first waves of U.S. soldiers to storm Omaha Beach. On Sunday, April 29, 1945, the U.S. Army received marching orders to liberate Dachau. Sherman led the first squadron, which consisted of eight soldiers. Robert described this experience in his memoirs, published posthumously.[1] He died on March 6, 2012.

Most Germans will not know Sherman by name, but most of them know the songs he and his brother Richard had written for Walt Disney, for *Mary Poppins* and *The Jungle Book*. *The Jungle Book* was the most successful animated feature film ever shown in Germany.

But little did Robert Sherman know that, shortly before the liberation, Dachau was not only the seat of an infamous concentration camp, but also the hoped-for center of National Socialist cartoon film production that was supposed to rival Disney and replace him on the European market. Originally there was a presumptuous plan to make occupied Crimea the central base of German and European animation, and barrack everyone who could hold a pencil there, but by that time the Germans were forced to evacuate the Crimea and abandon the project. So, instead Dachau.

After the fall of the Nazi tyranny, Karl Neumann, whom Dr. Joseph Goebbels, Reich Minister of Public Enlightenment and Propaganda, had appointed to helm the Reich's animation product (including trick film made in Dachau), was interned by the Soviets in a camp near Berlin. In June 1945, Neumann was found dead in the toilet where he had hanged himself.

As apolitical as German animated film may appear to be, it was always overshadowed by contemporary history. After what they termed *Endsieg* (final victory), by 1950, the Nazis planned a stream of feature-length animated films, and in fact one of their former artists finished a feature-length animated film exactly five years after Hitler's death, but it was a black-and-white film that looked cheap against the Disney competition in Technicolor and was graciously overlooked by German audiences.

The division of Germany, result of the Cold War, brought two rival puppet film *Sandmen* – bringing sleep and dreams to children in East and West, respectively (with the East being faster and overtaking the West). Much to the displeasure of the French creators, the first German translation of the *Asterix* comic books addressed the division of Germany into the Ostrogoths and Visigoths. The creators of *Asterix the Gaul*, one of them a Jew, made sure that the German publisher, who at one time even employed Hitler's former secretary, was deprived of the product.

West German advertising television caricatured the German Michel in a crowd of animated dwarfish *Mainzelmännchen* (Little Mainz Men) wearing stocking caps.

In all these years, however, Disney remained the dominant factor in the West German cartoon and merchandising market and, after reunification, in the German market as a whole. Full-length German animation films were soon available, but American distributors ensured that since the German output was mainly aimed at a preschool audience, they became limited to the afternoon run of the cinemas: reduced to the state of "local production." These films were very often not produced domestically, but, following the economic laws of globalization, outsourced to Asia, in one case even to Pyongyang, North Korea. (Even this author was asked by the North Korean embassy in Berlin if he could arrange assignments of this kind. He didn't.)

The impulses from short films produced, for instance, by the film schools in Ludwigsburg or Babelsberg, which were limited to festivals, were hardly taken up by commercial producers at all. Due to lack of funds, 3D animation in particular looked awkward. Totally dependent on public funding, in the midst of a turn of eras and the dramatic consequences of COVID-19 and the Russian invasion of Ukraine, German animation is getting into trouble. How will it reinvent itself in the environment of the new media? Actually, German animation is largely unknown in Europe. To him, it is incomprehensible that the biggest country in the European economy is still so weak in the animation industry, with all their competence and talents, Marc Vandeweyer, former director general of Cartoon Media Brussels, complained.[2]

Consequently, this book is not just about German animation, but about *Animation in Germany*, which includes foreign product that is predominant on the screens and on TV.

A personal remark is permitted: The author of this book was associated with the German animation film industry as screenwriter and consultant for almost 40 years. Some impressions and facts that were previously unknown can therefore be told from personal experience, insofar as this is not prevented by client's contracts and nondisclosure clauses.

NOTES

1 *Moose: Chapter from My Life*. Bloomington, IN: AuthorHouse Publishers, 2013.
2 Email to the author dated May 31, 2018.

1 The Golem Anticipates *Fantasia*

A GREAT SYMPHONIC FANTASY ANIMATED

Paul Wegener (1874–1948) was a famous German stage and film actor. He joined Max Reinhardt's acting troupe in 1906 and became interested in film before World War I. He understood that movies were more than a novelty, more than an amusement attraction. It was a new art form, and the manipulation of images was to be a part of it. In 1913, it was cinematographer Guido Seeber's trick photography that enabled Wegener to act in a dual role on screen with his own *doppelganger* in *The Student of Prague* (*Der Student von Prag*), but it was still Wegener's vision. One year later, Wegener originated the *Golem* character on screen. In a 1916 lecture, Wegener was the first stage actor to foresee new developments, interestingly not concerning live actors but animation, dreaming up an entirely new universe of synthetically created images that would transform images into a visual symphony of movement.

> You have all seen films in which suddenly a line appears, curves, and changes its form. Out of it grow faces and the line disappears. To me the impression seems highly remarkable. But such things are always shown as an intermezzo and nobody has ever thought of the colossal possibilities of this technique. I think the film as art should be based – as in the case of music – on tones, on rhythm. In these changeable planes, events unreel which are partly identified with natural pattern, yet partly beyond real lines and forms. Imagine one of [Arnold] Böcklin's sea paintings with all the fabulous tritons and nereids. And imagine an artist duplicating this work in hundreds of copies but with each copy having small displacements so that all copies revealed in succession would result in continuous movement. Suddenly we would see before our very eyes a world of pure fantasy come to life. Such effects can also be achieved with specially constructed little models animated like marionettes - in this field there are great achievements nowadays. One also can change the pace of different movements by shooting too slow or too fast, developing a fantastic vision which will produce entirely new associations of ideas. In addition, one can photograph microscopic parts of fermenting chemical substances, small plants, etc. in different dimensions in a jumble, so that the matter from which these visions arise is no longer recognizable. We are entering a new pictorial fantasy world as we would enter a magic forest. We are setting foot in the field of pure kinetics – or optical lyric as I call it. This field will perhaps be of major importance and will open new beautiful sights. This eventually is the final objective of each art, and so cinema would gain an autonomous aesthetic domain for itself.
>
> I don't want to describe this film to you any further. I just want to indicate to you what perspectives are given here. By using all imaginable forms and elements, such as artificial steam, snowflakes, electric sparks and so on, a movie could be created that would become an experience of art – an optical vision, a great symphonic fantasy! That it will happen one day, I am sure - and beyond that, I am certain, later generations will look upon our early efforts as upon childish stuttering.[1]

DOI: 10.1201/9781003375548-1

This was 4 years before Walt Disney, after his return from the battlefields of Europe, had decided to enter animation and 24 years (!) before *Fantasia* was released (Figure 1.1).

FIGURE 1.1   Paul Wegener as *The Golem*. (Author's Collection.)

It was a vision of a true parallel world created by the manipulation of a sequence of moving images, an illusion put together by the dream machine and mechanics of the cinema, by projecting a light beam, perceived by the human eye and transferred to the brain. Through the fog of his mind's eye, Wegener described a magic forest of optical lyricism, as he called it.

It is absolutely unique that an actor of all things and at that time embodied synthetic images. Georges Méliès found it easier to star himself in his films instead of hiring a comedian or an actor. These pictures were too tricky for "regular" actors. Wegener, a professional thespian on the other hand, became interested in trick film and played a key role in German silent cinematography.

A DYSTOPIAN WORLD WAR OF FLEAS, LICE, AND RODENTS

Wegener's peaceful vision was sadly overshadowed by the events of war.

Contrary to the myth of the Hooray patriotism that was spread by nationalist circles in August 1914, enthusiasm for war was understandably rather limited:

> …this phenomenon primarily affects the nobility, the bourgeoisie, many intellectuals, and, of course, the political leadership: In the working-class districts of the big cities and in the countryside, on the other hand, the mood is often very different. On their spy tours through working-class pubs in Hamburg, the agents of the political police note that those present ask aloud why they should be concerned about the [assassinated] Austrian heir to the throne and why they should give their lives for it. As early as August 1, a Social Democrat in Bremen observed the "most miserable mood" he had

"ever experienced": "Mothers, women and brides bring the young men to the train and cry. Everyone has the feeling: It's going straight to the slaughterhouse."

However, hardly anyone expects how fast times will become difficult. Most soldiers think they'll be home by Christmas, and the state isn't in any way prepared for a long war either. [...] With the first terrible experiences at the front, the "baptism of fire," disillusionment spread among the war volunteers. Theodor Reil from Oldenburg writes to his teacher from Belgium at the end of August: "After a 33-hour train journey and a seven-hour wait, our people had a strenuous march. On the way we saw the first destructions, the terrible fires of the war, burnt-out houses, villages completely destroyed.

At the latest with the defeat in the Battle of the Marne in September 1914, which made a quick victory against France impossible, many felt the same way as the grocer Johanna Boldt. At the beginning of October, she wrote to her husband Julius who was on the Eastern front: "People want nothing more than the end of this unfortunate war. And there is still no prospect of that."[2]

Millions of soldiers on both sides vegetate in trenches that zigzag through moonscapes torn apart by heavy gunfire. One of the soldiers, Adolf Mann from Stuttgart, describes the hellish noise of war in his letters from the front:

A simple infantry shell already reverberates like in a church, and now the artillery is constantly rattling. It is a plethora of the most peculiar noises: firing and impact of artillery shells, infantry shells, rifle grenades, mines. Then the muffled whizzing of the flares – all around comrades swearing, mice rustling.

Soon, the trenches are teeming with rats. The German soldiers call them "grave diggers."[3]

World War I conditions were horrific, and death was never far away. If the soldiers managed to survive enemy shelling and the sneaky sniper's bullet they could just as easily be defeated by an illness such as Trench Foot or Wiel's Disease. Fleas, lice, and rodents were rife and would plague the men with disease. [...] Lice sucked the blood of a host infected by trench fever and then spread the fever to a successive host.

Trenches often flooded with rain in which frogs swam. Red slugs would ooze from the mud. At night opportunist rats crept out. Discarded food cans would rattle as the rats crept inside to lick the remains. More horrifically the rodents were sometimes referred to as corpse rats. They bred rapidly in their millions and swarmed through No-Man's Land gnawing the corpses of fallen soldiers.

The rats would taut sleeping soldiers, creeping over them at night. There were long bouts of boredom and rat hunting became a sport. [...]

Trench conditions were ideal for rats. There was plenty of food, water and shelter. With no proper disposal system, the rats would feast off food scraps. The rats grew bigger and bolder and would even steal food from soldier's hand.[4]

THE ART OF SILHOUETTE PLAYS AND FILMS

In the meantime, with all these horrors going on, Wegener encouraged and supported one young actress who had listened to this lecture and became the first great female animator of film history, so to speak animating the shadows from the nightmarish realm of the dead as silhouettes. Her name was Lotte Reiniger (1899–1981) – and her art was in the line with the zeitgeist of the day. Lotte adored actors and particularly dancers who she had spent many hours watching perform. She even had access to the private box of Colonel Wassily de Basil for the performances of his *Ballets Russe de*

Monte Carlo. At a young age Lotte had entered the Theater School of Max Reinhardt but just wanted to join the boys-only classes, because they did gymnastics. It was at Reinhardt's school that she developed her paper cutting skills, producing tiny portrait figures with great accuracy, particularly of actors in order to attract their attention. Finally, she turned to the cinema and created the most wonderful silhouette films.

During Germany's postwar financial crisis and hyperinflation, Louis Hagen, a banker acquaintance, had invested in a large quantity of raw film stock as a shelter from inflation; but the gamble hadn't paid off. So Lotte was allowed to use it to make the *Thousand and One Night* fantasy of *Prince Achmed* in the magnificent tradition of the Shadow Theatre that originated from Asia, from China, India, and Indonesia, and is in fact one of the founding pillars of intercultural synergy between East and West.

Production on *The Adventures of Prince Achmed (Die Abenteuer des Prinzen Achmed)* started in 1923. The story is loosely based on the *Tale of the Magic Horse* from *The Arabian Nights*. At the court of the Caliph of Bagdad, an African sorcerer appears on a flying horse. He offers to exchange the miraculous animal for the hand of the Caliph's Daughter. The sorcerer tricks Prince Achmed, the brother of the princess, into mounting the magical horse and off the Prince rides to an enchanted island faraway. There he surprises the fairy queen Pari Banu at the bath and falls in love with her beauty. He takes her on an adventurous journey, but the insidious magician kidnaps her and presents her to the Emperor of China as a slave. The story has a happy ending, thanks to Aladdin's magic lamp and the friendly Witch of the Flaming Mountains who battles an army of monsters and demons, and the evil sorcerer himself in various animal forms.

The film was screened for the first time on May 2, 1926, as a matinee at the Volksbühne Theater at Bülowplatz in Berlin and then, in July, at the Comédie des Champs-Elysées in Paris, thanks to Jean Renoir's initiative. Distributed by UFA and Lothar Stark, it officially opened on September 3 in a Berlin cinema, the renowned Gloria Palace.

Silhouette film technique is very simple. As with cartoon drawings, shadow films are photographed movement by movement. But instead of drawings, silhouette marionettes are used. These marionettes are cut out of black cardboard and thin lead, every limb being cut separately and joined with wire hinges. A study of natural movement is very important, so that the little figures appear to move just as men and women and animals do. The backgrounds for the characters are cut out with scissors as well and designed to give a unified style to the whole picture (Figure 1.2).

First, Prince Achmed was drawn. After everyone was convinced that he should look like this, he was portrayed in silhouette. Then he was built out of wire, cardboard and rolled lead in such a way that he could perform flexibly and convincingly in the shadow play. He was disassembled into head, neck, shoulders, chest, abdomen, hips, legs, upper and lower arms, knees, hands and feet, then hinged together and jointed, hammered and rolled until he was a neat film silhouette. Masses of tracing paper were now bought to create the environment in which his adventures should take place. Sets upon sets, clouds, castles, forests and seas, landscapes and magical caves piled up around him. He himself was built in twenty different sizes for his world. Then finally he should come alive. To do this, the little puppet was placed on a sheet of glass and lovingly illuminated from below in such a way that all the hinges and joints could no longer be seen and it appeared as a free, independent being in its world of tracing paper, which was also lit from below. The camera patiently looked at both from above. Now Achmed who was nothing more than a flat puppet was supposed to play. He got help. Frame by frame, his limbs were moved to where they should be, every frame of his tiny movement photographed. He was given friends and enemies to fight with or against. The longer he was acting, the more demanding he became. Countless extras had to be cut out and animated. Sometimes there are fifty little characters in a single scene at the same time.

To give an idea of the length of the work: 52 individual frames are needed for a film strip that rolls by in two seconds before the eyes of the viewer. In all, during the more than three years of work, around 250,000 frames were photographed, of which ca. 100,000 were used in the finished film.[5]

If one considers – we read in a contemporary review[6] - that each of the acting characters must be flexible in all joints, one can get an idea of what a marvel was achieved. But the technical part alone is not what matters. The main thing is that the spirit of the fairy tale has been happily reborn in a series of cinematic images.

FIGURE 1.2 Lotte Reiniger in the 1920s at work on her (multiplane) animation stand. (Courtesy of Caroline Hagen Hall, Primrose Film Productions Limited, London.)

Reiniger's interest in silhouette films perfectly matched Expressionist filmmakers' fascination with shadows: Fritz Lang, Robert Wiene, Friedrich Wilhelm Murnau, and Albin Grau who had designed both *Nosferatu* and the eponymously titled *Schatten* (*Warning Shadows*). Yet she pointed out that there is a difference between a shadow and a silhouette (Figure 1.3):

> From the early days of mankind shadows seemed to men to be something magic. The spirits of the dead were called shadows, and the underworld was named the Kingdom of Shadows and was looked upon with awe and horror. [...]
>
> The essential difference between a shadow and a silhouette is that the latter cannot be distorted. A silhouette can cast a shadow. When you see trees or figures against an evening sky, you would say, not that they are shadowed against the sky, but silhouetted against it. The silhouette exists in its own right.[7]

FIGURE 1.3   *Die Abenteuer des Prinzen Achmed* (*The Adventures of Prince Achmed*). (Courtesy of Caroline Hagen Hall, Primrose Film Productions Limited, London.)

Lotte Reiniger was not only a storyteller but also an experimental filmmaker and well acquainted with the leading artists of the time. One of those was Walter Ruttmann:

> When the idea for Prince Achmed came up, we definitely wanted to have Ruttmann, whom we greatly admired, and he agreed to it. The scenes were always determined on a case-by-case basis. I wanted his special involvement for magical effects. On the climax of Prince Achmed, we worked together: mostly, when there were longer scenes, I animated my silhouettes alone and gave him the footage to compose his backgrounds, which he photographed at his home. Sometimes I also worked with him in his studio: While he painted, I was animating the characters for e. g. the opening title. That was very difficult because you play these little shadow figures on a glass plate. Glass is slippery. We had to place tracing paper on it to give the figures some resistance. And the figures had to be very small, too, because he only had a small camera field. And for

the last thing, he was always in the studio with us. We worked then on different [multiplane] sheets of glass, always watching what the other one did. We judged each other by each other. It was fantastic, it was wonderful! So if, for example, the sorcerer was going to conjure up a magic horse, I animated him in black and white, gave him [Ruttmann] the positive and calculated during the shot exactly where the sorcerer should be in the various moments of action according to the number of frames. Then Ruttmann composed the emergence of the magic horse. And I think it's the only time that two artists who are so different have worked jointly.[8]

At that time, Ruttmann had made the decision to set his painting in motion:

In his last paintings, the attempt to depict movement, based on futurism, becomes all too clear. [...] Ruttmann sees speed and tempo as the main characteristics of his time. This results in a different perception of the world: the frozen timeless moment is replaced by the dynamic, temporal happening – the movement.[9]

Ruttmann's Process and Device for the Production of Cinematographic Images was patented on June 27, 1920:

The aim of the invention is to provide a method for producing cinematographic images of non-moving objects based on non-moving frames that have changed between the individual shots. For this purpose, according to the invention, the successive frames belonging to the representation of a kinematic process are taken from several transparent image plates lying one behind the other in the light path, movable against each other, on which the necessary changes, e.g., the position, the lighting and the like; these changes can cover parts of the image or the entire image.[10]

Herbert Ihering, a well-known theater critic, had reviewed Ruttmann's *Lichtspiel Opus 1*, considered to be the first abstract or "absolute" work in film history, which was animated in 10,000 frames of colors and shapes in the course of nine months in 1921:

Colored triangles fought colored circles that swelled and shrank. Beams of ray swung. Suns circled. There was only one law that drove them against each other and apart, that allowed the forms to stretch and shrink: the rhythm. A movement game of rare purity. Basically, it was the archetype of the film play (to which only a late development came here): to show forms in rhythmic movement, independent of narrative inhibitions, independent of material stress. Visible music, audible light. This film was not photographed. It was painted. And was transferred directly.[11]

One thinks of Expressionist paintings, Ihering's even more renowned colleague Alfred Kerr wrote (and surpassed himself in the euphoric enumeration of verbs): But they [the paintings] are rather immobile. Chagall's luminous paradises remain rigid. The glittering futurisms of the latest Parisian petrify motionless – in their frames. But here things dart, row, burn, climb, push, glide step, wither, flow, swell, dawn, unfold, bulge, widen, decrease, ball up, narrow, sharpen, divide, curve, rise, fill, empty, crouch, flower and crumble.

In short: Expressionism in motion. A rush for the pupil – but not a film about and with humans.[12]

Lotte Reiniger: "I first saw Ruttmann's films in a night screening at the Marmorhaus Cinema in Berlin. We had heard that there was an artist coming from Munich who made abstract films. And since we were interested in this particular work, we went there and watched the films, and were tremendously excited. We were blown away by the musical rhythm of this thing, by the actual representation of a musical movement – visually – that was something completely new for us."[13]

Ruttmann's most famous work, however, was not animated. It was a documentary film, *Berlin: Die Sinfonie der Grossstadt (Berlin, Symphony of a Great City)*, made in 1927, which hit the nerve of the time. Finally, Ruttmann felt a call to become a director of feature films but failed. He spent making propaganda films during the final years of his life for the Nazis like *Deutsche Panzer (German Tanks*, 1940): *The devastating power of our armored divisions is due to the unique attacking spirit of the troops and the superiority of our combat material.* Not long after finishing this film, Ruttmann died of an embolism, on July 15, 1941, at the age of only 53.

When they saw Ruttmann's early work, other painters got interested in setting their paintings in motion too. On May 3, 1925, a unique matinee devoted to *The Absolute Film* was organized by the artists' association November Group in cooperation with the culture film department of UFA at U.T. Cinema, Berlin, Kurfürstendamm. Screened were films by Fernand Léger, Walter Ruttmann, and Dada artist Viking Eggeling (*Symphonie diagonal/Diagonal Symphony*). Eggeling, who was born in Lund, Sweden on October 21, 1880, used foils made to tinfoil that he cut into shapes:

> Lighting from below made them appear as if depicted brightly against a dark light. The camera's fading in and out conveys the impression of the shapes appearing and disappearing. The impression of the shapes getting closer or smaller is created by moving the foil and taking single-frame pictures or by adjusting the camera lens. [...] Through light-dark contrasts, changes in direction and a dramatized form of curves, lines, harps and triangles, Eggeling tries to clarify the aspect of time. At the same time, however, he tries to create shapes that should not be seen as just shapes, but rather as letters, as arabesque writing of a new universal language. An unusual novelty of the film is the jerky change of rhythm and forms, the meaning of which can only be grasped with the help of musical theory. Eggeling's intention, however, weas to make music of the eyes visually comprehensible.[14]
>
> The absolute film, on which Egeling [*sic!* Eggeling] worked for fifteen years and for which he produced tens of thousands of drawings and colored illustrations, was a preparatory work for a grammar of painting which Egeling [Eggeling] was going to edit. This work was intended to summarize the results of modern light and color theories.[15]

Alas, his work remained unfinished. Eggeling died nine days after the matinee of *The Absolute Film* on May 19, 1925.

Experimental filmmakers were lucky if they were allowed to use professional film equipment like Eggeling got from UFA. Otherwise, they worked at home, and the only chance to make some money was to get involved in advertising films.

One who saw the enormous possibilities of animated cartoons in advertising first was Julius Pinschewer (1883–1961). Pinschewer produced animated commercials from 1912 until 1933 when he left Germany. He even saw that his idea of producing advertising films was patented: "In 1910, when for the first time I attended a cinema, the hundreds of eyes fixed to the screen gave me the idea to use film for advertising." In 1917, he produced an animated anti-British propaganda film (titled *John Bull*) to promote the war effort and drum up the sales of war bonds. At one time or another, most German animators worked for him. Besides Lotte Reiniger, there were

Hermann Abeking, Harry Jäger, Hans Zoozmann, and Rudi Klemm who animated the silhouettes for the first German sound cartoon, *Die chinesische Nachtigall* (*The Chinese Nightingale*) based on a fairy tale by Hans Christian Andersen in 1929.

Even the highly acclaimed abstract animation done by Oskar Fischinger (1900–1967) ended as advertisement for tobacco manufacturers, like the marching and dancing cigarettes from *Muratti greift ein* (*Muratti Marches On*, 1934) and the experimental *Komposition in Blau* (*Composition in Blue*, 1934–1935), both produced in the beautiful three-color Gasparcolor process.

NOTES

1 Paul Wegener, *Die künstlerischen Möglichkeiten des Films*. Lecture at Berlin Singing Academy, April 24, 1916. Typewritten original. Collection Kai Möller, Deutsches Filminstitut, Frankfurt/Main.

2 Andrej Reisin, *Erster Weltkrieg: Vom Kriegsrausch zum Massensterben*. Norddeutscher Rundfunk, 2014.

3 *Die Feldpost von Adolf Mann: Nur die Ratten fühlen sich wohl*. In: Stuttgarter Zeitung, February 24, 2014.

4 *Rats and the Trenches of WWI*. Written by Pestie. https://www.rentokil.co.uk>Blog>Rats.

5 Program for the German premiere on September 3, 1926, Gloria Palace Berlin. Filed at Deutsche Kinemathek Berlin.

6 *Vorwärts. Berliner Volksblatt. Zentralorgan der Sozialdemokratischen Partei Deutschlands*, May 9, 1926.

7 Lotte Reiniger, *Shadow Theatres and Shadow Films*. London and New York: B. T. Batsford Ltd. and Watson-Guptill, 1970, pp. 11–13.

8 Heinz Steike, *Walter Ruttmann 1887–1941. Versuch einer Befreiung. Dokumentation über den Maler und Filmemacher*. TV feature, Bayerischer Rundfunk, Teleclub, May 5, 1977.

9 Jeanpaul Goergen, *Walter Ruttmann. Eine Dokumentation*. Berlin: Freunde der Deutschen Kinemathek, 1989, p. 21.

10 Deutsches Reich Reichspatentamt [Reich Patent Office] Patent No. 338774 - Class 57a, Group 37.

11 Herbert Ihering, In: Berliner Börsen-Courier, No. 201, May 1, 1921.

12 Alfred Kerr, In: Berliner Tageblatt, June 16, 1921.

13 Goergen, *Walter Ruttmann. Eine Dokumentation*, p. 23.

14 Susann Becker/Magdalena Pitt, *Viking Eggeling – Musik für die Augen*. Berlin, 2011.

15 Berliner Börsen-Courier, May 28, 1925.

2 Mickey Who?

TROLLEY TROUBLES

But not the Germans or other European producers were dominating the domestic market.

In cartoons, there is no other reality than appearances, wrote Béla Balázs, one of the few serious film theoreticians in Germany who would comment on animation – from America:

> Felix the Cat once loses his tail. He wonders what to do about it. This anxious question grows out his head in the shape of a large question mark, demonstrating by graphic means that he is torn by doubts. Felix now gazes pensively at the beautifully curved question mark. He has a bright idea, grabs the question mark and sticks it to his rump for a new tail. The problem is solved. Someone might object to such impossibilities that the question mark was only an abstract symbol! But it appeared in the cartoon as a line and as such subject to the laws of draughtsmanship and none other. The question mark was a line, just like Felix's body, their substance was the same. In the world of creatures consisting only of lines the only impossible things are those which cannot be drawn.[1]

KATER FELIX

die entzückende Trickfigur von Pat Sullivan, über dessen drollige Streiche Sie gewiß im Kino bereits oft gelacht haben,

FIGURE 2.1 1929 Advertisement for the irrepressible (UFA released) *Felix the Cat*. (Courtesy of J. P. Storm.)

DOI: 10.1201/9781003375548-2

Between 1924 and 1926, UFA imported 35 American *Felix the Cat* films (Figure 2.1).
But the character's fame faded with the onset of Black Friday and the advent of sound
films. Felix's place was taken then by *Mickey Mouse* and Walt Disney, whom Balázs
called "the undisputed king" in this field.

The story behind the first Disney short that ever screened in Germany involved
a man named Carl Laemmle. Diminutive Laemmle [Karl Lämmle] was born on
January 17, 1867, in Laupheim, in the Kingdom of Württemberg, to a Jewish family.
In 1884, he followed his older brother Joseph who had gone to America. In 1906,
Laemmle opened one of the first motion picture theaters in Chicago and subsequently became an exhibitor and film producer who fought and broke the patent
holding movie trust. Eventually he merged his IMP Company with other partners,
among them a certain Patrick Anthony "Pat" Powers (Powers Picture Plays), and in
1912 co-founded the Universal Pictures Manufacturing Company which he helmed
until he was ousted in 1936. Laemmle at that time had some hopes to purchase the
huge Berlin-based UFA Company (Universum Film Aktiengesellschaft) and its vast
theater chain. As a consequence of Fritz Lang's dystopian sci-fi epic *Metropolis* that
went way over budget and couldn't possibly recoup the risky investment, UFA was
financially shaken and had to look for fresh money and American investors. But
Paramount and MGM proved stronger than "Uncle Carl" and joined UFA for some
time in a wobbly venture called Parufamet (Paramount-Ufa-Metro-Verleihbetriebe
GmbH). Considering his strong ties with and his regular visits to Germany, Laemmle
decided to establish his own German distribution company. One of Laemmle's assets
was an animation series titled *Oswald the Lucky Rabbit* created by Disney and his
partner Ub Iwerks. Laemmle's Matador Film distribution company was based in
Berlin and sometime later would transform into Deutsche Universal AG (the German
branch of Universal) under the supervision of Austrian-born Paul Kohner.

On July 12, 1927, the first Disney cartoon passed the Berlin Board of Film
Censors: It was *Trolly Troubles*, retitled *Oswald und die Strassenbahn* (*Oswald and
the Trolley*) (Figure 2.2).

FIGURE 2.2 Advertisement announcing Oswald as the "crazy rabbit" in 1929: *Cartoons you've never seen before.* (Courtesy of J. P. Storm.)

When *Oswald* shorts became a success and the name of Walt Disney was noticed in the credits of the Universal releases, another distributor entered the stage. No, not UFA: UFA would stick with *Felix the Cat* by Pat Sullivan and artist Otto Messmer, the true creative force behind that character. Thanks to the support of British International Pictures, Disney's new distributor was Südfilm AG. Südfilm was a subsidiary of the Emelka Corporation. Emelka or MLK (Münchner Lichtspielkunst/Munich Film Art) was Bavaria's answer to the Prussian UFA. Südfilm released a variety of films, ranging from *Maciste in the Lion's Cage* to *Berlin-Alexanderplatz* starring Heinrich George. In 1928, Südfilm purchased a small package of 15 old Disney-made *Alice* comedies via British International, their London-based partner company, from F.B.O. (Film Booking Offices of America) and its successor, R.K.O. Radio. These cartoons were shown with Südfilm feature releases between 1928 and 1929.

In 1930, Gabriel Levy's Aafa (Althoff-Amboss-Film AG) secured more *Alice* cartoons for German distribution. Aafa lasted until 1934 when its assets were "Aryanized."

Besides *Felix the Cat*, *Alice* and *Oswald*, there was, up to that time, no other, especially no *German* cartoon star on German screens that would deserve that title.

When *Oswald* premiered on German screens, Disney had already lost the popular character due to copyright machinations of Charles Mintz, the husband of his original distributor Margaret J. Winkler. *Oswald* became a Universal property and was reshaped by Walter Lantz.[2]

But Walt Disney rebounded. He hit it big in Germany in 1930, when Charles J. Giegerich, since 1929 Disney's representative, was given the task to bring *Mickey Mouse* films to Europe. The Giegerich family originally came from Germany. Giegerich Jr. had tried his luck as an actor in silent films before he became a salesman. The first *Mickey Mouse* cartoons were sold to London in November 1929. Immediately they were recommended by British International Pictures to Südfilm. Although they created some important abstract and silhouette films, the Germans didn't have a comparable cartoon industry, just dozens of small outfits that produced advertising films. They seemed to be reluctant to create a cartoon star of their own or didn't trust themselves to do so, but they loved cartoons. Fortunately for them, German distributors found a way to circumvent the contingency of American short films. Südfilm was the first distribution company to secure the rights from Celebrity Pictures (owned by Laemmle's former partner Pat Powers) to show *Mickey Mouse* on German screens. The first *Mickey Mouse* sound cartoon to pass the Board of Censors on January 17, 1930, was *The Barn Dance*. As everywhere in the world, *Mickey Mouse* was Disney's breakthrough in Germany – in a time of financial and political ups and downs.

On January 10, 1930, the trade press announced *Mickey*'s arrival in Germany:

WHO IS "MICKEY"?

Mickey's creator is the American artist Walter Disney, the most inspired trick artist of our time. With his MICKEY MOUSE cartoons, he has edited the first sound trick films, because they are nothing else than one hundred percent sound comedies.

Mickey, the sound film mouse, is one up on his forefather FELIX, as he has the advantage of voice, sound effects, and musical accompaniment. In Germany, he sure will be soon as popular as Felix. The first MICKEY films are released by Südfilm.[3]

Then, on February 15, 1930, the first *Silly Symphony* came out: *Skeleton Dance*, in Germany released as *Die Geisterstunde* (*The Witching Hour*):

> Another hit from the *Mickey Silly Production*. An owl is having a conversation with its sitting tree, a ghost dog and two ghost cats intervene as the clock strikes 12, and a skeleton rises from its grave. Before you know it, it quadruplicates and a danse macabre of horrifying comedy begins, culminating – a splendid idea – in a xylophone solo which one of the skeletons plays on skull, vertebrae, and ribs of one of its companions. Then the crock crows, and the haunting is over; two forgotten feet remain lonely outside till a bone hand grabs out of the grave and collects the desperate parts to join it with the others – The End.[4]

Südfilm started a big, exceptional campaign on behalf of *Mickey Mouse* and placed ads in the trade magazines announcing the character as "MICKY DAS TONFILM-WUNDER" (MICKEY – THE SOUND FILM MIRACLE):

> Attention please! Here speaks Mickey on the frequency of sensational success!
>   What is Mickey? Who is Mickey? Answer: Mickey is the best of the best, the most terrific of the terrific! Mickey is simply unrivalled! Mickey can accomplish anything!

Mickey beats everything! Everybody loves Mickey! Everybody laughs himself to tears about Mickey![5]

In charge of *Mickey*'s German campaign was mainly Karl Ritter (1888–1977), a personal friend of Bayreuth's new first lady Winifred Wagner. Ritter started his movie career as a commercial artist for Südfilm in 1925. The same year he became a member of NSDAP. Between 1933 and 1945, Ritter was one of the leading UFA producer–directors of outspoken Nazi propaganda films: *Hitlerjunge Quex* (*Hitler Youth Quex*), *Unternehmen Michael* (*Operation Michael*), *Patrioten* (*Patriots*), *Legion Condor*, *Über alles in der Welt* (*Above All in the World*), the anti-Russian *GPU*, and the lost, unfinished *Das Leben geht weiter* (*Life Goes On*). (Interestingly enough, while producing special effects-laden pictures like *Stukas*, he became the first German film director to turn to storyboarding whole sequences and discuss them with his favorite process specialist, Gerhard Huttula, a former animation cameraman.)

This is how Ritter saw *Mickey Mouse*:

Mickey is born in the country of Black Bottom, Slow Fox, Nigger Songs, in the country of jazz, in a word: the U.S.A. Mickey is the sound film mouse. Father: Walt Disney, an American artist and cartoonist. A marvelous, ingenious, extremely witty, splendid guy! A whiz par excellence, a virtuoso of humor up to date, a universal genius in all things technical, obsessed by the sense of motion and rhythm as only few of his contemporaries are.

Mother: the animated drawing, like the *Silly Symphonies*, crazy jazz compositions from a strange, enlivened fairy tale nature! There are crickets and grasshoppers dancing, spiders playing dreamlike harp melodies on their webs, flowers and trees, birds and insects begin to live like human children, even clouds, lightning and rain begin to behave like people of today. Godfather: the sound film. One cannot imagine Mickey without sound. Everything Mickey does makes noise, tuneful or else. Mickey plays xylophone on the teeth of a cow, transforms a squeaking mother pig into a concertina, misuses cattails as singing saws, dances to the tunes of the newest hit songs on piano keys, plays the harp on macaroni noodles, hairs of the beard, spider webs. Even when Mickey hangs on a railroad car and thumps with his bottom on the railroad ties it sounds like clownish chimes that move your legs. […]

Mickey's language is international: Old and young, Chinese or Eskimo and Nigger, white or red, everybody understands him: a new Esperanto […] the divine language of the laughing human heart![6]

On Monday, February 17, 1930, 5:00 p.m., Südfilm invited all Berlin cinema owners to a trade show with *Mickey Mouse* and *Silly Symphonies* that took place in UFA's renowned *Marmorhaus* Theater (Marble House), where ten years ago *The Cabinet of Dr. Caligari* was premiered. Südfilm screened *Ein Schiff streicht durch die Wellen* (*Steamboat Willie*), *Das Dampfross steigt* (*Mickey's Choo-Choo*), *Jedermann seine eigene Jazzband* (*The Jazz Fool*), *Im Tiervarieté* (*The Opry House*) starring Mickey and the first *Silly Symphonies: Die Geisterstunde* and *Im wunderschönen Monat Mai* (*Springtime*).

The reviews were enthusiastic:

Even if the screening would have lasted six, eight, ten hours, one would have patiently stayed. It was that beautiful! It is no overstatement that this afternoon belonged to the most entertaining events of its kind. Screened were – one has to use superlatives again, but there is no other chance – the nicest, cutest animated films in the world. Maybe one or the other will now doubtfully shake his head and think for himself: My God, the man exaggerates, but that's the absolute truth.

There are big films that cost millions. Films with the best actors, but they are soon forgotten. And now comes a simple gentleman, Mr. Disney, and has nothing else than his pencil and white sheet of paperboard. But this pencil is a magic wand, it conjures up delightful creatures: Mickey the mouse and all the other quixotic quadruped creatures of the Silly Symphonies.

Even the erudite, academic film critic, a German phenomenon, was pleased:

What a gift for the masses of workers. The daily routine forgotten, one hour of joy and jauntiness. All this presented in a form that even the most subtle demands of art are satisfied.

If anything, then this Mickey and his cousins, the Sillys, are highly gifted symphonists of popular education. They teach us to understand visual and audio jokes. They are didactic, in the true sense of the word: and their vocation happens by virtue of true humor.[7]

The critic should have mentioned not only the masses of workers but also the masses of unemployed that suffered from the Great Depression. Without the Depression, Mickey might not have become a shining star neither in the United States nor in Germany. He clearly owes his stardom to the Great Depression.

Südfilm also released *City Lights* (*Lichter der Grossstadt*) at that time and promised that Mickey would soon be as popular as Charlie Chaplin.[8]

By 1930, Disney had left distributor Pat Powers, a tough Irishman. Thanks to a recommendation of Frank Capra who seemed to like Disney's early product, a new distribution deal was signed with Cohn Bros. Harry and Jack (who had learned the craft at Laemmle's company) and their Columbia Pictures outfit that grew from Poverty Row. Columbia sold its product to Germany via general agency Capitol Film AG., Berlin SW 68, Friedrichstr. 235 and announced the best short sound films in the world: *Mickey Mouse – Silly Symphonies – Krazy Kat*. Once again, the buyer was Südfilm.

At the same time, nine Disney *Wuppy* films turned up on the German market, but nobody had ever heard of *Wuppy*. Südfilm immediately checked with New York and notified the trade press that these films were silent cartoons and ten years old. A soundtrack was added, and a company named Stein-Film G.m.b.H. tried to cash in by releasing them. Our guess is that these shorts were Disney's first cartoon productions: from *Little Red Riding Hood* (1922) to *Martha* (1923). More serious were ads placed in the trade papers by Nowik & Roell Film G.m.b.H. in Berlin SW 48, Friedrichstr. 25–26. The company distributed Ub Iwerks' rival product *Flip the Frog* to Central, North, and Eastern Europe. Iwerks had followed an offer from Disney's Pat Powers. The German ads presented a tiny *Mickey Mouse* (!) introducing a huge *Flip* as his legitimate successor (Figure 2.3):

UB IWERKS, the brilliant creator and artist of "Mickey Mouse," takes the opportunity to introduce his latest sound film star *FLIP THE FROG*. *FLIP THE FROG* has already arrived in Berlin.

After the unparalleled success of little, capricious "Mickey Mouse" a new star has now risen on the sound film sky: Flip the Frog. Again, it is Ub Iwerks, the brilliant creator and artist of Mickey, who handled him so successfully. His "Flip" is even better than the graceful little mouse in imitating and parodying man's behavior and deeds. It is just a pleasure to watch and listen to the little frog "Flip".

Ub Iwerks who had worked for six years with Walt Disney was forced to part company with him. For sure this was no damage to the genial master of animated cartoons. Anyway, Flip will show up in May in Berlin.

Whoever delighted in "Mickey Mouse" will enjoy "Flip the Frog"![9]

FIGURE 2.3 Advertisement: Krazy Kat introduced as "the sister of Mickey Mouse." (Courtesy of J. P. Storm.)

Iwerks, by the way, had German roots. He was born Ubbe Eert Iwerks in 1901. His father, Eert Ubbe Iwwerks, had immigrated to the United States in 1869 from the village of Uttum in the western part of East Frisia, today part of the municipality of Krummhörn in the Aurich County in Lower Saxony. In ancient times, Uttum was a chief's home, the fortress of Uttum. The name Uttum is derived from Ottem, Otthem, or Ottheim and means home of the Utte or Otte. Farming was the main way of living in the village. There are still buildings left that Iwerks' father would have recognized: the church built in 1250 and the old mill from 1856. We checked the Krummhörn phone book and found people who probably are descendants and distant relatives: Anton Iwwerks, August Iwwerks, Christian Iwwerks, and Cornelius Iwwerks. Many men and women left Lower Saxony and the Hanover area in the 19th century. Population of Krummhörn today: 494.

Two other artists with German roots who later worked for Disney: Milt Kahl who animated Shere Khan in *The Jungle Book* and Wolfgang "Woolie" Reitherman who was born in Munich and directed it. John Hench (Johannes Hench), who dubbed the "German Baron" at the Disney Studio, was particularly close to Walt and contributed his skills to *Disneyland.* When this writer met Richard Williams in London over 30 years ago, Williams said, for some unknown reason, that Germans are the best animators and that they have a true understanding of movement. This quality doesn't show, however, in most German cartoons and seems to be lost to a great extent with the advent of 3D computer animation in Germany.

KING OF A LOST WORLD

In his sketchy, not too well researched book *Warum Hitler King Kong liebte, aber den Deutschen Micky Maus verbot* (*Why Hitler Loved King Kong but Forbade Mickey Mouse to the Germans*),[10] author Volker Koop talked about Hitler's enthusiasm for the 1933 *King Kong* that at the time was considered a technical marvel. According to files, Hitler saw *King Kong* at least 18 times, which is a record. *King Kong* is an animated character like *Mickey Mouse*, so why should Hitler have banned Mickey from Germany?

Ernst Hanfstaengl, in the beginning a strong supporter and confidant of Hitler who later turned his back on him and went to America, confirmed this strange passion for the giant gorilla: *He was captivated by this atrocious story. He spoke of it often and had it screened several times.*[11]

Despite Hitler's fondness of that particular animated film, *King Kong* faced some serious problems with German censorship before it became a giant hit on German screens, released on December 1, 1933. Ben Urwand did some research on the topic[12] and checked the files of the German Board of Censors: Oberprüfstelle No. 6910 dated September 15 and October 5, 1933[13]:

> Eleven men were sitting in a screening room in Berlin. Only a few of them were Nazis. At the front of the room was Dr. Ernst Seeger, chief censor from long before Hitler came to power. Next to Seeger were his assistants: a producer, a philosopher, an architect, and a pastor. Farther back were the representatives of a film distribution company *[Europa Filmverleih A.-G.]* and two expert witnesses. The movie they were about to watch came all the way from America, and it was called *King Kong.* [...]
>
> Dr. Seeger looked over at the first expert witness, Professor Zeiss from the German Health Office. "In your expert opinion," Seeger asked, "could this picture be expected to damage the health of normal spectators?"
>
> Zeiss was in no mood to cooperate. "First," he said, "I need to know whether the company trying to sell this film is German or American."
>
> Seeger replied that it was a German distribution company.
>
> Zeiss erupted. "I am astounded and shocked," he yelled, "that a G e r m a n company would dare to seek permission for a film that can only be damaging to the health of its viewers. It is not merely incomprehensible but indeed an impertinence to show such a film, for this film is NOTHING LESS THAN AN ATTACK OF THE NERVES OF THE GERMAN PEOPLE!"
>
> There was a brief silence. Then Seeger requested that the expert not judge the motives of the company in this way but confine his statements to his own area of expertise.
>
> Zeiss returned to the original question. "It provokes our racial instincts," he said, "to show a blonde woman of the Germanic type in the hand of an ape. It harms the healthy racial feelings of the German people. The torture to which this woman is exposed, her mortal fear... and the other horrible things that one would only imagine in a drunken frenzy are harmful to the German health.
>
> "My judgment has nothing to do with the technical achievements of the film, which I recognize. Nor do I care what other countries think is good for their people. For the German people, this film is unbearable."
>
> Zeiss had argued his case with all the zeal of a good National Socialist. No one could fault his motives. In response, Dr. Schulte, assistant practitioner at a mental hospital in Berlin, defended the film company's position. Unlike Zeiss, he was calm and composed, and he denied all of the previous charges.
>
> "In every instance that the film potentially seems dangerous," he said, "it is in fact merely ridiculous. We must not forget that we are dealing with an American film produced for American spectators, and that the German public is considerably more critical. Even if it is admitted that the kidnapping of the blonde woman by a legendary beast is a delicate matter, it still does not go beyond the borders of the permissible.

"Psychopaths or women," he added, "who could be thrown into a panic by the film, must not provide the criteria for this decision." [...]

Certainly no one wanted to get on the bad side of the new propaganda minister, Joseph Goebbels. Seeger therefore requested the Ministry's position on the case [...]

Finally, a letter arrived. After all the fuss, the Propaganda Ministry announced that *King Kong* did not harm the race instinct. [...]

Seeger announced the big news. "Because the specialist from the Propaganda Ministry stated that the film does not harm German racial feelings, the only thing left to determine is whether the film endangers the people's health."

Seeger did not stop to point out that there was something very odd about the Propaganda Ministry's position. He himself had just said that the blacks in the film presented a white woman to King Kong "instead of a woman of their own race." In other words, he was bringing up an obvious racial problem with the film. This image did not seem to offend the Propaganda Ministry, however. [...]

And so, instead of examining the obvious problems with *King Kong*, the committee simply returned to the original question of whether the film could be expected to damage the health of normal spectators. Zeiss had said that *King Kong* was "an attack on the nerves of the German people," and he had referred to particular images that he thought had a damaging effect. He had failed, however, to provide any justification for his view. The committee therefore rejected his testimony and found that "the overall effect of this typical American adventure film on the German spectator can be expected. The film was simply too "unreal" and "fairy-tale like" to be believable.

Thus, it was released, cut down to 76 minutes, as *Die Fabel von King Kong – Ein amerikanischer Trick- und Sensationsfilm* (*The Fable of King Kong: An American Trick and Sensational Film*). And it turned out, as everywhere in the world, a sensation on German screens.

MR. MOUSE STEPS OUT ON GERMAN SCREENS

There were, indeed, a handful of stupid Nazis who disliked not only *Kong* but Disney's animated mouse and its merchandising (Figure 2.4):

Blond, liberal German city youth on the string of the finance Jew. Youth, where is your pride? Mickey Mouse is the shabbiest, most miserable ideal ever invented. Mickey Mouse is mental enfeeblement of the Young Capital. Anyway, the good sense should tell every reputable girl and every honest boy that dirty, drecky vermin, the big bacteria carrier in the animal world, cannot be transformed to an ideal species. Don't we have something better to do than decorate our dress with dirty, dumb animal because American business Jews want to make money? Away with the Jewish stupefaction of the people! Away with the vermin! Away with Mickey Mouse, affix the swastika![14]

Bekanntlich haben die Nationalsozialisten auch die Mickymaus als „jüdische Er-
findung" mit ihrem Bann belegt. Warum wohl? Hitler ist eifersüchtig darüber,
daß man über die Mickymaus noch mehr lacht, als über ihn.

FIGURE 2.4   A 1931 caricature: Mickey banned by the Nazis as "Jewish invention." Hitler is
jealous because Mickey is more popular than him. (Courtesy of J. P. Storm.)

Another Mickey Mouse critic was one Walther Schneider, who in 1931 published
a sarcastic article in a respected liberal Berlin magazine in which he claimed that
Mickey is mentally retarded:

> The chronic movie image of Mickey Mouse displays unmistakable streaks of a para-
> noid mental illness of its originator. A diagnosis of the spindle-shanked, hydrocephalic,
> astigmatic and neurasthenic Mickey Mouse reveals particularly disorders in the sphere
> of face and hearing (commonly called mental delusions). On closer examination, con-
> cerning these "pathologically changed perceptions of real objects," one has to decide if
> this is a manic or paranoid case. [...]
>   Basically, this preposterous behavior (in kitchen, ice boxes, fortresses, and deserts)
> is a kind of paranoia that is characterized by right logic under wrong prerequisites. The
> "distortion of space, time and causal connections" (in the film plot), the "blurred blend-
> ing of various objects" (the car that transforms into a living being, the dancing piano
> stool), the "permanently erroneous repetition of perceptions" (multiplications of young
> Mickey Mouses) is indicative of youth madness.
>   A psychiatric surveillance of Mickey Mouse that lasted over several screenings
> leaves no doubt of a serious case of paraphrenia as described by [Emil] Kraepelin

(related to Dementia paranoids). The world of Mickey Mouse ideas, voluptuously equipped with fantasy and narrative streaks, represents a marginal case of lunacy psychoses that often leads to severe temper tantrums.[15]

This revealing "analysis" was published in 1931 in a respected Berlin magazine. Although it seems quite certain that it was meant satirically, there are some words of truth. Even Disney, when he became saturated and conservative, had doubts about Mickey's "mental disorder" and had the character changed in the course of years from anarchist *sturm und drang* (storm and stress) to *petit bourgeois*.

When *Flip the Frog* was announced, Südfilm hit back and countered the *Flip* advertisements with a full-page ad that made clear that Mickey and nobody else was the superstar:

To My People
Hail the day that I appeared to you!
It was a victory all along the line![16]

Due to the Great Depression, out of the 19,000 American cinemas, 6,000 had to close. So the export of films was an absolute necessity for any producer to recoup his investment. Europe and particularly Germany became an important market for American films and cartoons. Luckily, Disney's *Mickey Mouse* became an instant hit in Germany, not only in cartoon films but also in merchandising.

In the meantime, one short film was banned by the censors as the trade press reported: *Mickey im Schützengraben* (literally translated: *Mickey in the Trenches*).[17] This cartoon short is better known as *Barnyard Battle*: Mickey joins an army of mice dressed like the forces of the Confederate States of America in a war against Pegleg Pete and an army of cats who wear German World War I helmets while attacking the farm.

Who would have thought that the lovable little Mickey Mouse could be forbidden by the censors? Well – it has happened but not to the glory of the gentlemen with the red pencil. And why? Mickey Mouse dared to go into the trench – in a war between cats and mice – but "the artist of the cartoon has obviously imagined a combat operation from the Great War … while the victorious mice are marked by the cap of the Frenchmen *[sic!]*, the counterparty of the cats is clearly recognizable by an imitation of the German steel helmet and therefore identified with the German Army…" Thus reads the decision of the *Filmprüfstelle* [Board of Film Censors] so that the film was banned. The Board of Censors took the view that Mickey's excursion to the trenches might revive and keep alive the latent anti-German hatred (*Deutschfeindlichkeit*) that existed in foreign countries since the war. It further held that the film might offend the patriotic feelings (*Vaterlandsgefühl*) of the German audience and in effect must be detrimental to the German reputation. So, Mickey, lay down your rifle and don't join the soldiers; keep neat and spruce to the saxophone – war is a dangerous thing particularly if one has to fight the gentlemen of censorship![18]

Later, slightly changed, the cartoon was eventually approved by German censors.

Südfilm AG. qualified as a smart, engaged distributor of *Mickey Mouse* cartoons. After the Berlin premiere of a new Hans Albers picture titled *Der Greifer* Südfilm released on September 17, 1930, female patrons were given *Mickey Mouse* brooches. As a consequence of this sneaky cinema propaganda, one day later Mickey's image was seen all around Berlin.

One hundred cartoons made by Disney, beginning with the Universal releases, were screened in Germany before the war. Besides Disney products, there were also the *Betty Boop* and *Popeye* cartoons by Max Fleischer released by the German branch of Paramount Pictures, the *Hutzi Putzi* (*Bosko*) shorts from Warner Bros.-[First] National, and *Flock & Flickie* as the *Terrytoons* were named then.

While Südfilm should have done well and prosper thanks to Mickey, Karl Ritter's ads, and the expertise of the perseverant head of distribution, Gustav Berloger, Emelka, Südfilm's former parent company, did not. After UFA had experienced its commercial Waterloo with Fritz Lang's dystopian vision of a future *Metropolis*, Emelka had overdone it in 1929 with Karl Grune's *Waterloo* picture starring Charles Vanel as Napoleon and Otto Gebühr as Field Marshal Blücher. As a consequence, Südfilm got caught up in the maelstrom of bankruptcy and wouldn't last long.

TECHNICOLOR DREAMS

In 1933–1934, Germany registered 245 million moviegoers, a number that would triple until 1940. American film companies could use such a market for their products. In early 1933, Arthur W. Kelly, Vice President of the United Artists Corporation, visited several European countries, among them Germany. United Artists (UA), a film company founded by Douglas Fairbanks, Mary Pickford, Charlie Chaplin and D.W. Griffith in 1919, had become Disney's American distributor in 1932. On February 1, two days after Hitler's final rise to power, Kelly held a press conference and said that the American film industry couldn't ignore the potential German-speaking audience of one hundred million people in Western Europe. Kelly, therefore, intended to invite German partners to join him in coproduction:

> It is our sincere wish to tread a path towards a generous international cooperation. Having established local United Artists production in England, France and Italy we want to pay increased attention to the German market now. We would like to work with a German company if this would lead to the production of international films. We are looking for stars that are well known in the leading film countries. This way Jeanette MacDonald and Herbert Marshall will work for us in Great Britain and Dominions, and on this basis our further activity will develop.

As a good example for the quality of UA's product, Kelly decided to use Disney cartoons as a door opener and arranged a special screening of *Silly Symphonies* cartoons in Berlin's Paramount offices. These cartoons were not only talking and singing, they also had the advantage of the new three-strip Technicolor process.

Kelly: *"Our color Silly Symphonies will be released in Germany, and soon-to-be we will probably produce the Mickey Mouse films in color, in the Technicolor process too."*[19]

Some UFA representatives were present too. Still licking their wounds, they were not at all interested to enter coproduction with Americans, bearing their experiences with Paramount and Metro-Goldwyn in mind, but they sure liked Disney's Technicolor cartoons. On October 13, 1933, with Südfilm out of the picture, the UFA Board of Directors approved the purchase of five color *Silly Symphonies* and five black-and-white *Mickey Mouse* cartoons: *Die Vögelein im Walde* (*Birds in the Spring*), *Der Lenz ist da, Hänsel und Gretel im Zauberwald (Babes in the Woods), In der Werkstatt des Weihnachtsmanns (Santa's Workshop), König Neptun (King Neptune)* and Mickey Mouse starring in *Trautes Heim – Glück allein, Das grosse Micky-Mäuschen Fest (Whoopee Party), Micky's Galapremiere (Mickey's Gala Premiere), Die Maus im Sattel,* and *Der verrückte Urwald (Trader Mickey).* These shorts were far more attractive and commercial than anything that was seen on German screens before, and they had the advantage that leading Third Reich politicians liked them.

Most of these shorts, by the way, were granted a predicate by the officials. This meant tax reduction for the cinema owners: *künstlerisch wertvoll – artistically valuable.*

DISNEY TOYS AND MERCHANDISING

On April 10, 1930, the German branch office of George Borgfeldt, one of America's main suppliers of Disney products, received a patent re: *Mickey Mouse* and *Minnie Mouse* by Reichspatentamt (Reich Patent Office) for export business, but there were still German companies that tried to infringe the copyright. Disney's chief archivist Dave Smith recalled such a case in Germany:

> There were several products manufactured with the mouse attached without license. In order to stop that Walt and Roy decided to give a license to a single company. Together with that company they went to court and sued the other companies. As far as I know, the court procedure took place in a large cinema so that all parties involved could participate. We won the lawsuit and our claim became statutory.[20]

A glimpse into the files of the Reich Patent Office in Berlin shows the variety of available Disney merchandise. There were coffee bags, sewing needle etuis, food, chocolate, polish, stockings, fireworks, and even – inconceivable after the war – booze.

One German Disney postcard showed Mickey as an alcoholic ending up in the gutter:

> Klein Micky-Maus ist sehr vergnügt
> und trinkt, bis sie am Boden liegt
> Little Mickey Mouse is quite amused
> and drinks until he's down

Among Disney's official German licensees were:
Eisenmann & Co., Fürth, Bavaria:

tin toys

Heinz & Kühn, Manebach, Thuringia:

- Mickey Mouse hurdy-gurdy
- Mickey Mouse slate dancer
- Mickey Mouse drummer
- Mickey Mouse walker
- Mickey the musical mouse
- Mickey Mouse masks
- Mickey Mouse costumes

Richard G. Krueger, Bavaria:

- Mickey Mouse China
  The company-manufactured export articles
  Authorized by Walter E. Disney – Made in Bavaria

Rosenthal Porzellanfabrik Bahnhof Selb G.m.b.H., Bavaria (Figure 2.5):

- Mickey Mouse, China
  Only for the German market

FIGURE 2.5   Minnie Mouse porcelain figure manufactured by Rosenthal. (Courtesy of J. P. Storm.)

Margarethe Steiff G.m.b.H., Giengen an der Brenz:

- Mickey Mouse plush toys

In the beginning, there were disagreements over the design of Steiff's Minnie Mouse puppets. Borgfeldt's chief buyer Fred Wander was shocked when he saw Steiff's Minnie. He considered the first puppets ugly and complained to Disney himself. In a letter addressed to Steiff Wander wrote: *"…I am going to write you the exact words he [Disney] said to me: Regardless what Steiff thinks how my* Minnie Mouse *should be made: I insist it should be made the way I demand or not at all..."* Steiff backed down and redesigned Minnie.

Schuco, Schreyer & Co., Nuremberg:

The company was founded in 1912 by Heinrich Müller and Heinrich Schreyer, and belonged to the most popular and important manufacturers of tin toys. Schuco produced (Figure 2.6)

- a tin toy Donald Duck
- a tin toy Little Pig

FIGURE 2.6 Tin toy Donald Duck by Schuco, 1937. (Courtesy of J. P. Storm.)

W. Hagelberg AG.:

- Mickey Mouse postcards

COMIC STRIPS AND PICTURE BOOKS

From early on, Disney comic strips appeared in German newspapers. *Kölnische Illustrierte Zeitung* (Cologne Illustrated Paper) broke the first ground in its issue of December 27, 1930, which introduced *Mickey Mouse* with the following words (and Mickey's New Year's greetings on the title page):

> They have never lived but everybody knows them, they belong on the wish list of the folksy American: Mutt and Jeff, Winnie Winkle, Moon Mullins, "the Katzenjammer Kids" and so on, all the heroes of those funny comic strips that are, as if drawn for kids, the delight of the big children all over America. They appear in every newspaper, half a dozen daily, weekdays black, on Sundays in color: a bunch of funny people involved in situational and character humor, with speech balloons coming out of their mouth. You see mandatory punchable faces, unlucky devils and henpecked husbands, blatant philanthropists, little rogues à la Max and Moritz. Their newest adventures are devoured already at breakfast and evoke the Keep smiling in these days that are so arduous. These characters, however, are nowadays eclipsed by an animal that is different from all other animals: it doesn't appear in Brehm's zoological encyclopedia, his name is Mickey Mouse and he is the most famous of all mice. A distant echo of his black-and-white existence on the screen now appears in the newspapers. Here too bustles his lively, really mousy mobility, his fantastic play with reality; here, too, happen the heroic battles which a little David with mouse ears fights against the Goliath forces of man and machines and

all the big animals: awesome dances that are improvised for him by his creator Walter Disney and his twelve employees. A cartoon film that is unreeled in seven minutes consists of 10,000 little frames that have to be drawn individually let alone the precise sound mix. But this is blessed work: Mickey makes all people on earth laugh. Would there be a Noble Prize for the jesters of the world, then Mickey Mouse sure would deserve it.

The comics were based on *Mickey Mouse on Mystery Island* that appeared in U.S. papers from January 13 until March 31, 1930, distributed through King Features Syndicate. They were initially drawn by Ub Iwerks and inker Win Smith, who took over from Iwerks after he had left Disney to join the sirens of Pat Powers.

When time came for the Cologne carnival in February, the paper went so far as to commission an unnamed German artist to draw a strip just for that particular event.

Other papers and magazines followed the example of the publishers from Cologne:

Erfurter Allgemeine Zeitung (Thüringer Zeitung, Erfurth General Newspaper – Thuringia)
with *Micky Maus sucht eine Goldmine (Race to Death Valley)*, Floyd Gottfredson's first strip, and *Micky Maus als Boxer (Mickey Mouse, Boxing Champion).*
Das grüne Blatt offered *Micky Maus und die Flitspritze.*

J. J. Darboven, a Hamburg-based coffee roasting company, produced its own comic strips starring an anthropomorphic coffee bean gnome named Darbohne drawn by a female Jewish artist who, according to legend, left Germany with the help of Arthur Darboven, the head of the company. The truth is that Anna Cohen, who might have been one of the artists involved in creating the character, was murdered in 1944 in the Kulmhof/Chełmno extermination camp. In one of the Darboven comics, Darbohne met Mickey Mouse and rhymed:

Die Micky Maus liebt jedes Kind;
Darbohne geht hinein geschwind.
Und weil begeistert sie so sehr,
Ruft laut sie: „Mickey Maus, komm her!"

Und eh' sie es noch recht erfasst,
Kommt Micky Maus in grosser Hast
Herunter von der Leinewand.
Da sind die beiden durchgebrannt.

Every child loves Mickey Mouse.
Darbohne hurries
To call him with loud voice: "Mickey Mouse,
come here!"
And before he grasps,
Mickey Mouse comes in great haste
Down from the screen.
Then both of them elope.

In 1935, Williams & Co., a Berlin publishing house founded in 1924 by Edith Jacobsohn, edited a Disney picture-book based on the popular *Three Little Pigs*: Drei kleine Schweine, *a delightful funny picture book with many black-and-white and color illustrations. A world success as film – as book.* 64 pages, 26 illustrations.

Apparently not licensed was another picture-book titled *Murz der Kater und die Mickymäuschen* (*Murz the Cat and the Little Mickey Mice*), a fairy tale with morale by Hanns-Claus Roewer, 30 pages, published by Uhlenhorst Verlag in Hamburg and printed by Köbner & Co. Druckereigesellschaft m.b.H. in Altona (Elbe). The protagonists were a cat that looked like Felix with an oversized head and a smoking (!) Mickey Mouse with family in tow: Mother Mouse needs three hours to put her make-up on, and both kids, Mickey-Mutzi and Mickey-Schnutzi, don't obey.

Even more active in the late 1930s concerning Disney was Steinsberger Verlag in Vienna with its magazines:

> *Kiebitz: Schneewittchen und die sieben Zwerge* (*Snow White and the Seven Dwarfs*), *Adolar* (*Elmer Elephant*), and *Mickey Mouse*.
> *Der Papagei: Drei kleine Kätzchen* (*Three Little Kittens = Three Orphan Kittens*) and more.
> *Schmetterling: Henne Gluck und ihre Kinder* (*The Wise Little Hen*), *Emmerich der Gänserich* (*Emmerich the Gander = Donald Duck*).

The colored Viennese magazines were labeled customer's supplement and distributed by various companies with respective trademark imprint. These magazines were still published after the Nazi annexation of Austria, right into the war years until 1941.

With the Nazis' rise to power, however, the license for a popular series of German-language *Micky Maus Wunderbücher* (*Mickey Mouse Marvel Books*), based on Disney's American Pop-Up & Waddle Books, wasn't granted by Disney's European representative, Walt Disney Mickey Mouse S.A. in Paris, to a German publishing house. Instead, the German-language books were published by printing house Jacques Bollmann AG. in Zurich, Switzerland:

> *Micky Maus in Afrika* (*Mickey Mouse in Africa = The Adventures of Mickey Mouse – Book 2*)
> *Abenteuer der Micky Maus* (*Adventures of Mickey Mouse = The Adventures of Mickey Mouse*)
> *Micky Maus im Zirkus* (*Mickey Mouse at the Circus = The Pop-up Mickey Mouse*)
> *Minni Maus und das Entlein* (*Minnie Mouse and the Duckling = The Pop-up Minnie Mouse*)
> *Das Waldmännlein und König Neptun* (*Babes in the Woods and King Neptune = Silly Symphonies Pop-up*)
> *Micky Maus am Hofe König Arthurs* (*Mickey Mouse in King Arthur's Court*)
> *Das lebende Buch der Micky Maus* (*The Living Book of Mickey Mouse = Mickey Mouse Waddle Book*).

Unlike the original American books, the German-language editions contained more illustrations and text.

In early 1937, Bollmann followed with the first regular *Micky Maus Zeitung* (*Mickey Mouse Newspaper*, 8–10 pages), the German-language response to the Italian *Topolino*, the French *Le Journal de Mickey*, and the British *Mickey Mouse Weekly*:

> Mickey Mouse is more than a toy, he's not only entertainment. He wants to connect the youth of the whole world; he wants to lead this youth away from all thoughts of hatred, of arms and wars. All this is an anathema for him, because he loves only the good, the noble and the beautiful. If Mickey Mouse would have his way there would be no armament and conscription laws, people would understand each other in a peaceful way and joy and happiness would rule the world.[21]

In the Swiss editions, Pegleg Pete would become Peter Hinkebein, the Three Little Pigs a Trio Ringelschwanz (Trio Ring-tailed), and Donald Duck Schnatterich (*schnattern = quacking*).

In Germany, the Swiss-produced *Mickey Newspaper* was distributed by Gustav Brauns, a commissionaire from Leipzig. After 18 regular issues (plus specimen number) that appeared bimonthly, the publication ended. Mickey Mouse himself was asked to announce the sad news to the public:

> After all you have to consider that a newspaper costs a lot of money to produce and Switzerland is only a small country which offers more problems for the distribution of a newspaper in the form of taxes and police ordinances than other countries... Many parents have to save the money so that the little they earn will suffice for the daily bread...

SONGS AND RECORDS

Music was a key element in Disney films:

> What are these highly praised Disney films?
>   What are the basic principles of these works? There is only one answer: purely musical ones! At first the musical rhythm and the melody of the underlying music number is fixed. Based on the lines of the sheet music, Disney builds his "moving" drawings. Each rhythmic movement, change and flexion of the musical score is followed by the image with infallible delicacy of feeling. The music is the master of the film. There is no dialogue. Emotions of the acting persons are either expressed by singing or by the orchestra.
>   How are art pieces generally called that are based on these principles? We call them operas. And as Walt Disney is expressing himself cinematically, we have to call his smaller-scale performing arts cinema operas.[22]

Quite successful, therefore, were the German Disney records. German singers and orchestras re-recorded Disney songs and melodies. On April 5, 1930, the trade journal *Lichtbild-Bühne* published this note:

> A MICKEY HIT
>   The original foxtrot hit of the Mickey Mouse sound releases edited by Lawrence Wright Music Co., London, was purchased for Germany by Roehr Aktiengesellschaft, Berlin W8. The German lyrics were written by Bert Reisfeld. The Mickey Mouse Foxtrot will be published in short time in different adaptations and released on the records of renowned record companies, available in record shops.

Film-Kurier added on May 15, 1930:
A Mickey Foxtrot.
Mickey as foxtrot. The renowned music publishing house Roehr AG., Berlin W, Mauerstr. 76 has published a foxtrot *"Micky Maus"* (*Mickey Mouse*), with music by Harry Carlton and German lyrics by Bert Reisfeld. The Mickey hit song which one heard repeatedly in the broadcasts of Berlin Rundfunk was recorded by numerable record companies, with and without refrain: by Electrola (E. G. 1890), ODEON (Dajos Bela), Beka (Dobric) and Triergon (Harry Jackson).
New Mickey Record.
The Mickey Mouse Foxtrot, Verlag Röhr AG., was now recorded on Ultraphon record A 432. The orchestra (Theo) Mackeben plays, the refrain is sung by the Two Jazzers. The new record qualifies in the same way as the recordings by Elektrola, Beka, Orchestrola and is ideal for promotion in the lobby of a theater.

Bert Reisfeld, the Jewish lyricist, was born in 1906 in Vienna. In 1933, he left Germany and worked in France, then, five years later, in the United States. In 1941, he co-wrote the instrumental *Morning Mood* with Glenn Miller as a trombone solo with piano accompaniment. He was honored with a German Filmband in Gold in 1985 and died in 1991 in Badenweiler.

Equally, if not even more popular, were the German recordings of Frank Churchill's song of the Big Bad Wolf: "Wer hat Angst vor dem bösen Wolf?" – "Who's Afraid of the Big Bad Wolf?"

Carl Robrecht: CLANGOR T 4345
Willi Glahé: ELECTROLA E.G. 2986
P. Rebhahn: BRILLANT SPECIAL 246
Hans Bund: TELEFUNKEN T 2248

The German lyrics for "Wer hat Angst vor dem bösen Wolf?" were texted by Ch. Amberg. In 1942, the song was newly recorded in Germany, but this time with different lyrics for propaganda usage:

Bye, bye, Churchill, BBC, tralala,
Your tricks won't work with Italy…
Why not give us different news?
Skip those Soviets, skip those Jews.

NOTES

1 Béla Balázs, *Der Film. Werden und Wesen einer neuen Kunst.* Vienna: Globus Verlag, 1949, pp. 217–218.
2 Today *Oswald the Lucky Rabbit* is Disney property again. The Walt Disney Company purchased the rights to the character in 2006.
3 Lichtbild-Bühne, January 10, 1930.
4 Ton und Bild No. 37, 1930.
5 Südfilm Magazin, No. 1, January 1930.
6 Filmwoche No. 12, 1930.
7 *Kurzfilme, wie sie sein sollen.* In: Film Kurier, February 18, 1930.
8 Südfilm Magazin, No. 1, January 1930.

 9 Ad in: Film-Kurier, May 1930.
10 Berlin: be.bra wissenschaft verlag, 2015.
11 Ernst Hanfstaengl, *Zwischen Weissem und Braunem Haus: Memoiren eines politischen Aussenseiters.* Munich: Piper Verlag, 1970, p. 314.
12 Ben Urwand, *The Collaboration: Hollywood's Pact with Hitler.* Cambridge, MA: Belknap Press, 2013, p. 1.
13 Deutsches Filminstitut, Frankfurt/Main.
14 *Die Diktatur.* District organ of N.S.D.A.P. Pomerania, quoted from: Film-Kurier, July 28, 1931.
15 Walther Schneider, *Micky Maus ist geisteskrank.* In Der Querschnitt #10, Berlin 1931, p. 679. Printed with permission of J. P. Storm Collection.
16 Film-Kurier, February 1930.
17 Film-Kurier, May 14, 1930.
18 *Die verbotene Micky Maus.* In: Lichtspiel Rundschau, Supplement of Berliner Tageblatt, July 13, 1930.
19 Film-Kurier, February 4, 1933.
20 Klaus Strzyz and Andreas C. Knigge, *Disney von innen. Gespräche über das Imperium der Maus.* Frankfurt/Berlin: Ullstein, 1988.
21 Jacques Bollmann AG., Zurich.
22 Film-Kurier, 1935.

3 Puppetoons

THE ARTIST AS DON JUAN

All that Germany had to offer, on the other hand, were advertising films.

Market leader UFA released commercials by Wolfgang Kaskeline, who was more of an anti-Disney. Kaskeline was born on September 23, 1892, in Frankfurt/Main. Early, he developed an interest in painting and drawing. He was a war volunteer, seriously wounded in October 1914 and hospitalized for two years. He became a lifelong war invalid and sought employment as drawing instructor and art teacher in a Berlin middle school. At that time, he began work in animation and was joined by two former pupils, one of them Gerhard Huttula, who became his regular cameraman. First, both men worked in Kaskeline's home in Berlin Tempelhof. In the beginning, Kaskeline released his animated commercials through Mendelfilm and Epoche-Film [Werbekunst Epoche G.m.b.H.] in Frankfurt/Main. Epoche went into partnership with UFA for some time. As a consequence, in 1927, Kaskeline was able to negotiate a distribution agreement with UFA.

> Each cinema-goer will know the name of Wolfgang Kaskeline because he is credited with most of UFA's advertising films. If it appears on screen, one will know that now one of those amusing advertising films will unreel in which objectivity and humor, farce and fantasy will mix softly, in which color, form and sound, scene and schematic illustration evoke a general impression which will leave, apart from the propaganda effect, a pleasant artistic delight for each receptive eye.

In the article, Kaskeline himself is quoted as follows:

> I cannot freely and unconditionally express an artistic idea. The basic idea is always connected with the propaganda object. This is a specific thing, and believe me - for a true painter this reference to a subject, this responsibility to the real – is a delight. I'm not permitted to interpret something into an object which it doesn't tell me, otherwise it will become crooked and forced - not real. [...]
>
> As a painter - and only as a painter - [...] I am an enthusiastic Don Juan. That is, I love each object. Only the one who loves to explore the final secrets and only if I have put my ear and my eyes to these last secrets, I can reproduce the importance of an advertised object in a way that it will have an impact on the spectator: novel, thrilling, convincing.
>
> The wish to possess it must be awakened in him for this is the essential thing in all advertising.
>
> And now to the technique of the art of advertising films - no, I better shouldn't begin. It is like a country's government - the better, the less one has to talk about.
>
> I have approximately 20 employees. It is they who transform my sketches and pre-production art technically with remarkable diligence and - this is the key to the art of animation - accuracy.[1]

DOI: 10.1201/9781003375548-3

He still had one leg in Expressionism:

> Since I have been the first who has created a sound image in color, I constantly endeav-
> our to vary the use of sound in all of my advertising films. The expressionist, allegori-
> cal film requires different sound, different score than the grotesque cartoon where all
> objects will become living beings and all living beings will become creatures of magic
> and jugglers.

Above all, Kaskeline avoided Disney's style of series characters and anthropomor-
phism. The only interest both shared was music.

GEORGE PAL'S CIGARETTE PARADE

At UFA, Kaskeline had become the undisputed successor of George Pal, who had set
up his own business and later would become a personal friend of Walt Disney. George
Pal was born Gyula György [Pál] Marczincsák on February 1, 1908, in Cegléd, then
Austria-Hungary, and died on May 2, 1980, in Beverly Hills. He had worked in four
countries: in his native Hungary, Germany, the Netherlands, and the United States on
short and feature films, animation, and live action.

> Having graduated from the Technical High School in Budapest, one day George Pál
> happened to stray into a film laboratory, where he learned the technique of trick film-
> ing. Confident of his ability to succeed in this field, he later formed a company of
> his own and produced advertising films for home and foreign firms. To increase his
> chances, he transferred to Germany and obtained in Berlin a situation as trick film
> designer, and was eventually engaged by UFA as Chief Animation Designer. In eigh-
> teen months, he produced here 23 advertising films and also worked during this period
> for the Scherl Publishing House that published his *Habakuk comic strip* series.

UFA wanted him to rival the popular stop-motion animation made at Julius
Pinschewer's advertising film studio. In March 1930, Pinschewer Film
Aktiengesellschaft had released a puppet advertising film for Nestlé's Milk
Chocolate, *Kirmes in Hollywood Ein Puppenspiel* (*Kermess in Hollywood:
A Puppet Show*). Puppet duplicates of actors Emil Jannings and Buster Keaton face
each other in a boxing match. Buster wins thanks to delicious Nestlé chocolate,
and receives the $1,000 prize money from the hands of Miss Arabella. Hedwig and
Gerda Otto, mother and daughter, had produced this short. Both were experts in
puppet making and animating. Pinschewer had already secured their services to
film two other stop-motion shorts, *Im Filmatelier* (*Inside a Film Studio*, 1927) and
Das Wetterhäuschen (*The Weather Box*, 1929).

On October 15, 1931, joined by Berlin businessman Paul Wittke Jr., Pal founded
Trickfilm-Studio G.m.b.H. Pal & Wittke. He maintained four units animating
in 2D and 3D. After some time, however, he decided to switch completely from
2D to 3D technique. But keeping the fundamentals of 2D animation, became the
basic principle of his later replacement series, produced to great critical acclaim
in Eindhoven, Netherlands (for Philips Radio) and Hollywood, USA (for release
through Paramount Pictures).

A trade article announced Pal's independent venture in 1931:

MICKEY MOUSE
GETS COMPETITION

The lack of good funny short films that match European taste has brought about the overnight establishing of a trick film studio in Berlin. Oswald the Rabbit, Felix the Cat and the wonderful Mickey Mouse have played their part.

Two young artists have reacted to the emergency call: Pal and Wittke. On the fourth floor [note: according to American counting: 5th floor] of the new Nürnberg Haus [Nuremberg House], four units are operating. For the first time, the unbound [*entfesselt*] trick film camera is used. It is attached to a subtly conceived crane construction. It can move upwards, downwards, right and left, float, gyrate or stand still, it can do somersaults and pirouette.

A second device is also used for the first time. The individual animation images are no more drawn on paper but on transparent cells. This saves the painstaking process of cutting out templates.[2]

The new trick film studio will release in the near future the first film of its series "*Der Herr Kollege*". This "colleague" – the figure of a dotty, philistine and overly pedantic clerk – will be introduced in a funny little film: one will see and hear – "colleague" speaks of course – one day of his "busy and eventful life".

Pal and Wittke will release their star in all language versions.[3]

H[ugo] O[tto] Schulze, who was the cinematographer, recalled the process of Pal's filmmaking. I interviewed him about his participation in the photographic effects of *Metropolis* (shooting the light rings around the robot), when he suddenly mentioned, en passant, his involvement with Pal and Wittke:

I became acquainted with George Pal at UFA Werbefilm where I was responsible for model animation photography and for the photographic quality of the cartoons. In 1932, when he decided to leave UFA and establish his own company, Pal asked if I was interested in joining him. He told me that he had something really unusual in mind and that he wanted to equip his new studio in a very up-to-date manner. Always interested in experiments, I accepted. Our first commission was an advertising film for Oberst Cigarettes [a tobacco brand belonging to Waldorf Astoria]. Pal didn't want to have it drawn frame by frame in the common cartoon fashion but to do it instead with dimensional animation. A blade of tobacco would fold up by itself, glide into a paper husk, stand up, get legs and a head and so on. Then the twenty cigarettes from one package would form a squadron, with an Oberst (colonel) commanding in front, and would march through a futuristic setting which consisted of cigarette packages. The main street of our set was about thirty feet long and ran the whole length of the studio. The cigarettes for each animation step were mounted on boards. All in all, we had approximately sixteen or eighteen boards with squadrons of cigarettes in various walking positions to complete one single walking step which, repeatedly used, resulted in a walking cycle.[4]

For a long time, the footage was considered lost – until a few years ago a badly damaged print resurfaced in the vaults of the German Cinematheque in Berlin:

A cigarette tobacco leaf standing on two legs, complete with plasticine mouth movements, is going to introduce the process of cigarette production that is shown in live action scenes.

The humanized lead tells the audience that the tobacco leaves keep moist, not by drinking (from a small milk bottle) but by generating moisture from the air to keep themselves smooth.

We see female workers sort out leaves.

From the process of shredding, the leaf returns, from the netherworld so to speak, in ghostly 2D animation, to continue its narration. Then it is rolled into the paper.

Finally, we have a humanoid cigarette, with wire legs and wire arms and clods for feet and hands.

This stop-motion cigarette takes over as Colonel "Oberst" with paper mouth movements and a small paper hat as a helmet. He then proceeds to command a small army:

> *Stand at attention!*
> *Eyes front!*
> *Count off!*

Gold filter soldiers count off and form a marching column: six cigarettes in front, six in the middle, two behind, with the colonel marching ahead to Prussian and Bavarian march music.

The camera mounted on a track above follows them.

Finally, they slip into cigarette packs.

In early 1933, when Pal, a Jew, saw Nazi troopers storm his studio and arrest one of his employees, he decided on the spot to leave Germany. He knew such pogroms already from his native Hungary. Eventually, he settled in Eindhoven and set up a new studio with the support of Philips Radio. With the outbreak of World War II and Hitler invading the Netherlands as well as the rest of Western Europe, George Pal escaped a second time and became an award-winning puppet filmmaker in Hollywood. Like Disney, he realized that short films were becoming too costly to provide enough revenues, and so, in the late 1940s, he switched again, this time to feature filmmaking for Paramount and MGM. Pal worked on science fiction and fantasy special effects films like *Destination Moon*, *When Worlds Collide*, *War of the Worlds*, and *The Time Machine*. He would return to Germany only once for a film production: doing location shots (in Rothenburg ob der Tauber and Dinkelsbühl, near Munich) for Cinerama's lavish but sentimental *The Wonderful World of the Brothers Grimm* in 1962.

NOTES

1 UFA Feuilleton #8, February 25, 1931.
2 In Germany and other parts of Europe up to that time they often cut out 2D animation and placed it frame by frame on the background.
3 Newspaper clip from Pal's German scrapbook. Source unknown.
4 Rolf Giesen, *Der Trickfilm: A Survey of German Special Effects.* In: Cinefex No. 25, Riverside/California, 1986.

4 A German Fairy Tale "Disneyfied"

DISNEY IN MUNICH

UA's Kelly was the first to come to Germany and promote Disney. Then Disney came himself. Europe and Germany were the destination of the Disney Brothers Walt and Roy in 1935. They wanted to strengthen ties with these countries and do some research for a future production that would be decisive for the fate of their studio.

Disney scholar Didier Ghez has meticulously recorded the trip of the Disney Brothers to Old Europe in his book about *Disney's Grand Tour*[1]:

They traveled by train from California to New York, where they boarded a ship (the *SS Normandie*) to England and Scotland, from there to France, and by car to Germany. They came to Baden-Baden and drove through the Black Forest via Freiburg, Ulm, and Augsburg to Munich. The Disneys and their wives arrived on Sunday, July 7, 1935, in the Bavarian capital. Obviously, they were mainly interested in Southern Germany. They also had some business in Munich.

On July 8th, the brothers met with the Board of the newly founded Bayerische Film- und Verleihgesellschaft (Bavarian Film and Distribution Company). This company was sort of a receiving company for Emelka and Südfilm and soon to be called Bavaria. Bayerische had recently become Disney's new German distributor.

Disney and United Artists had received several offers from German distribution companies. Disney was not pleased about the UFA deal because the German major had purchased the shorts for a fixed price. Disney preferred a percentage in relation to Germany's market power. In May 1934, Tom P. Mulrooney cabled new offers from Germany to Roy O. Disney: Europa Filmverleih A.-G., the company that had released *King Kong* and made it a major hit all over Germany was prepared to pay each RM 8,000 for six *Silly Symphonies*. Bayerische Filmgesellschaft followed with a better offer: 15 *Silly Symphonies* and *Mickey Mouse* cartoons, the Technicolor *Silly Symphonies* for RM 7,000, and the black-and-white *Mickey Mouse* cartoons for RM 3,000 each. But Disney asked for more. In a telegram dated May 21, 1934, Roy Disney informed Mulrooney that regarding the release of their cartoons in Germany they were against the one-time sale because they were interested in the long-term development of the territory for their products. Each territory that Disney dealt with should be developed in such way that it would recoup expenses. Generally speaking, Roy Disney was right, because old Disney cartoons that still played interfered with the release of the new ones. Disney had also big things in mind.

For the first time Roy spoke about a new project:

We are working definitely on the release of a feature-length cartoon. It should be finished at the earliest in twelve to fifteen months. This would open wonderful options,

DOI: 10.1201/9781003375548-4

particularly in Germany. Cartoons which at that time would be handled by other distributors might seriously spoil the release of our feature-length cartoon.

For these reasons we wish that [foreign] sales will be closed for the shortest terms possible. I guess three years are the minimum that is asked for in general. It shouldn't last any longer. You know this: People would like to take seven years once they are offered. But a cartoon usually has only three active, profitable years, and so to our mind there is no reason to release cartoons any longer.

The French branch office of United Artists, Les Artists Associés continued its negotiations with Bayerische and tried to find the best solution for all parties involved, because the Munich company already released other UA films. On August 6, Mulrooney informed Disney that Bayerische had agreed to release the cartoons on a percentage, and Disney was pleased.

On September 12, 1934, the deal with Bayerische and Les Artists Associés was signed. The Munich company purchased a new package of Technicolor *Silly Symphonies*. The first program consisted of *Three Little Pigs* (*Die 3 kleinen Schweinchen*), *Father Noah's Ark* (*Die Arche Noah*), *The Night Before Christmas* (*Die Nacht vor dem Weihnachtsabend*), *The Pied Piper* (*Der Rattenfänger von Hameln*), and two black-and-white *Mickey Mouse* cartoons: *Mickey's Mechanical Man* (*Die mechanische Micky Maus*) and *Giantland* (*Micky im Lande der Riesen*). Bayerische committed itself to release three *Mickey Mouse* cartoons and three *Silly Symphonies* per month. Eight to ten percent of the box office receipts for a feature film went into the cartoon supplements and were split 70:30 between United Artists and Bayerische. This meant approximately 16,600 Reichsmark per *Mickey/Silly* supplement for Disney. Only one *Mickey Mouse* cartoon was rejected by the German censors, the nightmarish—*The Mad Doctor* in which a mad scientist tries to cross Pluto with a hen. It was substituted with another cartoon—*Playful Pluto*.

When the meeting with the Disneys took place in Munich, the Bayerische board was represented by Franz Beltz and Wilhelm Kraus. Head of distribution was, as in the case of Südfilm, Gustav Berloger. The Bayerische representatives told the Disneys that the revenues of their short films would be even better if UFA would stop the competition and not continue to release their Disney shorts. This was what Roy Disney had feared! The brothers assured the Munich board that Bayerische was first choice for all the German releases, including their projected full-length feature film. The Bayerische board also suggested that Disney should release one *Silly Symphony* in the German language. The Disneys promised to give this idea some thought. In Hollywood, they said, there was enough German talent to handle such a task.

But Walt wouldn't have been Walt, if he hadn't used his spare time to do research. He strolled through the city and bought numerous books at two Munich bookstores: Christian Kaiser located in the town hall and Heinrich Hugendubel at Marienplatz. One hundred forty-nine books were purchased in Germany and shipped to Hyperion Avenue Studios as reference material for the artists and animators who had started work on a new project. It was originally going to be another entry in the *Silly Symphonies* series, but it transformed into the first feature-length cartoon Roy Disney had mentioned in his telegram: *Snow White and the Seven Dwarfs*. A German fairy tale sure should make an ideal release on the German market.

The books and research material boxes arrived on August 5, 1935, in Los Angeles, California.[2] There were

- **German legends and fairy tales.**

Particularly the Scholz edition of the Grimm fairy tales proved a true treasure trove for the animators:

> Since 1904 the series Das deutsche Bilderbuch [The German Picture Book], including "fairy tales," was published by the well-known publishing house **JOS. SCHOLZ in *Mainz*.** With these editions the publisher made a move to color lithographs of Jugendstil [art nouveau]. These picture books which are traded today at very high prices were not only the peak of Jugendstil illustrations in picture books but also exquisitely printed. All illustrators (for instance Kreidolf) and picture book publishers struggled for optimal printmaking. **Karl Scholz,** the head of Mainz publisher Jos. Scholz that specialized in lithographs, had developed a special flat screen-printing process around 1890 called algraphy.[3]

The algraphy used paper impregnated with an aluminum salt and was forerunner of offset printing.

- **Stories about Gnomes, Imps, Dwarfs, and Brownies**

One of them, Ernst Kreidolf's 1902 tale of the *Die Wiesenzwerge* (*The Grassland Dwarves*) was made into a Gasparcolor cartoon by Gerhard Krüger in 1940–1941.

Another, *Des Wiesenmännchens Brautfahrt* (*The Honeymoon of the Little Meadow Man*), was written by Will Vesper. In 1931, Vesper became a member of NSDAP. Thomas Mann called him one of the most atrocious National Socialist fools. Vesper's son Bernward dissociated himself from his father. He married Gudrun Ensslin, who became a partner of Andreas Baader and a leading terrorist in the tragic events of German Autumn. Bernward Vesper committed suicide in 1971.

- German Song Books and Rhymes
- Picture Books

The names of two female illustrators pop up throughout Disney's shopping list: Else Wenz-Viëtor (1882–1973) illustrated 11 books by Adolf Holst. Her work was acknowledged by the National Socialists. Ida Bohatta (1900–1992) had attended the Kunstgewerbeschule, the Vienna School of Arts and Crafts. After the Anschluss, the annexation of Austria, she became a member of Reichsschrifttumskammer, the Reich Chamber of Literature. During the Nazi regime her books were as highly recommended as those illustrated by Wenz-Viëtor.

- Children's Tales
- Reading Primers
- Books celebrating Easter and Christmas
- Books about Birds and Animals
- Flowers and Trees
- Books by Wilhelm Busch and other Artists

Busch (1832–1908) was a humorist, illustrator, and painter, and his work were a fore-runner to comic strips. He certainly would be a subject for animation films (as we will see). Rudolph Dirks' *Katzenjammer Kids* were clearly modeled after Busch's *Max und Moritz*.

The bulk of Disney's selection consisted of children's books, although he didn't intend to make a children's film but a movie for the whole family. Nevertheless, he wanted to see the family with a kid's eyes.

Disney, mainly influenced by American popular culture, cinema, music, and comic strips, wouldn't forget the roots of Old Europe, art, and music. He found his sources in Scandinavia, France, England, Italy, France, and Germany, which he soaked up like a sponge and tried to Americanize. That way he kept the old tales alive for modern mass audiences. Bruno Girveau, a French art historian, called him truly transatlantic.[4]

During their stay in Munich, the Disneys attended a congress of Reichsfilmkammer [The Reich Chamber of Film] and a screening of *Die lustige Palette – Im Reiche der Micky Maus* (*The Funny Palette: In the Kingdom of Mickey Mouse*) that was released as a United Artists program by the Bavarian Film Company. It was a compilation of four *Silly Symphonies* and two black-and-white *Mickey Mouse* cartoons the company had just purchased. Compilations like this one were already released in Sweden and in France, but in Germany they played to house record.

Marmorhaus in Berlin was sold out for weeks with five screenings per day, when it booked *Lustige Palette* in December 1934 for the Christmas season. Theater management had gone out of their way to please young customers and their parents:

> Long before the screening started masses of children flocked into the room, admired the shining Christmas tree and the large Mickey Mouses and Little Pigs that were placed in front of the stage. Immediately after the lights went out and the beaming face of Mickey appeared on the screen the first guffaws of laughter rolled through the cinema…[5]

Bayerische Filmgesellschaft received a grateful telegram from the theater management: SILLY SYMPHONIES *biggest box office since existence of this house. Congratulations to the incredible success. Tolirag – Marmorhaus.*

The souvenir film brochure edited to the *Funny Palette* revealed Disney's great plan to the general audience:

> Walt Disney who develops the ideas for all his films in his own studio works with a large number of artists, primarily young people who were trained by him particularly for his animated films. But still the creator of the animated films isn't satisfied with his achievements. Mickey Mouse has great plans for the future. After sound and color, he [Mickey] will expand his sphere of activity in other ways. Walt Disney intends to produce feature-length cartoons.[6]

Unfortunately, theater owners took great satisfaction in conceiving their own short film programs and combined Disney shorts with lower quality films.

Roy Disney wanted Bavaria to only release Disney shorts with first-class feature films, not with second rate features, as had happened in the past. But there were problems in the background: the shortage of foreign currency in Germany and a restricted contingency of films. Despite the huge success, Disney didn't make any big profits from his German releases. On February 19, 1936, UA informed Disney that there weren't itemized records from the Munich film showings. There were only statements that listed the total sale profits for the showings, instead of itemized statements which listed the individual earnings for each short. Roy Disney was not pleased with this information. Suddenly a lot of Disney money was stuck in Germany. The Disney brothers would reject a new offer from a Luxembourg-based, apparently German outfit named Continental Film to buy more cartoons for the Reich. In July and August 1936, the Disneys received at least Reichsmark 18,000 out of the Bavarian releases, but it was not what they had hoped for.

However, in 1935, during their European trip, the sun was still shining bright for Disney's European activities. Leaving Munich, the Disney party traveled to Neuschwanstein, mad King Ludwig's castle, built on a rugged hill against a backdrop of picturesque mountain scenery, the symbol of idealized romantic architecture. This fairytale castle and Copenhagen's Tivoli inspired Disney to build his own Magic Kingdom in Anaheim, California 20 years later.

From Austria and Switzerland, the trip continued to Italy where Disney was welcomed like a state guest. The Foreign Minister of Fascist Italy, Count Galeazzo Ciano, and his wife, Mussolini's daughter Edda, paid court to him. Disney met Mussolini's wife and children, and – Didier Ghez isn't sure about it, Diane Disney Miller denied it – the Duce himself, who (like Hitler) was a great film enthusiast. According to Mussolini's son Romano, there was "an amiable meeting": "He [the Duce] invited him to his official residency, the Villa Torlonia, where they talked about Mickey Mouse, Minnie, and Donald Duck."[7]

NOTES

1 Didier Ghez, *Disney's Grand Tour: Walt and Roy's European Vacation, Summer 1935.* Theme Park Press, 2014.
2 Ibid., pp. 96–102.
3 Lies Staechelin. Traumstadtmuseum Wissen. www.pasttimes.de/Grimms-Maerchen-Scholz-Kuenstler-Bilderbuecher.
4 Bruno Girveau (ed.), *Once Upon a Time: Walt Disney: The Sources of Inspiration for the Disney Studios.* Munich: Prestel Verlag, 2007.
5 Deutsche Allgemeine Zeitung, December 22, 1934.
6 Illustrierter Film-Kurier No. 962: *Silly-Micky-Wunderwelt.*
7 DER SPIEGEL No. 41/1995, October 9, 1995.

5 Herr Hitler and Mister Mouse

A MEETING THAT NEVER HAPPENED

There was some speculation if Disney had met his most ardent German fans too: Hitler and Goebbels.[1] John J. Powers, an American playwright, suggested that such a meeting took place at least in his play *Disney in Deutschland*, but there is no evidence to be found in the files of the former Reich Chancellery that it took place. In the play, a fanciful political satire, Disney meets Hitler in the presence of Leni Riefenstahl and Joseph Goebbels. The time seems to be a mix of 1935, 1939, and 1941 (the strike at Disney Studios).

Well, I've been traveling through Europe and, as we're here, Lilly and I, my wife, we thought I should come to see you, Disney says casually. Hitler offers him a glass of sherry.

Herr Hitler, Disney tries to make some conversation, *I can't tell you how impressed I am. I know the economic situation took a lot out of Germany, and now – it's remarkable to see what's happened in the last couple of years.*

He enthuses about what they have seen, the Black Forest, Munich. Hitler remains monosyllabic: *We have our standards.*

And everyone is so healthy too, Disney continues to schmooze.

Physical health is the cornerstone of our social order, Herr Disney, Goebbels splutters.

They don't have to say much to each other until they find out that both had served during the Great War at Alsace-Lorraine in France.

Disney: You don't say.
Hitler: I am saying this.[2]

Of course, nothing like that ever happened:

> ...playwright and director John J. Powers' production never ignites. The 20-minute history lesson that starts the 90-minute play fails to build up the excitement before the big get-together. Once Disney and Hitler are in the same room, along with Hitler's right-hand man, Joseph Goebbels; and his personal filmmaker, Leni Riefenstahl; there is hardly any dramatic action to push the play along. There are occasionally tense moments, such as when Hitler wonders how much of a Jew-hater Disney really can be if he works in Hollywood. But most of the hour is spent sitting around a big oak table...[3]

Nevertheless, fact is that Hitler adored Disney films.

The diary of Dr. Goebbels, Wednesday, December 20, 1937:

DOI: 10.1201/9781003375548-5

As a Christmas present, I gave the Führer 30 top movies of the past four years and 18 Mickey Mouse films. He is pleased to no end. Glad to have that treasure which hopefully will give him joy and relaxation.[4]

One document re: deposal of Disney shorts to the Führer reads:

Reichsministerium	*Berlin W 8, 27 July 1937*
für Volksaufklärung und Propaganda	*Wilhelmplatz 8–9*
	Phone: A 1 Jäger 0014

To
Adjutant of the Führer

By order of Herr Obergruppenführer [Lt. General Wilhelm] Brückner,[5] we herewith deliver film prints for your archive

1. *Italian movie* **Mario**
   (Italian original with no German subtitles)

2. *Five Mickey Mouse films*
   Romeo und Julia
   Käsepiraten
   Feuer und Traumland
   Das grosse Rennen
   Jägerlatein

Invoices over RM 501.50 and RM 199.64 are attached. May we ask you for immediate payment on behalf of Deutsch-Italienische Film-Union GmbH. resp. Deutsche Fox-Film AG.
   Heil Hitler!
   Signed,
   Seeger

MISSION IMPOSSIBLE: GET *SNOW WHITE* BACK TO GERMANY

Of course, the Nazi film industry had high expectations to present Disney's most Teutonic entry, his first feature-length production *Snow White and the Seven Dwarfs*, released in the United States in December 1937. The film's budget was $1.2 million, not really that expensive for a Technicolor feature at that time but still a high financial risk for Disney who up till then had only produced short films, *Mickey Mouse* and *Silly Symphonies*. To make a decent profit or just to break in the Depression, Disney and other American producers badly needed the European market, including Germany.

The vast majority of German reviews enthusiastically reported about Disney's new release:

On Christmas Eve[6] the first feature-length fairy tale color cartoon, *Snow White and the Seven Dwarfs*, was premiered in Hollywood. It was a premiere event Hollywood hasn't seen for years. The most famous directors and actors attended the screening which took place in Hollywood's noble cinema Carthay Circle. The surroundings of the cinema were changed into a fairy tale kingdom with elves and gnomes which attracted many curious onlookers. During the screening and at the end the movie was met with great enthusiasm by the patrons.

The film runs approximately one and a half hour at a cost of 3,000,000 Mark. 570 artists have worked on it since 1934. [...]

The brilliant success, however, compensated for the high costs. The movie promises to become a global box-office success.[7]

No other American movie received that much attention in the National Socialist Press. The Germans tried to import it and show it in their theatres as quickly as possible.

On February 5, 1938, the Führer himself ordered his adjutant to get him a print of Disney's hottest release for his private cinema on the Obersalzberg, Hitler's mountainside retreat situated above the market town of Berchtesgaden. Three weeks later, Hitler was able to screen and view it. Without any doubt, it became one of the most favorite and cherished treasures of his film collection.

Considering the high costs, certain columnists of German trade papers remained skeptical:

We already have pointed out that the immensely blown-up coverage of the Walt Disney picture *Snow White and the Seven Dwarfs* represents extremely dangerous premature praise. Apart from that it is questionable if this picture will be released in Germany at all; apart from the fact that the costs of this movie amount to the whole annual production budget of a medium-sized German film company; apart from the fact that the number of contributors on this picture equals approximately the whole staff of UFA Neubabelsberg; apart finally from the fact that Disney thanks to global release chances can work unrestrictedly while German animation artists Lotte Reiniger and [Oskar] Fischinger have left Germany and went abroad for lack of opportunity in Germany – who will guarantee that in this picture the greatest goods of German fairy tale have been preserved faithfully and were not changed into a drawn American revue? This doubt seems likely for one learns from England that the picture was passed by the Board of Censors into A category, i.e., juveniles under age 16 only allowed with parental guide. According to the judgement of the English censor, the film contains several passages which are not suitable for children. And this in a *Snow White* film!!![8]

Nevertheless, the Minister of Enlightenment and Propaganda, Germany's number one Disney fan, Dr. Goebbels, ordered his staff to buy *Snow White* for the Reich. Immediately, not only one but also two German distribution companies set out and tried their luck.

CLASH OF THE TITANS: UFA VERSUS BAVARIA

Ernst Walter Herbell, Fritz Klotzsch, and Hans Schweikart were managers resp. production heads of Bavaria Filmkunst G.m.b.H., newly founded on February 11, 1938, in Munich, which now occupied the former Emelka Studios in Geiselgasteig and owned a releasing arm that included Disney's former distributor Bayerische Film- und Verleihgesellschaft. It seemed obvious that they would be awarded the contract as Disney had promised during his brief stay in Munich. The negotiations on behalf of Bavaria were conducted by authorized representative Dr. iur.[9] Helmut Keil who had the power of procuration.

The Office of Dr. Max Winkler apparently had given the green light to go ahead. Dr. h. c.[10] Max Winkler was kind of éminence grise of Nazi press and film. For a short time in 1918 Winkler had been mayor of Graudenz in West Prussia, today Grudziądz, Poland, which made him a mayor ret. by title through all the time he served Dr. Goebbels and Nazi Germany. Consequently, he insisted on being addressed by this title. Since 1920, he had successfully acted as trustee on behalf of all German governments. As a "master of tactical dodges and evasions," he had found influential patrons in Hitler's and Goering's entourage before both men came to power. In early March 1933, he became acquainted with his new superior, Joseph Goebbels. Goebbels found warm welcoming words for Winkler: "You don't know how much I am going to appreciate your services and how intimately we know you."

In mid-1937, Goebbels promoted Winkler and made him *"Reichsbeauftragter"* (Reich commissioner) in charge of the German film industry. This title included privileges that nobody else had. His decisions were, of course, always agreed with and approved by Goebbels. He not only brought the German press into line, but also arranged and contrived the *Gleichschaltung* (enforced conformation, nationalization) of Germany's leading film companies in 1937 which put them under the Reich's control.

Disney no longer distributed his films through United Artists. Disney's new distributor, RKO Radio Pictures, responsible for the production of one of Hitler's favorite movies, *King Kong*, had exported their last pictures to Germany in 1935. After that they had closed their Berlin branch located at Friedrichstr. 225, as it didn't seem profitable any more. For this reason, Bavaria Filmkunst believed it would need an experienced mediator. Although these mediators worked from much smaller offices, they had good business ties with domestic and foreign partners. Bayerische Film- und Verleihgesellschaft had acquired their Disney shorts with the assistance of such a mediator. This practice saved large companies lots of business correspondence and, of course, the big ones hoped, as a smaller company was involved, there would be lower fees to pay.

To purchase *Snow White* and circumvent the direct way via New York, Bavaria approached Deka Film G.m.b.H. Deutsche Kampffilm had been involved in the production of National Socialist "documentaries" (for Alfred Rosenberg and others) and also made an expensive Emil Jannings film *Der alte und der junge König* (*The Old and the Young King*) in 1934/1935. Rüdiger Freiherr von Hirschberg (1907–1987), son of a lieutenant-general, had founded the company in 1933. Some of his productions were released by Bavaria. After the war, as production manager, he supervised the making of a heroic Nazi Luftwaffe film, *Der Stern von Afrika* (*The Star of Africa*), on the Bavaria lot. Being doubly sure, Bavaria also commissioned another Berlin-based company to try and make a deal with RKO: Otzoup Film. Otzoup Film maintained good relations with film companies in Spain and South America. The owner, Serge Otzoup, was Russian and served the Nazi film policy as did Hirschberg. He later settled in Franco's Spain, where he died in 1974.

But UFA, the almighty German film company, was eager to get *Snow White* too. Both companies, UFA as well as Bavaria, were state owned. In an odd way, German film industry competed with itself. In June 1937, two UFA representatives traveled to the West Coast to participate in the Congress of the Society of Motion Picture Engineers. The two gentlemen were Paul Lehmann, board member of UFA AG, in charge of financial assets, and George Nitze, President of the U.S. branch office UFA Films Inc. They met with Roy Disney and suggested a joint venture releasing Disney films not only in Germany but also in other European countries too, including Belgium, Czechoslovakia, the Netherlands, Hungary, Yugoslavia, and Switzerland. Disney showed some interest, but he asked for guarantees. Naturally for the German Ministry of Finance an export of foreign currency totaling the (at the time unheard-of) sum of one million Reichsmark for an American cartoon feature would have been an incalculable risk, as at this point average production costs of German features were far lower.

Despite their best efforts, Bavaria's attempts to have a distribution deal signed failed, and the members of the Bavaria board saw their hope dashed when Goebbels and Winkler seemed to prefer UFA.

The most important film event of this summer was *La Biennale di Venezia*, the Venice Film Festival in 1938. RKO was going to screen two new Disney shorts, *Farmyard Symphony* and *Brave Little Tailor* (Mickey Mouse in another adaptation of a Brothers Grimm tale) and the feature-length *Snow White and the Seven Dwarfs*. Eventually the heads of the German film industry could view *Snow White* themselves. Some enthused over the picture, while others remained doubtful as we know from various reviews in German trade papers and played it down (especially since they already assumed that the film would not be shown in Germany anyway):

> In these days the Walt Disney cartoon feature, *Snow White and the Seven Dwarfs*, which was expected with bated breath, was screened here. For many months the picture is shown to great acclaim in the capitals of the world. The film won't come out in Germany and one has to say that, in spite of many exceptional ideas, not all too much is lost for the German audience.[11]
>
> The evening performance was in the focus of the much-anticipated feature-length cartoon *Snow White and the Seven Dwarfs* (*Schneewittchen und die sieben Zwerge*) which got preliminary laurels as outstanding and which (besides *The Adventures of Tom Sawyer*) counts for the Americans' prize possession. One has to admit that Walt Disney and his employees have achieved something amazing technically as well as artistically.
>
> The German fairy tale by the Brothers Grimm provided the original source out of which much could be formed because it is inexhaustible. It is anyone's guess why and if at all our old fairy tales should be used to create color cartoons which are exclusively reserved for a humorous approach and in some countries are even not allowed for juveniles because they might frighten the young minds too much like the horror scenes in this movie do.
>
> Without any doubt Disney accomplished really magnificent film parts which are stylistically and visually not only beautiful but also stuck in the memory because they are unique. Such as Snow White's flight through the cave where she is pursued and hunted by some beast, the image of dwarfs working underground, the rescue of Snow White (with her body laid out) by the handsome, brave prince, the transformation of the evil stepmother into a witch just to mention a few parts which in the long work attracted special attention.

After all what one has read and heard about this film a certain disappointment had to follow. Despite plot, colors, and clean, technical and artistic effort by Walt Disney's artists the movie could not hold, because of its length, the interest until the final frame with unchanged intensity. At least the work booked a relatively big success for itself which, however, shouldn't seduce to make more feature-length films along the same lines but to keep the Mickey Mouse and other cartoons as supplementary. It would be better.[12]

At the Venetian Lido, the German films in the competition were awarded two cups, four medals, and two short film prizes. In recognition of its outstanding technical and artistic achievement, Disney's *Snow White* received the Great Art Prize of the Festival sponsored by the Partito Nazionale Fascista. The same year, 1938, *Snow White* started its triumphal run through all of Europe: United Kingdom (February–March), Belgium (March), France (May), Norway (September), Czechoslovakia (September), Sweden (September), Denmark (September), Croatia (October), Yugoslavia (October), Finland (October), Slovenia (November), Netherlands (November), Portugal (December), Switzerland (December), Poland (December), and Italy (December). To Spain, it came in 1941.

Between December 15, 1938, and January 18, 1939, Bavaria's Dr. Keil who had not given up hope repeatedly visited the offices of Otzoup Film in Berlin's Kaiserallee 55. The Ministry of Public Enlightenment and Propaganda, however, intervened and prevented Otzoup from further negotiations, because the Third Reich officials only considered Ufa strong enough to bid for *Snow White*. After all hard work, Bavaria was out.

On the other hand, the Ministry was forced to take more stringent measures against American film production and criticize the activities of an Anti-Nazi League that had been founded in a wave of Hollywood films with anti-German tendency. On January 17, 1939, board member Max Witt, an Ufa vice president since 1937, issued a decree that American movies shouldn't be screened in premieres and first-run cinemas. Without any doubt, however, the Ministry and German film experts regarded *Snow White* as a high-calibre film for which an exemption clause should be made.

Protocol Board meeting of UFA on January 20, 1939
Herr [Wilhelm] Meydam reports on the submission re: the offer resp. the acquisition of German distribution rights of the American color movie *Snow White* on January 19, 1939.
The German release rights are for the time being reserved for Ufa by Office Dr. Winkler.
Licensee is Herr Schmeling.
The board authorizes Herr Meydam to continue negotiations resp. the acquisition of the movie for German distribution.
The board agrees to accounting on the basis 50:50.
The guarantee will be between RM 300,000 and RM 500,000 to be paid in Reichsmark. Included in the guarantee is the shipping of 100 prints, the costs will total roughly RM 75,000 inclusive.

The Herr Schmeling mentioned in the protocol was none other than German boxing champion Max Schmeling (1905–2005) who acted as licensee on behalf of RKO for *Snow White*. How did this come about? On August 19, 1936, Schmeling had fought Joe Louis in New York City's Yankee Stadium. RKO had offered him the exclusive screen rights for the match, which was only expected to last a few minutes. But when the fight entered the annals of boxing history as "The Fight of the Century," RKO lost millions and sadly realized its mistake. All attempts by RKO to rebuy the world rights to the picture failed. The movie was successfully launched in German cinemas under the title *Max Schmelings Sieg, ein deutscher Sieg* (*Max Schmeling's Victory, a German Victory/Great International Heavyweight Boxing Contest between Joe Louis amd Max Schmeling*). In late June 1938, Max Schmeling had a rematch against Joe Louis. This time RKO obtained all rights, but Schmeling was knocked out after only two minutes. Schmeling was not only an internationally renowned boxing champ but also an intelligent, shrewd businessman. He agreed to act on behalf of RKO to sell *Snow White* to the German Reich.

> Board meeting of UFA on January 24, 1939
>
> Mr. Zimmermann reports that as a result of negotiations concerning purchase of picture *Snow White* for German distribution licensee Schmeling is asking 60% of gross revenues for his shares, deducting the usual costs, with a guarantee sum of RM 500,000. Included in the guarantee, however, are 100 color prints valued at about $50,000 (=RM 125,000). According to German regulations, a German version of an American movie produced in a foreign country is not allowed here. Therefore, it shall be re-dubbed. The costs for dubbing exceed to about RM 40,000. This sum, however, can be deduced from gross revenues. The board will get an official confirmation in letter that there are no objections against purchasing the film nor against later exhibition. Seller's previous demand to include two Anny Ondra films[13] in the release deal has been dropped.
>
> Because this is an extraordinary color film, the board approves the aforementioned conditions of sale.

The Walt Disney Company, of course, had high expectations for the European market. Germany was still a key element in this marketing strategy. Even by 1940, at least one American distributor, Paramount Pictures, was still able to release four films to the German territory. Others, however, were less fortunate. They were involved in anti-Nazi films, so-called *Hetzfilme* (agitation and campaign pictures). Goebbels expected more insight from Leni Riefenstahl who visited Hollywood in November 1938. Although she was granted a lukewarm reception, she soon realized that most studios ignored her. Only Walt Disney, still interested in releasing *Snow White* in Germany, invited her to his studio.

Riefenstahl recalled that meeting in her memoirs (although more than once in her life she seemed to confuse facts with fiction, so her memoirs should be treated with caution):

> Walt Disney received us already in the early forenoon in his studios and spent the whole day with us. Patiently, but proudly as well, he showed us how his animated characters were developed and explained his unique technique and let us see the sketches he had made for his new production – *The Sorcerer's Apprentice* [segment from *Fantasia*]. I was fascinated – for me Disney was a genius, a sorcerer himself whose imagination seemed to be unlimited. At lunch he got on to the Biennale [in Venice] where *Snow White* and *Olympia* were screened in competition. He would have loved to see both parts of *Olympia*. No problem. The prints were in the hotel, they only had to be brought here. Disney pondered it for a while, then he said: "I am afraid that I cannot afford to do that."
>
> "Why?" I asked bewildered.
>
> Disney: "If I would see these films, it would be known tomorrow throughout Hollywood."

"But," I tossed in, "you sure have your own screening rooms. So nobody would know it."

Disney resigned: "My projectionists are members of the union. They would learn from their gossip. Although I am an independent producer, I have no distribution and no cinemas of my own. It could happen that they would boycott me. The risk is too much."

How powerful the Anti-Nazi League was I could read in the U.S. press three months after I had left America. Walt Disney was forced to give a statement that at my visit he didn't know who I was.[14]

At the end of January 1939, Riefenstahl returned to Europe and was interviewed by a French reporter from *Paris-Midi*:

Three months in America: everywhere lustrous reception except Hollywood where she only was received by Walt Disney, but otherwise was boycotted at the instigation of the Anti-Nazi League.[15]

Film-Kurier reported about Hollywood's Anti-Nazi League under the headline "Filmhetze in Hollywood":

An Anti-Nazi League has been established in Hollywood which was termed by Vittorio Mussolini [Benito's son] returning home from his research trip a "center of political agitation against the Fascist Idea."[16]

According to recent reports, for the time being they [the Anti-Nazi League] want to support needy emigrees before, with might and main, they are going to pursue their true objective of launching film agitation against Germany.

After all, they have worked on a film in which Charlie Chaplin satirizes the Führer and hence wants to make a laughing stock of him.[17]

On February 5, 1939, Joseph Goebbels noted in his diary:

"Question if one should remove the American films. I am not quite sure about this matter."

"This evening Leni Riefenstahl told me her exhaustive impression which is not pleasant. We have no chance over there. The Jews rule with terror and boycott. But how long?"

Filmamerika 1938

The anti-National Socialist and anti-fascist angle of the mainly judaized [verjudete] American film industry emerged from several agitation and campaign films [Hetzfilme] which we have pointed out repeatedly in FK (Film-Kurier).

The Jewish Anti-Nazi League in Hollywood has a pressure upon all who have a different opinion (Andersgesinnte) so that, for instance, nobody else except Walt Disney recently dared to welcome Leni Riefenstahl publicly in the American film town.[18]

The Minister reacted with a ban of most American films (although behind closed doors he screened and adored them, including *Gone with the Wind, Swanee River* or *Mrs. Miniver* which he considered high art of propaganda), but was still willing to make an exception for *Snow White*. American producers, however, refused to cooperate any longer. Goebbels told one Mr. Peters, who did some business for Metro-Goldwyn-Mayer *and* Twentieth Century-Fox in Berlin that not only was *Snow White* too expensive to buy but would also demonstrate the superiority of Disney animation compared to German animation.

HOW DISNEY WAS GERMANIZED AND BECAME DISTLER

The ban was not in Disney's interest. The company had already prepared a German dubbed version of *Snow White* in Amsterdam, supervised by Kurt Gerron, Marlene Dietrich's[19] co-star in *The Blue Angel* (*Der blaue Engel*). For some time, it was believed that famed Austrian actress Paula Wessely, another Hitler favorite, dubbed Snow White. This wasn't true; German film historian Joseph Garncarz discovered that it was actually Hortense Raky. The dwarfs were dubbed by Gerron, Otto Wallburg, and Siegfried Arno; the latter in better days hailed as a German Chaplin. Dora Gerson, another exiled actress, voiced the evil queen. Gerron, Wallburg, and Gerson were murdered in Auschwitz. Dora tried to ask her ex-husband Veit Harlan for help, but he had "better things" to do: In fulfilment of an order from the very top, he directed the notoriously antisemitic *Jud Süss* (*Jew Suss*). Arno survived the holocaust in Hollywood, where he mainly acted in bit parts, including Chaplin's *Great Dictator*. In 1939, the German-dubbed *Snow White* ended up listed as deposit no. 3828 in Berlin's Reich Film Archives and at Hitler's Obersalzberg retreat.

With negotiations at an end, the official party language started to diminish Disney and his work for being too American for German taste. German fairy tales, official reviewers said, are strictly "German matter,"[20] while behind the curtains there was some speculation about Disney's family background and even an attempt to "Germanize" him: Was he American or European? On inquiry by Dr. Günther Schwarz, Reichsfilmkammer, in a letter dated May 5, 1941,[21] documentary filmmaker Dr. Hans Cürlis (falsely) assured that he had heard Walt Disney was born in Germany: baptized **Walter Distler**. He even had worked for some years in Germany. Others located the place of Disney's birth in Spain. And there were even speculations that he wasn't what they called "Aryan"!

The tug of war between Ufa and Bavaria helped a small distributor, Willy Wohlrabe's Jugendfilm Verleih in Berlin, and Hubert Schonger's Naturfilm Company to issue their own low-budget, live-action version of *Snow White* in 1937, starring declared Nazi actress, Marianne Simson. Simson later shared some scenes with Hans Albers in a high-budget special effects fantasy about the Baron of Lies, *Münchhausen*, released on Hitler's order without any screen credit given to the author: the banned Erich Kästner. That lavish extravaganza in the Agfacolor process was produced to celebrate the 25th anniversary of Ufa in 1943. It was destined as a show piece to demonstrate that German films were on a par with Alexander Korda's Technicolor production of *The Thief of Bagdad* as well as *The Wizard of Oz* and the Disney epics that were secretly screened, analyzed, proverbially dismantled, and scrutinized by Dr. Goebbels and his movie machinists.

TOCCATA AND FUGUE

When a Zurich cinema dared to screen Disney's *Fantasia*, the Nazi reviewers fumed and criticized it as

> a malpropism of sublime German cultural goods, of Bach, Beethoven, and Schubert, that in this grotesque form is only possible in the mental state of North-Americans who

are going to deliver Germany's greatest musicians to colored trick film drawings of the most stupid substance.[22]

Maybe they would have liked it better if Disney had included, as originally planned, Richard Wagner's *Ride of the Valkyries*. Among the artists who worked on *Fantasia* was German émigré animator Oskar Fischinger (1900–1967) who was known as a pioneer in experimental animation. Contrary to Disney, Fischinger, who was a trained organ builder, never wanted to just illustrate music. He wanted more! He wanted to provide a visual equivalent:

> The Disney Corporation's official account of the origins and making of *Fantasia* has appeared many times, but the name of Oskar Fischinger does not figure large in any of them. It should have. Oskar Fischinger was a year older than Walt Disney. Even before sound film became available, Oskar synchronized his abstract films to phonograph records and live musical accompaniments, because he found that the analogy with music (i.e., abstract noise, a well-developed and widely-accepted non-objective art form) helped audiences to grasp and accept the nature and meaning of his "universal," absolute imagery. Oskar never meant to illustrate music, and often screened his "sound" films silently for already sympathetic audiences.[23]

In November 1938, the agent of Oskar Fischinger, once a renowned experimental filmmaker in Germany, arranged a job for him at the Walt Disney Animation Studios. Fischinger had already been in touch with Leopold Stokowski, the conductor in *Fantasia*, before the Disney job. Both had talked about an animated feature with him conducting, but then Stokowski suggested that the project might be too big to execute for Fischinger alone, and that it would be better to secure the assistance of a studio, mainly Disney. Fischinger found himself hired by Disney for $68 per week as "*motion picture cartoon effects animator*" – and was unhappy. He spoke very poor English. He couldn't voice his opinion. Some Disney staffers even pinned a swastika on the office door of the refugee artist. Fischinger usually avoided talking about this his Disney tenure. Once he wrote a friend and was pretty harsh discussing the situation at Disney's:

> I worked on this film for nine months, then through some 'behind the back' talks and intrigue (something very big at the Disney Studios) I was demoted to an entirely different department, and three months later I left Disney again, agreeing to call off the contract. The Film "Toccata and Fugue by Bach" is really not my work, though my work may be present at some points; rather it is the most inartistic product of a factory. Many people worked on it, and whenever I put out an idea or suggestion for this film, it was immediately cut to pieces and killed, or often it took two, three or more months until a suggestion took hold in the minds of some people connected with it who had their say. One thing I definitely found out: that no true work of art can be made with that procedure used in the Disney Studio.[24]

Fischinger went so far as to screen some of his work to the staff. Walt Disney was aware of that, but he didn't want his movie to be abstract. He wanted it to be commercial and reach a large audience:

> Everything that has been done in the past on this kind of stuff has been cubes, and different shapes moving around to the music. It has been fascinating. From the experience we have had here with our crowd -- they went crazy about it. If we can go a little further

here and get some clever designs, the thing will be a great hit. I would like to see it sort of near-abstract, as they call it -- not pure. And new.[25]

But back to Germany: Time and again, the German-speaking press still runs brief, sometimes odd articles that mentioned Disney and/or *Mickey Mouse*:

Fatal Shot at Trick Shooting
  Eugen Galaune, a trick-shot artist who is known beyond the borders of France, has been arrested in Paris. He had killed fellow artist Andre Robert by heart shot. The trick-shot artist was going to shoot a Mickey Mouse figure out of the hand of his colleague without grazing the skin. The bullet hit Robert right in the heart and killed him immediately. When he was arrested, Galaune claimed that Robert must have moved an inch.[26]

THE STORY OF THE CHILDREN'S BARACK OF AUSCHWITZ

Collector J. P. Storm once phoned Hitler's projectionist and was told about the Führer's enthusiasm for that particular movie – while others claimed to have found no evidence that Hitler had a print of *Snow White*. Anyway, Hitler knew *Snow White* almost inside out. William Hakvaag, the director of a war museum in northern Norway, even told the press that he unearthed four watercolor paintings of Disney's dwarfs that were hidden in the frame of another Hitler painting:

He found colored cartoons of the characters Bashful and Doc from the 1937 Disney film *Snow White and the Seven Dwarfs*, which were signed A.H., and an unsigned sketch of Pinocchio as he appeared in the 1940 Disney film.
  Mr Hakvaag, who said he had performed tests on the paintings which suggested that they dated from 1940, said: "I am hundred percent sure that these are drawings by Hitler. If one wanted to make a forgery, one would never hide it in the back of a picture, where it might never be discovered."
  The initials on the sketches, and the signature on the painting, matched other copies of Hitler's handwriting, he claimed.[27]

That story, however, was too good to be true and turned out to be a complete hoax. Nevertheless, papers round the globe published it eagerly.
  As a kid Albert Speer, Jr. (1934–2017), the son of Hitler's chief architect and Minister of Armaments, was often to the Berghof. Before his death, he was interviewed by Falko Hennig:

Do you remember your childhood on Obersalzberg, for instance Hitler posing with
        children?
Yes, I sure do.
Your father wrote that Hitler's magic didn't work on children. Can you confirm this?
I don't particularly remember him, just as a nice uncle. But it was great when we were allowed to the mountain without [having to follow the rules of] protocol. That was different from official occasions, such as a birthday. Hitler had a cinema, and there were for instance Mickey Mouse films. This was fascinating stuff for kids of course.

So you have seen Mickey Mouse films with Hitler together?
I would have to lie if I would claim that Hitler was present. But these films belonged to him.[28]

And talking to TV author Heinrich Breloer[29]:

Breloer: Did you see films at the Berghof?
Albert Speer, Jr.: Yes sure, Mickey Mouse.
Breloer: Did the "Führer" see them too?
Albert Speer, Jr.: I don't know if he was present.
Breloer: Fräulein Braun?
Albert Speer, Jr.: Yes, Fräulein Braun and some other people were present.

Frank Schirrmacher, the late co-editor of *Frankfurter Allgemeine Zeitung*, wrote a comment:

> Kids who had at times a family relationship with Hitler don't remember him but Mickey Mouse.[30]

There are other tales of *Snow White*. Dinah Gottliebová was one of Hitler's victims, a concentration camp prisoner in Auschwitz. She was an artist and recruited by the infamous "Angel of Death," SS garrison physician Dr. Josef Mengele, to do portray studies. There was a children's barrack, where Mengele's test subjects slept, decorated with a mural on one of the walls. As she had seen Disney's *Snow White and the Seven Dwarfs* in a Prague cinema before the Wehrmacht occupied Prague Castle, Dinah chose to paint the Princess, the dwarfs, and scenery from the movie. In the children's imagination, the characters even might have come alive and given them a bit of hope in their dire situation.

Gottliebová escaped the Death Mills, and, in 2010, she was interviewed by Rafael Medoff, head of the David S. Wyman Institute for Holocaust Studies:

SZ: Why did you paint Snow White?
Babbitt: I wanted to paint the happiest scene I could imagine. The animated film
         Snow White was very popular in Europe in those days. I had seen it in
         Prague seven times in succession. I was that fascinated by the anima-
         tion technique. For that time, it was very elaborate. While I painted Snow
         White, the kids stood around me and asked me to paint more, the seven
         dwarfs and the animals, which I did.[31]

Gottliebová later married one of *Snow White's* animators, Art Babbitt. She died in 2009 in Felton, California. In 2021, without contacting Dinah's heirs (she had two daughters), a German producer received project funding for a falsified version of the story: *Snow White in Auschwitz* became *Hansel and Gretel in Auschwitz*. The menacing embers of the fiery furnace in which the witch was burned to death didn't have to be mentioned. In Auschwitz, it was always present...

Else Baker, as a young girl deported to Auschwitz and Ravensbrück: "I couldn't understand. I knew the fairy tale of Hansel and Gretel. But you don't burn people. You burn wood and coal."

NOTES

1 *When Walt visited Munich in 1935, Nazi newspapers warmly welcomed him as a hero who stood up to the Jews in Hollywood.* https://www.jewishpress.com. July 11, 2019.

2 *Hitler in Deutschland* by John J. Powers. A full length one act drama. Copyright May 2013 John J. Powers Off The Wall Plays. http://offthewallplays.com

3 Molly Rhodes, Disney & Deutschland. SF Weekly, 02/13/2008.

4 Goebbels, Joseph, *Die Tagebücher von Joseph Goebbels.* Edited by Elke Fröhlich on behalf of Institut für Zeitgeschichte Munich. December 1937 to July 1938. Berlin: De Gruyter Saur, 2000, p. 64.

5 Brückner was Hitler's personal adjutant until 1940.

6 Actually December 21, 1937.

7 Film-Kurier, December 27, 1937.

8 Lichtbild-Bühne, February 16, 1938.

9 Doctor of Canon and Civil Law.

10 Honorary doctor.

11 Lichtbild-Bühne, August 26, 1938.

12 Film-Kurier, February 15, 1939.

13 Actress Anny Ondra was Schmeling's wife and became known as *The Mickey Mouse Girl* through one of her film roles (1930, release in Austria under that title).

14 Leni Riefenstahl, *Memoiren 1902–1945.* Berlin: Verlag Ullstein GmbH, Frankfurt/M; Berlin, 1987, pp. 323–327. English edition: *A Memoir.* New York: St. Martin's Press, 1995.

15 Film-Kurier, January 28, 1939.

16 Film-Kurier, January 30, 1939. For a brief time, Mussolini's son had become partner of Hollywood producer Hal Roach in a company called *RAM* [Roach and Mussolini] with the idea of producing opera films in Rome.

17 Referring to Chaplin's new production *The Dictator,* later to be called *The Great Dictator.*

18 Film-Kurier, January 30, 1939.

19 Marlene had attended the Hollywood première of *Snow White* accompanied by Douglas Fairbanks Jr.

20 Bundesarchiv/Federal Archives.

21 Ibid.

22 Film-Kurier, December 1941.

23 William Moritz, *Fischinger at Disney, or Oskar in the Mousetrap.* In: Millimeter, February 1977, Vol. 5:2.

24 Ibid.

25 Transcript from storyboard meeting that took place on February 28, 1939.

26 Alpenzeitung, October 4, 1938.

27 Did Adolf Hitler draw Disney characters? In: The Telegraph February 23, 2008.

28 "In Berlin hatte ich immer Nachteile." taz.de online, May 9, 2006.

29 *Speer und er.* TV mini-series. 2005.

30 Frank Schirrmacher, *Der Engel fährt zur Hölle - Breloers Film über Albert Speer...* In: Frankfurter Allgemeine Zeitung, March 18, 2006.

31 Überleben durch Talent - Schneewittchens Albtraum. In: Süddeutsche Zeitung, May 17, 2010.

6 The German Sense of Humor

THE NEW OBJECTIVE: WORLDWIDE RECOGNITION FOR GERMAN TRICK FILM

Twelve months before the American premiere of Disney's *Snow White*, *Lichtbild-Bühne* had speculated under the headline "Deutscher Trickfilm weltmarktfähig" (German Trick Film ready to enter the world market) about the question why German animation hadn't achieved worldwide recognition: *Weltgeltung*.

> Doesn't the German animator have imagination? Does he have only inadequate technical equipment? Don't exhibitors want to see his films or don't they want to pay for them? Or are there other invisible resp. unknown factors? How did it come that Mickey Mouse and Felix the Cat delighted us so much, that the *Silly Symphonies* amazed us, cinemas brought us whole series of Betty Boop, the spinach-eating sailor Pop [a.k.a. Popeye] or the little pigs and have booked them mainly for box-office? Was it only a single factor or was it a combined effect?
>
> Well, the German is known for his imagination, for his artistry. German animation stands differ only outwards from the equipment used in Hollywood and other movie capitals whereas the aerial-view camera operated by a single-frame motor including lighting of the glass by incandescent lamps, the film stock and the tracing paper including cels and ink is the same all over. But don't they watch in Paris, London and Rome Reiniger's silhouettes (for instance the marvellous *Prince Achmed*)? *[At this point the author reminds us of the many successfully animated commercials with objects and advertisements that moved frame-by-frame and sometimes created more excitement among the patrons than the feature film.]*
>
> Do they think they don't have enough talent, or don't they dare to "sacrifice" a few hundred feet of film and the fee for the trick film trainees? Animation stands are relatively inexpensive to buy or to produce in the facilities of a big production company. Camera and lighting equipment one will get inexpensively. So that's not an issue. Do we have to blame the cinema owners? Well, they wouldn't be smart if they would pay good money for stupid, boring trick films, but – that is for sure – for good, attractive little supplement films they are gladly willing to pay. The reason is quite obvious! One has not only to rely on adapting the irrepressible Wilhelm Busch (although he has invented downright film types): Our fairy tale characters are numerous; one can also turn to animals, for instance a cute terrier, a duck, a parrot etc., give the animal an attractive name and throw it into all kinds of adventures. In the USA and England, they have begun with well-known comic strip characters as they still run them in the big magazines etc. in inexhaustible sequence. May it be a cart horse or ape, a duck or pelican: it always has to do with enchanting sense of humor, skills and inventive mind to bring the artificial character to life. We sure have enough of such talented men and women among our filmmakers. Let them work, all who are obsessed with trick film. Then, in brief time, German animation will be *weltmarktfähig* and ready to enter the world market. Then it will compete - supported by German color film techniques and

DOI: 10.1201/9781003375548-6

the art of German music – with Felix, Mickey Mouse and all the other film animals from the United States, the "country of the already limited possibilities."[1]

And also in terms of humor, so the National Socialists claim, they have increased – albeit a very special German humor:

> Where in all of the world is a government that rewards those who teach to laugh and makes the gift of smiling? Where are administrations, authorities, statesmen, and partisans who are not afraid to express this publicly? Three years ago, many people in Germany thought the time of laughing was over. Yes, indeed it was over with *that* kind of laughing! With that slimy, obscene and disgusting grinning that drooled from nude revues, which leaped over from dirty jokes. The jokes of those days were tense, the humor was greasy, the funny caprice was suggestive. In the new Germany one can laugh again![2]

A MIXTURE OF THE SUBLIME AND THE BANAL: THE FIRST DOCTORAL THESIS ON ANIMATION IN GERMANY

Research had to be done. An in-depth study was needed to fully explore the differences between American cartoons and European and German culture.

Result was *The Phenomenology and Psychology of Trick Films: Analytical investigations (analysis) of the phenomenological, psychological, and artistic structures of the trick film group.*

This was the title of Reinhold Johann Holtz's thesis, written in 1939 and published in 1940. He called the subject matter *trick film*, because the term animation wasn't used in Germany that often. Holtz was born June 19, 1913, in Hamburg Harburg. He first gained college admission Easter 1933, and after a brief guest performance at *Freiwilliger Arbeitsdienst* [Voluntary fatigue duty], he was allowed to enroll at the Philosophical Faculty of Hanseatic University in the winter semester of 1934/1935: *In addition to historical, literary, and linguistic (English, Japanese) research, my main areas were psychology, philosophy, and psychopathology.*[3]

His thesis evolved in cinematographic colloquia and lectures held by Professor Georg Ernst Anschütz (1886–1953). Inspired by Anschütz's color-sound research and congresses, Holtz attempted to explore the category *cartoon* within the context of its phenomenology, and psychological and artistic significance to the phenomenon film. Doctoral supervisor Anschütz was psychologist, and worked in the field of music psychology and synesthesia. From 1939 to 1945, he was Führer of the Lecturers' Community at the Hamburg University and Federal Leader of all Lecturers at Gau Hamburg.

As reviewers next to Prof. Anschütz Holtz named Dr. Joachim Ritter und Prof. Dr. Hans Bürger-Prinz: Hans Bürger-Prinz (1897–1976) was a physician and psychiatrist, a descendant of German poet Gottfried August Bürger who wrote the original adventures of *Münchhausen* published in 1786. From 1937, he was Professor of Psychiatry and Neurology, since 1933 member of both NSDAP and SA, also member of the National Socialist Teachers' Association, the National Socialist Physicians' Association, and the National Socialist Lecturers' Association. As an honorary judge at the Hereditary Health Court, he was involved in decisions on forced sterilization.

The role of the clinic [University Hospital Hamburg-Eppendorf] and its medical director Bürger-Prinz in cases of "euthanasia" and forced sterilization has not been completely clarified to this day. His own statements about this after the war are questionable. The patient mortality rate was extremely high during the war. The existing documents and death certificates are currently being examined. There is a suspicion that killings took place inside the clinic.[4]

Dr. Joachim Ritter (1903–1974) was lecturer in philosophy and appointed adjunct professor. On May 11, 1933, he belonged to the signers of the Confession of Professors at Universities and Colleges to Adolf Hitler and the National Socialist State, since 1937 member of the NSDAP, the National Socialist Student Combat Aid, the National Socialist, the National Socialist Lecturers' Association, and the National Socialist Public Welfare.

There are 26 works of filmic literature[5] that Holtz quotes in his thesis, but only three books that explicitly deal with (the technical part of) film animation: *Der gezeichnete Film. Ein Handbuch für Filmzeichner und solche, die es werden wollen* by E. G. Lutz, the German translation of an American book (*Animated Cartoons: How They Are Made. Their Origin and Development*, 1913) edited by Dr. Konrad Wolter, *Film-Tricks und Trick-Filme* (1933) by Alexander Stüler, and *Der Trickfilm in seinen grundsätzlichen Möglichkeiten. Eine praktische und theoretische Darstellung der photographischen Filmtricks* (1927) by Guido Seeber who was Paul Wegener's favorite cinematographer and had created the first matchstick animation in Germany in 1909/1910: Matches form different patterns and caricatures until they finally burn down in a windmill made of matchsticks. Before shooting began, Seeber meticulously drew the individual images that were to be animated with the matches in a small notebook: an early example of a storyboard. But otherwise, as a feature film cameraman and expert in photographic effects, Seeber was not that much interested in the tedious, rather static, little varied work of animation photography.

The main sources quoted by Holtz were articles published in the trade journal *Lichtbild-Bühne* founded in 1908 by Karl Wolffsohn, a Jew: *Busch-Sullivan und Mickey-Mouse* (*Wilhelm Busch, Pat Sullivan, and Mickey Mouse*), *Mickey-Mouse farbig* (*Mickey Mouse in Color*), *Amerikanische Tricktechnik* (*American Trick Technique*), *Drei kleine Schweinchen* (*Three Little Pigs*), *Deutscher Trickfilm* (*German Trick Film*), *Trickfilm und Reklame* (*Trick Film and Advertisement*). The filmography[6] lists 76 films, including two feature-length: *Prince Achmed* and *Snow White*. Most of the titles are Disney productions, plus a little bit from Max Fleischer (a Jew, born Majer Fleischer in Cracow, then Austria Hungary) and Paul Terry. Among the Germans listed are Lotte Reiniger, Kurt Stordel, Schwab, Schonger, and the Diehl Brothers. Even some abstract artists are mentioned: Walter Ruttmann, Viking Eggeling, Max Endrejat, Man Ray, and Oskar Fischinger.

The political aim of the thesis was to contrast the content of American animated film with a *German* one the trade press kept postulating for years.

Following the spirit of the times, the work and its method are introduced *weltanschaulich – ideologically:*

> The diverse manifestations of film in the cultural environment of ethnic life have long required comprehensive scientific processing. Even before the National Socialist upheaval there were individual attempts at analytical classification, but their scientific importance was seldom recognized and acknowledged. The reason for this is

primarily found in the assumed irrelevance of film itself. One saw something only casually important, the contents of which only revolved around sensation and which were of no importance whatsoever. This completely ignorant view was only changed when the values of the new ideologically formed Germany permeated general contemporary life. So today, after a few years, we see in the movies a highly significant part of our culture.[7]

In his introduction, Holtz kowtowed Joseph Goebbels, Reich Minister of Public Enlightenment and Propaganda, and mentioned the impulses emanating from him in the film production since 1933:

The big, significant change in the perception of film, however, was brought by the upheaval in the whole public thinking and feeling thanks to National Socialism. This does not mean that German film production has suddenly reached an unimagined height of ideological and artistic expression since 1933. In the beginning the opposite was the case, the cause of which can be found in the obvious economic interests of the old producers. After this crisis was overcome, however, some films appeared which, inspired in their aim by the trend-setting speeches and publications of the patron of German film, Reich Minister Dr. Goebbels, revealed a previously unimagined purity of ideological and artistic intentions.[8]

Holtz welcomes the upheaval of peoples' collective minds, feelings about National Socialism, and the state's recognition of valuable films. He names the most popular cartoons from America, notably Disney's *Mickey Mouse* and *Silly Symphony* series as well as his "imitators," Fleischer and Paul Terry. Compared to these global market leaders, European trick film seems to be weak and inconsistent:

A variety of outward forms inside the group of trick film in Europe is contrasted by a single American manifestation.[9]

A particular advantage of American cartoons of *Mickey Mouse* und *Silly Symphonies,* Holtz saw in the innovative use of sound and in the "racial and peculiar language structure of the North American *Völkergemisch [ethnic mix]* and the resulting difficulties of non-verbal communication on a spiritual level."[10] Especially comic strips, poor in text and clarification, are an indicator for the *Einsprengungen [influence] of alien people and races.*[11] Holtz determines an "incredible brutality" in American cartoons that one finds only in areas that are populated by cruel psychopaths.[12] One has to protect children from such products.

The laughter evoked in American films is of explosive nature and consists of an intense amount of spitefulness evoked by a reaction of primitive functions. Compared with this, German trick film, such as silhouette film, doesn't provoke violent effects. Our laughter is quieter, inwardly and often warmer.[13]

Then Holtz tried to define the term *trick film* which is used in Germany instead of animation:

The word "trick," borrowed from the Anglo-Saxon, means the use of technical or psychological devices – usually only known to the performer – to achieve an effect, which is intended to amaze the passive part of the audience. [...]
    The designation of what is meant by a trick film is a mixture of factual-formal and content-ideological meaning. On the one hand, the trick film technique is in the technical

focus, and on the other hand, the limitation of this technique to the photographic record-ing of non-human actors is decisive for the naming of this group of films.[14]

Basically, Holtz distinguishes the following two types:

The American cartoons: *The American cartoons have found the greatest distri-bution and thus the largest share within the overall group of trick films, gen-erally, albeit incorrectly, called "Mickey Mouse films." This special form is characterized by very direct features that are unmistakably American, have also been successfully copied in the States and from there spread across the continents, but have found no significant imitators in other countries.*[15] As "inventor" Holtz names the "press artist" Walt Disney, as imitators [sic!] Curt [sic! Max] Fleischer and his hero Popeye the Sailor and [Paul] Terry with his characters Farmer Falfa [Al Falfa] and Kiko the Kangaroo.

A weak European production: On the European continent there is no similar cinematic phenomenon neither in the Nordic states nor in Russia, England, or among the Romanic people are cartoons widespread.

In Germany, too, there is no sign of significant increase in any type of trick film. Holtz mentions the synesthetic abstract films of the Brothers Fischinger (Oskar und Hans), the silhouette films of Lotte Reiniger, the drawn fairy tales of Kurt Stordel, the puppet fairy tales by the Brothers Diehl, and more.

The most diverse forms within the trickfilm group in Europe are opposed to a single American type.[16]

The real heyday of trick film began shortly after World War I, around 1920: *It was the time when Expressionism let its paper blossoms grow rampant in the incompetent minds of some hysterics.*[17]

Holtz consistently dedicates some sections of his work to

The abstract film: He particularly refers to Walter Ruttmann's *Opus 1924, which as single-frame style and compositional element has the continuous use of vibration or waves*, the *Symphonie Diagonale* by Viking Eggeling and *Rhythm 21 (Rhythmus 21), and Film Study (Filmstudie)* expressly avoid-ing the name of Hans Richter, a Dadaist, who left Germany in 1933, and only mentioning Richter's cameraman Max Endrejat.[18]

The abstract musical trick film, which includes the work of two brothers, Oskar Fischinger's *Composition in Blue (Komposition in Blau)* and Hans Fischinger's *Dance of Colors (Tanz der Farben)*.

In contrast to *Film Study*, which mainly uses meandering moving lines and smaller dashes, dots, etc., *Composition in Blue* mainly shows large colored circles, rectan-gles, cylinders, and pyramids:

What is essentially new is the movement of these elements in the sense of a change of size, a change of color, a reversal of direction and a transition to the rhythm of the music and in sync with it. The color and the impression of the dimensional reserve a preferential position for Composition in Blue compared to the others.[19]

The other trend in European trick film lies, according to Holtz, in fairy tales: *In fairy tales, the predominantly epic-lyrical form of folk art, a number of racially, ideologically and symbolically important content is shaped, which was disseminated from generation to generation exclusively by the word.*[20] Holtz lists Lotte Reiniger, the puppet films (Holtz: "fairy-tale object films") by Ferdinand and Hermann Diehl, Starewicz, finally the drawn films from by Kurt Stordel, a one-man company.

Then the author talks in detail about the American cartoons, particularly Disney's *Mickey Mouse* and *Silly Symphonies* series. The latter are color cartoons with a strong emphasis on sound:

> Whereas the first *Mickey Mouse* films had no sound [sic!], and sound only later found a meaning in the predominant accentuation in the sense of more noisy illustration, the color *Silly* films without sound are unthinkable. The color and melodious music make these films appear as an undoubtedly different from of American cartoons altogether. The drama of the black [sic! black and white] films has given way here to a lyrical mood.[21]

To please Bürger-Prinz, Holtz included a section on the *Psychology of American cartoons, the morphological structure of its viewer, and its artistic significance.* He comes to an astonishing conclusion that fits perfectly into the context of National Socialist ideology:

> The American cartoon owes its origins to its present-day significance to the peculiar racial and linguistic composition of the North American ethnic mixture and the resulting difficulties of a non-linguistic understanding in the spiritual realm. It should be noted that with regard to the genesis of the trick film that it is most likely to be derived from the comic strips, which occupy a large space in the American daily press. What is striking about these drawings is the lack of textual explanations. The drawn situations are understood without comment from the pictures themselves. Only very occasionally does one find interspersed short exclamations. It is evident that only this species could find general distribution within the United States, with their hundreds of thousands foreign people and races.[22]

Accordingly, there is a rich but uncomplicated and undifferentiated variety on a predominantly mental basis, which excludes from the outset any inclusion of somehow higher mental functions that could raise a certain request for emotional education.

On closer inspection of a trick film, it is immediately apparent that the quasi-human behavior of the characters is portrayed in an extremely crass, downright cruel manner. Considered by itself, for example, such a scene represents outrageous brutality in the human realm that can only be found in the context of affect crime or in emotionally weak psychopaths.[23]

No food for kids: When compiling children's programs from black-and-white and color American cartoons, it was found that children between the ages of six and puberty had absolutely no understanding or even any experience concerning black-and-white trick film, e. g., *Popeye* films. This is different with color and object/puppet films, which are based in most cases on fairy tales or lyrical sources. Otherwise, it is wrong to define the world of cartoons as a world of children: *Rather, the term infantile should be used here.*[24]

The question arises:

> In which way and through what contact with psychic functional groups can the extraor-
> dinary effect on the one hand and the extensive spread of American cartoons be made
> understandable? The fact already that this kind of film has found such extraordinary
> sympathy among the more or less emotionally educated masses of America and the
> rest of the world gives reason to assume that here, to speak with [Carl Gustav] Jung,
> primarily not rational circumstances, but collective mental areas are addressed. When
> critically reviewing trick films, it is inevitable that the logical, rational mechanisms of
> apperception must perform at a minimum.[25]
>
> A question that is particularly important in this context concerns the ecstasy as
> a relapse into the state of the instinctively acting animal: as theme of the plot, such
> ecstatic states can be shown in many ways in cartoons (*The Goddess of Spring*, *The
> Golden Touch and Mickey Playful Pluto*, e.g., Mickey Mouse cartoon *Playful Pluto*).
> Primitive, magical customs are addressed here, which as such are immediately under-
> stood by the viewer, but cannot arouse any emotions in him with regard to his own
> ecstatic experience. However, we believe that for some viewers, provided they are
> "carried away," the ecstatic element is a co-determining and supporting factor in this
> experience.[26]

The most conspicuous emotional reaction triggered in the watcher by drawn trick
film is laughter. Especially when it comes to humor, it's about being rooted in
Weltanschauung:

> We too are of the opinion that, from a higher point of view, what we call humor in the
> best sense of the word requires an ideological sobriety. [...]
>
> The higher points of view shown are undoubtedly not useful to explain the phe-
> nomena of comedy found in trick film. We even consider that the term humor is not
> acceptable. What is shown in drawn trickfilm are primarily caricatures, grotesques and
> situation comedy. Even the wide distribution and the demand for general comprehen-
> sibility exclude the addition of finely oriented mental references. The grotesque, which
> in European culture is to be found mainly in the Nordic countries, experienced its real
> heyday in cartoons in America.[27]

Holtz confirms a logical contradiction here, a mixture of the sublime and the banal,
a cheerfulness caused by the strong dynamic differences:

> The laughter evoked by the American film is explosive in nature and contains a strong
> element of malicious joy, as the reactions it triggers stem from primitive functions in
> the viewer, which in no way means that educated personalities are inaccessible to this
> stimulus. In contrast, German trick film, such as silhouette film, does not trigger such
> violent effects. Rather, the laughter is quieter, more inward and usually warmer, which
> seems clear from the ideology of our films. Here the term humor is much more justi-
> fied than in American films. It is nevertheless striking that in Germany, the country
> of [Fritz] Reuter and [Wilhelm] Busch, such a small number of laughable films is pro-
> duced. We would like to explain this from the specific talent of the Germans for humor
> and the difficulty of presenting it in film, just as the special talent of the Anglo-Saxons
> for the grotesque and situational humor (Twain, Swift, Jerome) is the prerequisite for
> the emergence of comic strips and cartoon films of the American type.[28]

The Germans, Holtz concludes, simply lack the talent for American exaggera-
tion, which is ultimately a product of American racial mixing. *But the products
of the northern European countries, such as the Danes and Swedes, are deeper,*

more abysmal, and sometimes more malicious in their humorous works than those of the Americans...[29]

In his work, Holtz did not have any clue how to improve Nazi German animation. The first German dissertation on the subject of cartoons had no consequences. Reinhold Johann Holtz died on November 12, 1989.

LET THE PUPPETS DANCE

It was speculated that one way to make Germany an animation producer to rival Disney would be to turn to alternative animation techniques: puppets and stop motion. In that technique Europe, especially Germany, had far more experience than Hollywood. And, by the way, wasn't *King Kong* an animated puppet too?

In September 1938, film journalist Frank Maraun [Erwin Goelz] visited Władysław Starewicz in Paris. The Russian exile, born to Polish parents in Moscow, was a famous puppet filmmaker and creator of the feature-length *Story of the Fox*. Starewicz claimed he had discovered a movie formula that could beat Disney. That sounded interesting for the Germans, since the import of Disney films during the war was out of question:

> Contrary to Disney, the animals are no little machines but living entities, almost human.
>
> Anyone who has seen *The Story of the Fox* and who knows Disney will find this differentiation very affecting. Starewicz's film, compared to Walt Disney's animal grotesqueness, has the advantage of an unlikely higher level of liveliness and naturalism. In his finer, tender, saturated tone of fairy tale, he is closer to our feeling. Against the saucy, clean step of civilisation of the American, the Pole convincingly represents old Europe with its culture grown in emotion and rich in tradition. About Disney one can laugh and marvel, but Starewicz one has to love.[30]

One producer, Jürgen Clausen, who knew the puppet filmmaker, tried to promote Starewicz's ideas. He approached Tobis Filmkunst company on May 30, 1941, and offered to produce color puppet films as well as establish a color film studio. Clausen was an expert in both fields due to his work as a business and production manager at both Gasparcolor Werbefilm G.m.b.H. and Gasparcolor Naturwahre Farbenfilm G.m.b.H. Clausen re-issued Oskar Fischinger's abstract *Composition in Blue* in a special screening of *Color Advertising Films* on October 30, 1938, in Hamburg's Waterloo Cinema. And as he had been involved in processing stop motion films, particularly George Pal's shorts for Philips in Eindhoven, Clausen seemed to be the right choice for Tobis heads Ewald von Demandowsky and Karl Julius Fritzsche. They offered him a one-year contract, beginning on July 1, 1941, with a monthly payment of RM 2,500.

During the war, Clausen, together with Herbert Pohris, provided a memorandum for Tobis Filmkunst in December 1941. Herbert Pohris, co-author of the memo, was a Berlin painter and a member of NSDAP since 1931 (membership no. 724 929). For a monthly fee of temporarily RM1,000, he was hired as consultant, writer-director, and artist-designer. With their memo, both men wanted to talk Tobis into setting up a puppet film studio (if only to please the animated ambitions of the Minister of Public Enlightenment and Propaganda and his many children). They claimed: We can do better with animated puppets than Disney with animated drawings. In the end, the plan, however, failed, but what was suggested is, beyond all propaganda, still food for thought:

> Is one allowed today, as German people not only fight for their economic and political existence but even more for the culture of the Occident, to bring up such question? Namely, as in this case, for the direct purpose of founding and systematically establishing a very special and in Germany only little noticed let alone acknowledged production, the production of feature-length color puppet trick films?
>
> Well – if you are allowed to do so or not, government is going to decide. And that here we got order to hoist the colors of the art even – and even the more – during the war is prerequisite of our planning and working.
>
> *Art is Food – Joy is Strength*
>
> Art often is more important to war than army bread: every soldier who left the trenches and got into a front theatre will confirm this. In this – and only this – regard every discussion is superfluous.
>
> And it includes the right acknowledgment of the puppet trick film. [...]
>
> *Only in Germany!*
>
> The puppet or dimensional trick is located in the European cultural space, and no other country can be its more natural home than Germany. The German is deeply dimensionally-romantic, profoundly imaginative, he is dreamy and contemplative. None other succeeds that well in <u>humorous</u> grotesque (see Wilhelm Busch) so definitely that one can count it almost into classic art – classic in a sense of perfection of expression. All of this means a splendid, not to say decisive predestination for the dimensional trick film and – an obligation. Space and depth oblige the German-Nordic identity. Therefore, important results will be accomplished much faster with the German dimensional trick film than hand-drawn animation which is burdened with Disney's virtuoso style.

Jürgen Clausen demanded that the German puppet films follow the *Puppetoon* replacement animation technique of émigré producer George Pal. Animated feature films, Jürgen Clausen wrote in his memo, are expensive, but they make a lot of money not only from cinema revenues but also from merchandising:

> *Puppet Trickfilm and German Toy Industry*
>
> In reference to American animation film, a unique insemination of the toy has occurred, which results for instance in the fact that after release of the Mickey Mouse or Pig films and later after *Snow White* and *Pinocchio* not only children's books were published in millions of copies based on the artwork and characters of the Disney production, but also toys, puppets and records invaded European countries (bijouterie: necklaces, buttons, stickers etc.). In Paris, for instance, many shop windows were decorated with characters of the *Snow White* picture. The same is true for the George Pal production in Holland. Here, too, the most prominent characters from various Pal films were absorbed by the toy industry and were exploited.
>
> The German toy industry up until now was leading in the whole world, especially the German children's puppet industry. We are absolutely sure that out of German puppet film production an equally extensive as well as necessary insemination of German toy industry will result, so that later an interaction will occur: puppet trick film will support toy industry and vice versa. Add to it that Pal's technique (use of simple work forms like cone, ball, cylinder etc.) is well suited for mass production. This is the technically best prerequisite for animated film featuring plastic color bodies and on the other hand simplifies the transfer into efficient production methods of the toy industry.

The toy industry will have to learn from color dimensional trickfilm if it wants to play the role again, particularly as an export industry, in the wide world as it has done before. –

The document indicates that Pal himself had already moved to America two years previously, but that his collaborators, mainly from the Netherlands, and their know-how were still available. Some were working in the movies. Others had returned to their original craftsman jobs. As a special coup, Clausen had hired some of them to build the nucleus of future production. Clausen's clear objective was to create feature-length puppet films in color. He estimated RM1,5 and 1,7 million per puppet feature, but in August 1942 Clausen's ambitious plans for puppet animation were vetoed by the Film Department of the Ministry of Enlightenment and Propaganda for reasons caused by the war. On March 14, 1944, *Film-Kurier* reported Clausen's death as combat newsreel cameraman.

GOLD-DONKEY AND CUDGEL-OUT-OF-THE-SACK

The producers of German puppet films were a different breed. They were slow in mind and animation. When Pal left Germany in 1933, the only noteworthy creators of puppet films were the Brothers Diehl. The Diehls made a rather portly 53-min-ute version of Grimm's *Die sieben Raben (The Seven Ravens)* that was theatrically released but to no great acclaim.[31] In 1985, on the occasion of the Berlin International Film Festival, I arranged a meeting between Ray Harryhausen, a protégé of *Kong's* chief technician Willis O'Brien, and Ferdinand Diehl who passed away in 1992. They seemed to like each other, but once he had left George Pal, Ray Harryhausen didn't think in terms of puppets or dolls anymore. On the other hand, the Diehls never tried to do something like *Kong* or even what Ray Harryhausen did in his teens in his parents' garage. They survived by releasing puppet films for education and for the front commissioned by the state-controlled Reichsanstalt für Film und Bild in Wissenschaft und Unterricht (an institution devoted to release films and slides to schools and universities) (Figure 6.1):

FIGURE 6.1 Ferdinand Diehl. (Author's collection.)

In our front cinema which regularly screens cine-films from local film rentals we have seen two films from the German fairy tale world: *Tischlein deck dich (Table-Be-Set)* and *Stadtmaus und Feldmaus (The Town Mouse and the Country Mouse)*. At the beginning my comrades smiled a little bit. But then there was evidence that the fairy-tale pictures had to offer a lot more for the soldier. Not only was it an hour of entertainment, forgetting all sorrows and trouble of our battle. Many thought deeper. Since the days of our childhood for the first time something plastically rose before our very eyes. We recalled the long-forgotten days of our childhood and youth. Our comrades who are family fathers thought about the content of the pictures and at the same time were reminded of their wives and children at home. Because of that the fairy-tale films touched anybody notwithstanding the deeper meaning behind the plot. We said to ourselves that these, too, are cultural treasures of our people which we must preserve for a future generation by defending our native country, even by risking our life. War last not least is fought not only for material but for cultural goods. And therefore, these films have conveyed to the soldiers the meaning of their present life task and have awakened their enthusiasm...[32]

The soldiers weren't alone in their opinions of the films, Hitler Youth members also found something in these fairy tales that deeply touched them. An eighth-grade pupil, who saw the Diehls' version of *Tischlein deck dich,* wrote a school essay:

Yesterday to much laughter of the undergraduate class we saw the picture *Tischlein deck dich (Table-Be-Set/The Wishing Table).* For us grown-ups the fairy tale, however, provided more than entertainment and joy. For in every fairy tale there is a deeper meaning. Today we discussed with our teacher the deeper meaning of this fairy tale.

Two tailor's sons acquired, according to the fairy tale, by hard work prosperity and wealth. One got a Table-Be-Set with magic properties: "Tischlein deck dich," the other a Gold Donkey: *"Eselein streck dich."* Happily, they returned home. But the evil and envious landlord robbed them of prosperity and wealth. Luck seemed to have deserted them.

The third brother, however, put an abrupt end to the fraud of the host through the *"Knüppel aus dem Sack"* (Cudgel-out-of-the-sack). This demonstrates that for the maintenance and security of prosperity and wealth a strong Wehrmacht [German military] is necessary, just a Cudgel-out-of-the-sack. It alone is able to regain for the others the lost treasures.

The three sons of the tailor come, as the fairy tale tells us, from Dingsda (Dingbat). *Dingda,* however, is somewhere in Germany, it can be anywhere. So the three brothers represent our whole German nation which has to master life as the three apprentices do. The little goblin, however, that lives in fairy-tale land and gives the brothers work and pay, represents the luck that everybody needs. For a time, it seemed as if luck had abandoned the good three brothers; but then it returns to them forever.

The treacherous host, who hoped to get rich by employing swindle and meanness, faced the fate of punishment. He resembles the eternal Jew who wants to profit from the work of the diligent and capable without moving a single finger. He is a *Schmarotzer* [parasite] who only wants to suck the others and exploit them. In spite of his smartness, he can't escape punishment; for there is the Cudgel-out-of-the-sack.

So at the end of our review, we have come to the conclusion:

1. By work German people acquire prosperity and wealth.
2. The evil Jew wants to rob the German people of prosperity and wealth.
3. German people, however, secures its prosperity and wealth by a strong army.
4. Only a hard-working nation is lucky in the long run.

This fairy tale strengthens and invigorates us in our unruly belief in the *Endsieg* [final victory] of Germany in this war. Its "Cudgel-out-of-the-sack" drums heavily on the back of our enemies until all who have called upon the cudgel will buckle like the malicious host did.[33]

Nonetheless, business-minded officials were asking for 2D animation Disney-style, not for 3D Diehl puppets and dimensional animation. Germany was going to challenge Disney in his own field: 2D animation, not with the wooden heads of dolls.

Concerning this objective, the main question was: Were there any artists and animators in Germany who would fill the bill?

NOTES

1 Lichtbild-Bühne, January 1, 1937.
2 Review of the Heinz Rühmann comedy *Wenn wir alle Engel wären*, 1936.
3 *Die Phänomenologie und Psychologie des Trickfilms. Analytische Untersuchungen über die phänomenologischen, psychologischen und künstlerischen Strukturen der Trickfilmgruppe.* Doctoral Thesis by Reinhold Johann Holtz. Hamburg: Hansische Universität, 1940. 1st Referee: Prof. Dr. Georg Anschütz. 2nd Referee: Prof. Dr. Hans Bürger-Prinz.
4 Universitätsklinikum Hamburg-Eppendorf: *Geschichte der Klinik. Vom Mittelalter bis zu ersten Irrenanstalt in Hamburg.*
5 Holtz, *Die Phänomenologie und Psychologie des Trickfilms*, pp. 53–56.
6 Ibid., pp. 56–58.
7 Ibid., p. 5.
8 Ibid., p. 8.
9 Ibid., p. 11.
10 Ibid., p. 20.
11 Ibid., p. 29.
12 Ibid., p. 30.
13 Ibid., p. 52.
14 Ibid., pp. 8–9.
15 Ibid., p. 10.
16 Ibid., p. 11.
17 Ibid., p. 12.
18 Ibid., p. 13. Endrejat later worked on propaganda films such as *Klar Schiff zum Gefecht. Ein Film von der deutschen Flotte* (1936), *Der Westwall* (1939) and as combat cameraman on *Kampf um Norwegen* (*Battle for Norway*, 1940).
19 Ibid., p. 15f.
20 Ibid., p. 16.
21 Ibid., p. 20.
22 Ibid., p. 29.
23 Ibid., p. 30.
24 Ibid., p. 30.
25 Ibid., p. 41.
26 Ibid., p. 45.
27 Ibid., p. 51.
28 Ibid., p. 52.
29 Ibid., p. 39.
30 September 1938: Der deutsche Film: *"Poet am Tricktisch" Besuch bei Starewitsch.*
31 There was a limited American release of that picture in 1952 by M & A Productions Inc.
32 *Märchenfilme bei den Soldaten.* In Film und Bild, Reichsanstalt für Film und Bild in Wissenschaft und Unterricht, Issue 4/5, May 1, 1942.
33 July 4, 1941 Deutscher Kulturdienst: *"Knüppel aus dem Sack"* School essay – recorded by Ferdinand Josef Holzer. Collection of J. P. Storm.

7 The Dangerous Freedom of a Quarter Jew in Magicland

THE STRUGGLE FOR ARYANNESS

The first choice of a Disney challenger would have been Wolfgang Kaskeline, but Ufa had renounced his services.

On November 1, 1933, the National Socialists revised the Reichskulturkammer [Reich Culture Chamber] *Law*. According to §4, all artists and technicians involved in the making of animated films were requested to register their company with Reichsfilmkammer. Their employees had to apply for membership in the section Reichsfachschaft Film [Reich Film Department].

Wolfgang Kaskeline did so on January 25, 1934,[1] but he had serious problems to produce documents to prove his so-called Aryan background.

On September 17, 1935, the Ufa Board of Directors discussed this issue:

> Herr Grieving announces that Reichsfilmkammer has prohibited animator Kaskeline from continuing work as non-Aryan. The Board assents to pay his fee until end of this month. Also Kaskeline should receive an interest-free loan up to RM5,000 on October 1, 1935.

On September 23, 1935, *Reichsfachschaft Film* reported to the President of Reichsfilmkammer and denounced Wolfgang Kaskeline:

> Subsequent to our letter of December 19 we have to tell you that it was determined post hoc that Wolfgang Kaskeline (advertising film cartoonist and director) is n o n - A r y a n.
>
> In the marriage certificate his father is registered as Jew.
>
> Kaskeline has suppressed this fact in his application to Reichsfachschaft Film on January 25, 1934, and indicated parentage as: German Protestant.
>
> We request herewith the expulsion of said person from Reichsfilmkammer resp. Reichsfachschaft Film.

On October 1, 1935, Reichsfilmkammer wrote to Wolfgang Kaskeline and asked him for his comment within three days.

Nevertheless, the manager of Reichskulturkammer, Hans Hinkel, allowed to employ Kaskeline *"bis auf weiteres"* [for the time being] until the fundamental question how to deal in the cases of so-called *Halb- & Vierteljuden* [Half- and Quarter-Jews] has been resolved.

On June 5, 1939, Reichsfilmkammer forwarded a petition signed by Kaskeline to Reichsstelle für Sippenforschung (Berlin NW 7, Schiffbauerdamm 26):

DOI: 10.1201/9781003375548-7

Wolfgang Kaskeline   *Berlin S 19, 11/6/34*
Universum-Film   *Krausenstr. 38/39*
Aktiengesellschaft

To Reich Ministry of Interior,

Bureau for Racial Research, Berlin.

The undersigned asks for recognition of his Aryan descent according to §2 decree for the screening of foreign films dated June 27, 34, next-to-last passage, because he, as he explains below in more detail, is not able to submit documents about the actual Aryan descent of his father and grandfather who both came from Finland.

I was born as German citizen on September 23, 92 in Frankfurt a[m] M[ain] and baptized Protestant as son of merchant Viktor Samuel Kaskeline and his wife Katharina née Scherf. My father, who already as a young man had immigrated from Finland and was German citizen, died in 1931 in South Italy. My mother lives in Berlin. I have forwarded the hitherto missing documents concerning the parents of my mother to the contingency office for information.

Despite of all my efforts, I myself, my brother who lives in Rome, and my brother-in-law Bruno von Alt-Stutterheim were not successful in collecting any document concerning the birth of my father and grandfather Kaskeline, and such concerning the marriage of my parents in Genoa. The Kaskeline family origins, as the name says, from Finland and, as is known to my family, generations ago immigrated from Toscana. Any two generations in Finland were glass painters and glass burners, and due to their profession had traveled frequently around the world.

Because of the political change of system in Finland, research regarding the Russian time is extremely difficult, especially as my father, who died in a foreign country didn't leave any documents, because he wasn't interested very much in family history. However, it is certain that there is no evidence of Jewish blood in our family. I leave this issue to an expert assessment. My only brother who entered the war as volunteer, became a pilot and left as lieutenant, is living in Rome for 8 years. I myself entered the Elizabeth Guard Grenadier Regiment on August 1, 14 as war volunteer, was transferred to Infantry Regiment 203, 11th Company, and was severely wounded on October 26, [19]14 in the battle of Dixmuiden. I was made private and received the E.K 2 [Iron Cross 2nd Class]. After a two-year stay in the military hospital, I was released as 70% war invalid because of my wound (stiffening of the knee joint, shortage of the right leg, Peronnaeus paralyzation and Fascialis paralyzation) and received a pension from relief organization.

The past 7 years I worked for Universum-Film-Aktiengesellschaft as an artist and now have to attest my Aryan background according to the mentioned contingency decree. Therefore, I ask politely to certify that I am of Aryan descent.

I am married to Minna Kaskeline née Berg since 1917. She comes from Buchwald i. Riesengebirge [Giant Mountain range in Silesia] and is of pure Aryan descent.

Mit deutschem Gruss
Signed with German greeting, Wolfgang Kaskeline.

But nobody believed what Kaskeline said. Attached to his letter was the following official comment:

> Regarding the origin of his father, the testee explains that he is not able to prove and submit records of the actual Aryan descent of his father and grandfather who both come from Finland. His father (Viktor Samuel Kaskeline), who already as a young man immigrated from Finland and was German citizen died in 1931 in South Italy. Despite of greatest efforts, the testee writes, he, his brother, who lives in Rome, and his brother-in-law, Bruno von Alt-Stutterheim, were not successful in collecting birth certificates of his father and grandfather Kaskeline and the marriage certificate of his parents from Genoa. The Kaskeline family origins, as the name says, from Finland and shall have immigrated, according to a tradition only known to the family, generations ago from Toscana. Any two generations were glass painters in Finland and glass burners and have travelled due to their profession all over the world. "Certain, however, is only that there is no evidence of Jewish blood in our family. I leave this issue to an expert assessment." "Therefore, I ask politely to certify that I am of Aryan descent."
>
> These statements of the testee are lies. The same false statements were also made concerning the pedigree paper of Reichsfilmkammer. The father Viktor Emanuel Kaskeline comes not from Finland; he was actually born on December 28, 1858, in Teplitz/Bohemia as son of the **Jewish** couple Ludwig Kaskeline and Linna Schlesinger. The marriage of the testee's parents was not contracted in Genoa but on March 30, 1887, in Frankfurt/Main (according to marriage certificate No. 336 of the register office in Frankfurt/Main, district I, issued on August 3, 1935). This certificate was located by the Pedigree Office of Reichsfilmkammer without any problems and with it the statements of the testee disproved. The mother of the testee, Mrs. Katharina Kaskeline née Scherf, who lives in Berlin, could have told her son and son-in-law if asked about day and location of their marriage.
>
> The request of Wolfgang Kaskeline (dated November 6, 1934) addressed to the Office for Race Research, to confirm that he is of Aryan descent, is, considering the (false) statements, a manifestation of greatest audacity. [...]
>
> You will have to check the petition and decide if regarding the poor and doubtful material the application for hereditary and race file of Wolfgang Kaskeline can be approved. We have refrained from asking the testee to submit more means of evidence as requested.
>
> *Heil Hitler!*
> *REICHSFILMKAMMER*
> *Pedigree Office*
> *signed by proxy, Dr. Jacob.*

By special permission of the Reich Minister dated July 25, 1939, at any time revocable, Wolfgang Kaskeline was allowed to continue in his profession, until conclusion of the current investigation of his descent by Reich Office for Hereditary Research. On February 1, 1940, *Reichsfilmkammer* reported to Fachschaft Film:

RE: WOLFGANG KASKELINE

The Reich Ministry for Public Enlightenment and Propaganda announces by decree from January 27, 1940, as follows:

After receiving now pedigree paper from Reichsstelle für Sippenforschung [Reich Office for Family Research] which has arranged for a hereditary and race investigation at the Poliklinik für Erb- und Rassenpflege [Polyclinic for Hereditament and Race

Cultivation], Berlin-Charlottenburg, in the case of Wolfgang Kaskeline, the above
mentioned is Vierteljude [One-Quarter Jew].

Thus, there are no objections against his registration as fully-valid member of your
Chamber.

Nevertheless, Kaskeline's career in the Third Reich had virtually come to an end, at
least for some years to come.

PURZEL THE DWARF BINDS A FAIRY-TALE WREATH

Next in line were Kurt Stordel and Luis Seel. Stordel was a graphic artist and
book illustrator. Although he had no experience in animation, he was commissioned by a Hamburg-based advertising company to try and draw a trick film.
With an old camera equipped with a stop frame device, Stordel began his first
experiments.

The initial spark was provided by a *Felix the Cat* cartoon, but the idea to found
his own animation company came to Stordel after attending the screening of an early
Mickey Mouse cartoon in a Hamburg cinema. Due to the Depression, he failed to
make any profit. The year 1932 was not a prosperous one, neither for society nor an
animation studio. Stordel mainly did advertising to survive but refused to do por-
nographic cartoons, which in those days were sold to (and via) South America. His
objective was the family-friendly animated fairy tale.

Finally, in mid-1935, he opened a studio for documentary, advertising, and animation films. Together with his wife he developed the idea of a *German Fairy Wreath*
(*Deutscher Märchenkranz*) and announced that the first cartoon would be *Graf
Habenichts*—an adaptation of *Puss in Boots* (*Der gestiefelte Kater*): *Reference to
the grotesque style of Walt Disney was consciously avoided. Stordel's films shall be
funny, romantic, folksy. The background of the individual sequences is rendered in
grey water colors to evoke soft color tones.*[2]

Moving his small family enterprise to Berlin-Charlottenburg, he turned out more
entries in his *German Fairy Tale Cycle*, and produced a number of black and white
animation films with *Sleeping Beauty* (*Dornröschen*), *The Bremen Town Musicians*
(*Die Bremer Stadtmusikanten*), and *Hansel and Gretel*.

A journalist of a trade paper visited Stordel and his wife in their Berlin apartment:

> In the big city of Berlin, in Moabit, the young artist Kurt Stordel lives with his wife in
> a middle-class 4 room flat. The young couple, however, doesn't belong to those quiet
> people for whom the Sunday chicken in the pot means the fulfilment of all earthly
> wishes. They are imaginative people who on top of it are in league with film. [...]
>   Clearly contrary to foreign animators, who mainly focus on gags and for whom the
> idea is essential, Stordel proceeds from content and from strong romanticism. This
> shows in his work. Instead of sharp outlines he prefers soft watercolor, instead of hard
> color, stains and blots the more effective but more difficult nuances. The key frames he
> draws himself. His wife supports him in tracing them onto cels.[3]

One of Stordel's creations was Purzel, a dwarf in Magicland (Figure 7.1). *Völkischer
Beobachter*, the newspaper of the Nazi Party, hailed the product as a first-rate
German cartoon:

Nobody should ask which fairy tale shall be filmed. There is no answer to this question. Nothing will be turned into a film what German people possess in treasures of fairy tales. Stordel loaned his creatures from cartoonists, draughtsmen and painters and one should let them go as they were conceived by their creators. If we wouldn't be able to newly invent nice and funny plots, things would be looking bad for us. The trick film is an absolutely modern invention and so the contents which he deals with have to be new and topical.[4]

One should be anxious to see if Stordel will succeed in breaking Walt Disney's present autocracy over the "German fairy tale forest." In fact, in the interest of German filmmaking it should be wished that this gap in the field of short films will be filled if one considers the many excellent attempts for instance in the advertising films.[5]

FIGURE 7.1   Kurt Stordel's *Purzel the Dwarf* starred in two shorts. (Courtesy of J. P. Storm.)

In another interview Kurt Stordel stressed that, good heavens, he didn't want to become a Walt Disney.[6]

In March 1940, after a nonpublic screening of Disney's *Snow White* in the cinema of the Propaganda Ministry in Jägerstrasse, Kurt Stordel received an offer from UFA to join their newly established trick film studio. Although he was interested in staying independent, in July 1940 he eventually signed a contract primarily to avoid getting drafted. Stordel was selected to helm UFA's prestige project *Quick macht Hochzeit* (*Quick Marries*), but a year later, in July 1941, the production was canceled. Stordel was too much a self-made man to stomp a German Disney Empire of the ground, and he was obviously burdened by (nonproven) rumors to be unreliable (Figure 7.2).

FIGURE 7.2 *Quick macht Hochzeit* (*Quick Marries*), unfinished UFA project supervised by Kurt Stordel. (Courtesy of J. P. Storm.)

More experienced than Stordel was Luis Seel, who was in charge of another Berlin-based trick film studio funded by Tobis Filmkunst—the company that had rejected Clausen (Figure 7.3). Seel and his associate Bernhard Klein planned a color cartoon:

> Rübezahl, the folkloristic ghost in the decisive battle of existence for the nation, not only maintains the unabated standard of production in peacetime, but above that is going to break new ground and make it fertile out of European tradition and spiritual outlook for Europe.[7]

FIGURE 7.3 Original artwork from Luis Seel's unfinished *Rübezahl* project. (Courtesy of J. P. Storm.)

Luis Seel was allegedly a true animation pioneer who had worked in North and South America. At the end of August 1939, he was summoned back to the German capital from Rio, Brazil. 25 years ago, he had been involved in cartooning in New York, and had joined Bud Fisher in the production of *Mutt and Jeff* cartoons (Figure 7.4).

FIGURE 7.4   *Rübezahl.* (Courtesy of J. P. Storm.)

Seel and his unit worked for almost a year, but suddenly a rival turned up the idea of forming a German animation film company controlled by the Ministry of Enlightenment and Propaganda. Subsequently, the Tobis company was closed down. Seel was sidelined and worked for some time for a company in Prague where his trace is lost (Figure 7.5).

FIGURE 7.5   A look into the Tobis Studio: Animation under the portrait of the "Fuhrer." (Courtesy of J. P. Storm.)

The throne of the top German animation expert did not go to an animation expert but to a Nazi bureaucrat who had previously worked in meant and sausage factories.

BLOWN TO DEATH WITH A JAZZ TRUMPET

As Nazi Germany was not able, and finally not willing to raise the high costs and foreign currency to buy and release Disney's *Snow White and the Seven Dwarfs*, and Stordel, Seel, and others were not up to the task of truly becoming a German version of Walt Disney, Goebbels decided to enter the ring himself. In the midst of World War II, he took the bull by the horns and established his own cartoon factory. However, it was not Disney that gave the impetus to create a German animation industry, but rather the feature-length animation film of a Jewish producer: *Gulliver's Travels* (1939) by Max Fleischer. Money would be no problem. To head the new company, Goebbels selected a member of his own staff. Only qualification: devout Nazi.

Karl Neumann, a councillor, was a long-time trusted official of Goebbels' and a party member since 1931, but had had nothing to do with art or animation. In fact, as usual with Nazi parvenus, he was a complete layman. Neumann's career was based on accounting, meat, and sausages. On October 15, 1934, Neumann became referee in the Reich Ministry for Public Enlightenment and Propaganda. He helped to prepare Hitler speeches and reorganized Deutsche Kulturfilmzentrale—the German Culture Film Department. Goebbels was satisfied with Neumann's activities: "Neumann has whipped this into shape."[8] Neumann seized the opportunity and found himself a trickfilm producer, the German equivalent of Walt Disney (Figure 7.6).

FIGURE 7.6 Karl Neumann, a protégé of Dr. Goebbels. (Courtesy of J. P. Storm.)

Goebbels believed that Disney's days were numbered. He and Neumann began to pay attention to rumors that Disney's studio in Burbank was on the verge of bankruptcy after a 1940 European export deficit of $1,259,798. Immediately, Goebbels saw a chance to fill the bill and Neumann reinforced him. On May 15, 1941, Goebbels noted in his diary that he had examined Neumann's memo about German cartoon film production: "I will support this, because it is a good and useful matter." A day later he was prepared to give Neumann free rein in building a production company on an even larger scale.

On August 7, 1941, the entry Deutsche Zeichenfilm Gesellschaft mit beschränkter Haftung (DZF), the German Animation Company Limited was published in the commercial register of the Berlin-Charlottenburg court district.

Because Neumann and his right-hand man, scenarist Frank Leberecht, who was a journalist and had been involved in cultural films, were novices to trick film making, both sought the advice of a specialist whom they found in Dr. Werner Kruse. In 1934, Kruse had established an animation company in Berlin. Kruse had successfully studied Disney's early "rubber hose and circle" formula style, as practiced in the basic creation of the *Mickey Mouse* to design and build cartoon characters.

In a memo Neumann, assisted by Kruse, stated:

> The distribution head of a big state company explained that one could not reach what Disney had achieved as he is a unique genius. When Disney would die, it would be over with animated films. In defeatist manner mouth-to-mouth propaganda has been employed that it (namely the establishment of an animation film production with the goal of producing feature-length films) never would come true. The working methods would be too expensive and would schedule for much too long preproduction. The whole issue was begun with too much grandeur. *Against such "defeatism" Neumann demanded:* Instead of an alienated trick film proletariat of technical supporting forces that without any passion stolidly draws its lines, a special professional type of responsible and creative artist craftsman must develop in German animation. [...]
>
> If one considers that Disney has worked on the movie *Snow White* for two years with 500 men after training and expanding his employees over 15 years in the production of short films, one easily will understand that until the start of production of feature-length cartoons in Germany there is still a long way to go. It will be even longer if one approaches the clearly manageable solution of the assignment less determined and less goal-directed.
>
> Of course, Deutsche Zeichenfilm G.m.b.H. can skip many of Walt Disney's years of apprenticeship provided one will not force upon it a narrow-minded, limited, purely capitalist amortization afflicted with deadlines that are too short.
>
> In this sense I have understood the Minister's remark in the personal meeting on July 18, 1941, in which you took part and in which he said that in Germany it doesn't need to last so long as in Walt Disney's case. [...]
>
> The past week we negotiated with the famed Norwegian commercial artist [Harald] Damsleth [9] who could make exact specifications about the state of Disney production at the beginning of the war. Disney worked then in his old facilities with 1,500 men. Included in this number are 300 men who exclusively work for non-film exploitation of his characters in picture books, for promotional campaigns and so on.
>
> By that time his new studio [in Burbank] was built which is laid out for 4,000 employees. One has to have in mind that Disney too, without any doubt, would need for the expansion up to 4,000 men several years if he will not do damage to the quality of his work. Disney himself confirmed this in earlier statements about his trainee school. Already in 1937, he annually trained 200 graphically skilled young people for his demands and integrated them due to their skills into his practical production.
>
> Regarding Disney's large-scale planning there is evidence that he intends to release in the future several animated feature films per year.
>
> If German Reich will approach the establishment of its animation film production with less initiative than private entrepreneur Disney, we will fall behind even more than we already are.
>
> This fact would be less than supportive for the reputation of German film especially in Europe which shows a big demand for American cartoons. For the German cultural propaganda, it would be essential if we succeed to fill the existent gap in the foreseeable future and provide German cartoons to the open market. [...]
>
> According to a message by Vice President [Karl] Melzer, the animated feature film *Snow White* has recouped between Dollar 1.5 and 2.5 million in Europe alone excluding Germany.[10]

The Ministry of Public Enlightenment and Propaganda ordered several research groups to collect information about Walt Disney and his working methods. One of these groups found out that DZF [Deutsche Zeichenfilm G.m.b.H.] would have to rely heavily on foreign talent to guarantee *kriegswichtige* (strategic) production. Animators and artists from France and the Netherlands would volunteer and offer their services. Of course, before being hired, they were checked for their Aryan background. As a special bonus, a return trip [*Heimaturlaub*] was offered, which a few used for courier services on behalf of various underground organizations (Figure 7.7).

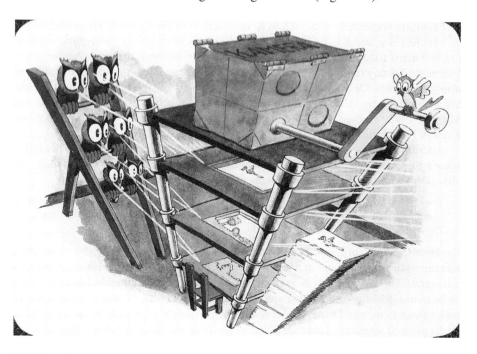

FIGURE 7.7 Multiplane technique was used by DZF during the making of *Armer Hansi* (*Poor Hansi*) in a vain attempt to rival Disney. (Courtesy of J. P. Storm.)

In the beginning, Dr. Werner Kruse acted as a mastermind and talent scout. In the summer of 1942, he went to Paris to secure animation equipment and Disney material. The German occupying forces showed high interest in continuing ties with Disney. After doing some business at the French branch location of the German Filmtechnische Zentralstelle (Central Office for Film Technique) located at 104 Champs-Elysees in Paris, which collected the requisitioned film material (here Dr. Kruse bought drawing paper, cels, paints, and cameras), he immediately visited French Disney representative Raoul Wallace "Wally" Feignoux. Feignoux literally shared his offices with Gestapo at 52 Champs-Elysees in Paris. He had joined the Disney company in 1936, after meeting Roy and Walt through a mutual friend. Feignoux was responsible for a staff of 10 and supervised RKO's distribution of Disney films throughout Continental Europe.

Disney's daughter Diane remembered him fondly:

During the German occupation of France Dad's French representative, Wally Feignoux, stayed in Paris. He was forced to continue proceedings because they wanted to prove that in Paris life was as usual.[11]

When Hitler seized Paris in the fall of 1940, Wally took all the Disney film prints and buried them to keep them out of Nazi hands. After the war was over, Wally returned the films. He managed to keep the Disney office open during the occupation by cooperating to a certain degree, but at a great personal risk. After 35 years with the company, Wally retired in 1971 and died 10 years later.[12]

Feignoux pretended to be open to Kruse's requests. He even recommended an artist who just was about to be conscripted by Arbeitsdienst (fatigue duty) and serve as graphic artist for Siemens in Berlin. His name was Robert Salvagnac. According to Feignoux, Disney had been prepared to hire Salvagnac a few months ago and bring him to America. Dr. Kruse was able to get Salvagnac off the list, and have him and his wife signed by DZF. Neumann welcomed the French artist with open arms. On May 15, 1942, his boss, Dr. Goebbels, had noted in his diary: "Exceptionally gifted artist in French film must be hired by us as soon as possible."

André Salvagnac, the son of Robert, differs with Kruse on one point—his father wasn't going to work for Siemens. He was drafted as foreign laborer for railroad construction commissioned by Reichsbahn and was called out of a transport:

> They all were assembled for transport [to Poland]. Then a German came: They should line up again. And he asked if among them was a graphic artist with film experience. They were looking for somebody for Ufa. And he reported immediately.[13]

Suzanne Claire Kaufmann, Feignoux's secretary, spoke German. It was most likely Suzanne who told Kruse, at the instance of Feignoux, about Salvagnac. Besides Salvagnac Dr. Kruse took as many Disney papers and documents back to Berlin as he could. Most of it was destroyed during the war: stills, books, designs; but one paper describing the Disney process and organization survived. It was translated by Kruse and secretary Libertas Schulze-Boysen, who was murdered by the Nazis as a supporter of the anti-Fascist resistance group *Rote Kapelle* (Red Orchestra) on December 22, 1942.

> Die Welt des Zeichenfilms ist die unserer Einbildungskraft, eine Welt, in der Sonne, Mond und Sterne so wie alle lebenden Dinge unseren Befehlen gehorchen. Wir schaffen eine kleine Figur unserer Einbildungskraft und beseitigen sie wieder, wenn sie nicht gehorcht, mit dem Radiergummi. Kein Diktator hat eine so absolute Gewalt.
>
> The world of animation is the world of imagination, a world in which sun, moon and stars as all living objects listen to our orders. Out of our imagination we create a little character and let it vanish by using an eraser if it doesn't obey. No dictator has such absolute power.[14]

The Gestapo itself took care that the remaining Disney papers be dispatched to the DZF in Berlin for further research and translation.

In order to have enough stories to follow, DZF ran an artistic working group. There were cartoonists, journalists, and critics who submitted ideas and concepts, among them Ernst Keienburg, Friedrich Luft, Hans Kossatz, Dr. Kurt Kusenberg, Will Halle, Horst von Möllendorff, and the unfortunate E. O. Plauen (Erich Ohser from Plauen who committed suicide in Nazi custody on April 6, 1944, to avoid the death sentence).

Manfred Schmidt, another member of the group, who satirized after the war Sherlock Holmes in his *Nick Knatterton* comic strips, suggested an anti-American fable:

Wenn Columbus heute... (*If Columbus today...*) was to be a cartoon against the American Way of Life filled with racist stereotypes. Like almost all other projects of DZF, it was not realized, but the treatment survived.

We hear the *song La Paloma* in a tight foxtrot rhythm with saxophone flourishes: Columbus sees the silhouette of skyscrapers. His ship docks in New York harbor, where Columbus is greeted by a huge crowd. The people descend on the caravel like a swarm of locusts and tear it apart.

> Locked in by the crowd, Columbus runs up Broadway, into a skyscraper. An elevator door slams behind him and with a long, drawn-out whistle the elevator rushes to the 20th floor in one go. Due to the upward speed, the people in the elevator are compressed to half their size. The elevator stops with a jerk, people grow again and slam under the elevator ceiling, then spill out of the elevator. Columbus, green and swaying, is the last to leave.
>
> He staggers opposite in an elevator downstairs, which also covers the 20 floors in one go and whistle. Except that this time the people are stuck under the elevator ceiling due to the downward speed, with their feet freely hanging in the cabin. With a halter jerk, the opposite effect as above.

Next, Columbus goes to a dance hall. There he is dragged onto the floor, and *La Paloma* is beaten to death with a jazz trumpet.

> The Americans can stand it. Only bold sailor Columbus is not used to such stresses. He staggers out and sinks into a chair in front of the door. This chair belongs to a shoe-shine boy. Ten shoe-shine niggers pounce on him, smear his feet, which are only clad in sandals, and while singing a wild nigger song, polish every single toe to a high-gloss black finish. [...]
>
> Columbus is relaxing in a chicken bar. He sits next to a piano at which a negress with a deep voice is moaning. A European tune, syncopied beyond recognition. When her voice descends low, trembles Columbus all over, and the table bends with it. The furniture changes into a tremulous African jungle. The pale inmates become their own negative: niggers in white tuxedos.[15]

Finally, Columbus gathers his crew on the quarterdeck, puts a finger to his mouth, and admonishes them not to tell anyone that they have discovered America (Figure 7.8).

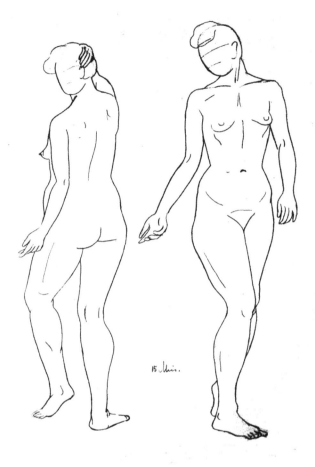

FIGURE 7.8 Female nude by DZF apprentice. (Courtesy of J. P. Storm.)

Eventually, Frank Leberecht decided in favor of a bird tale. The original idea was submitted in October 1941 by Hermann Krause titled *The Story of a Little Canary that Flew into Freedom.* In his cage, a canary named Hansi listens to the voice of freedom, love, and adventure. He hears the song of a chickadee and carelessly leaves the birdcage. The canary's wings, however, grow weak, a metaphor that freedom is elusive and dangerous. Hunger, thirst, rain, and finally an ugly street cat drive Hansi back to the safety of prison. In the end, it all turns out to be a dream.

Technically *Poor Hansi*, released in 1943, was a poor man's Disney. Anneliese Klemm was an assistant animator at DZF. She recalled that she had to base her drawings off Disney artwork and was told to copy entire scenes (Figure 7.9):

> We had the chance to see the most beautiful American movies, in the middle of the war. Goebbels had brought these films to Germany via Sweden to show German actors and directors how they worked in foreign countries.[16] They should learn from it. [...]

My task was to rotoscope for *Armer Hansi*. I rotoscoped from the American *Snow White*. Frame by frame I traced a dwarf with watering eyes, this little dwarf who was a little weepy.[17] The same situation we had in *Armer Hansi*: Hansi, lost in the forest, is yearning for his Hansine, terrible, and his eyes are filling with water. That was done frame by frame.

FIGURE 7.9   Original cel *Armer Hansi* (*Poor Hansi*). (Courtesy of J. P. Storm.)

There was another scene Anneliese Klemm was asked to "borrow" and rotoscope from *Snow White*:

> ...when she runs through the forest and – a very creepy atmosphere – branches are grabbing her like hands with long claws. [...] Rotoscoping means: There is a projector with a film strip, maybe 65 feet or so, that can be projected frame by frame, like a slide projector. And then they prepared a frame, very primitive, a ground glass and then a pegbar with standard hole punch. You took for each frame another sheet of tracing paper and pushed the button for the next frame which was then projected, and then you traced the outline on the paper.[18]

The parable of a weak canary, a typical pet bird, feeling safe only in his bird cage prison was outrageously stupid, but it seemed to please the Nazi powers-that-be who had prisoned a big part of Europe, at least ideologically, and send millions to the concentration camps. The very thought of freedom, on the other hand, certainly wouldn't appeal to them. It was not part of their brainwashed way of thinking. Having read the basic idea of *Hansi*, cartoonist Horst von Möllendorff, who belonged to the company's staff of freelance writers, seemed to have been the only who realized this matter. He suggested immediate changes and tried to introduce ideas of his own (Figure 7.10):

I want to comment on two important issues:

> The canary who only dreams about the flight into freedom leaves an unsatisfied desire.
> The ending leaves an unfree feeling, the cage becomes a prison as the canary returns, because he is unable to live in freedom.

Therefore, I suggest:
> Leave the desire for freedom as core of the plot, but give the whole another basic idea as follows:

The wish to swap with the life of another

> 1. This would give a different meaning to beginning as well as the ending.
> 2. The canary wants to swap his life with a sparrow, and this not in dream but in real life.

After they have lived the life of the other, they are happy to become their old self and change again.[19]

FIGURE 7.10 Original cel *Poor Hansi* and Hansine. (Courtesy of J. P. Storm.)

Neumann and his stubborn dramaturge Leberecht wouldn't listen. They were resistant to Möllendorff's advice, and he left the company soon after.

THE APPRENTICES AND THEIR MENTOR

In the beginning, Dr. Kruse acted as mentor of eight apprentices who were the first to enter the newly founded *Lehrwerkstatt* [training workshop] of the company. As teacher Prof. Sommer was hired, a former member of Moscow Art Academy, but he delved and plunged mainly in water colors and not in animation.

When the company moved from Rosenthaler Strasse to Kaiserstrasse, the number of apprentices increased to 30, and then to 60 youngsters. A good number of trainees already became involved with finishing *Hansi*. Finally, a new training ground was found on the second floor of Kaufhaus Horn, a department store located at Alexanderplatz 2. Three classes (A, B, C) were arranged and, from April 1, 1943, instructed by teachers Heinrich Zernack (who supervised nude drawing, and had models on disposal who even included forced laborers and war invalids), Max Lingner, Max Kaus, Wilhelm Hübner-Lauenburg, Egon Stolterfoht, and others.

Heinrich Zernack used constantly changing models for nude drawing: elderly people, war-disabled people, forced laborers. The best works were awarded at the end of each month. Sigrid Vogt, apprentice: "There was actually a very relaxed, casual tone. [...] I can only remember one Russian prisoner of war who was a nude model with us."[20] When a visitor from the Propaganda Ministry saw one of the sacred Fuehrer portraits among nude models, Prof. Rudolf Schoen was called in and asked to remove it immediately. Hitler was not supposed to oversee nudism.

On November 1, 1943, Deutsche Zeichenfilm G.m.b.H. published a fact sheet re: choice of employment:

> Boys and girls who can prove their aptitude for drawing will be accepted once a year for a three-year training period. Ten teachers instruct in object and figure drawing (including nude study and anatomy), perspective, culture and style research, animation and stop-frame technique, rhythmic education, aural training and handicrafts. Objective is the development of sight and motion, to master a character and the laws of movement as well as free design within the context of the language of animation.

One of the first to apply was Horst Alisch: "I was hired by Dr. Kruse. He was a very handsome man, always looked tanned. He conducted an admission interview with me, and I don't know who else was there, which gentlemen they were. In any case I was the only male apprentice in this studio, and I was the fourth or fifth apprentice at all. We had nature studies, we had color theory, we had architecture, but also drawing lessons. We went out into the streets, painted brewery horses, there were still some on the street back then. We went to Grunewald [the largest forested area in the western part of Berlin], still lifes were painted, in other words everything that you actually learn at an art school."[21]

By that time, when already 200 employees worked at DZF (120 of them apprentices), "Aryan" Kruse who was married to a Jewish wife was no longer staff member of DZF. On August 27, 1942, *Reichsfilmkammer* reported to *Fachschaft Film*:

Re: my inquiry at Gau Staff Council of NSDAP., Gauleitung Berlin, I today receive the following note:

Volksgenosse Kruse is a member of both, NSV and Reichsfilmkammer. For the efforts of NSDAP, he shows no interest, however participates in social activities of party and state. His wife is first grade Jewish half-breed. There is no guarantee for his political reliability on my part.

On November 13, *Fachschaft Film* phoned Neumann. Neumann already had talked to Kruse. Both agreed to terminate their contract. The pilot disembarked from the sinking ship. Kruse, however, was allowed to continue at UFA. There he was assigned to a project *Brot für Europa* (*Bread for Europe*). All involved were married to Jews and agreed that this project should not be finished before the end of the war. Thus, Kruse was able to save his wife from arrest and deportation.

NOTES

1   All following documents from Berlin Document Center (BDC), File Wolfgang Kaskeline.
2   Film-Kurier, November 27, 1935.
3   Der Film, December 10, 1938.
4   Völkischer Beobachter Issue Munich April 30, 1939
5   *Konkurrenz für Micky Maus? Gespräch mit Kurt Stordel.* In: 12 Uhr Blatt, December 22, 1938.
6   *20 000 Zeichnungen – ein Film. Interessante Versuche mit bunten deutschen Märchentrickfilmen.* In: Hamburger Fremdenblatt, December 24, 1938.
7   Frank Maraun in: Der deutsche Film, Special Issue 1940/1941.
8   Goebbels' Diary, August 6, 1940.
9   Damsleth was a Norwegian Nazi collaborationist.
10   December 18, 1941. Files of Bundesarchiv/Federal Archives.
11   Disney Miller, Diane, *Mein Vater Walt Disney.* Gütersloh: C. Bertelsmann Verlag, (1960), p. 165.
12   Trahan, Kendra, *Disneyland Detective: An INDEPENDENT Guide to Discovering Disney's Legend, Lore, and Magic!* Mission Viejo, CA 200, p. 110.
13   André Salvagnac interviewed by J. P. Storm. 72 *"Mickey-Maus zeigt..." von Walt Disney. "Mickey Mouse presents..." by Walt Disney.*
14   Collection of J. P. Storm.
15   *"Wenn Columbus heute..."* Idea sketch by Manfred Schmidt. Munich City Library: Monacensia Literary Archive.
16   The Ministry of Enlightenment and Propaganda maintained its own cinema in Berlin, Jägerstrasse. Employees of Deutsche Zeichenfilm G.m.b.H. were allowed to attend special screenings of foreign films, notably Disney animation.
17   Bashful.
18   Anneliese Klemm interviewed by J. P. Storm.
19   Document made available by J. P. Storm from his collection.
20   Sigrid Vogt interviewed by J. P. Storm.
21   Horst Alisch interviewed by J. P. Storm.

8 Somersault to Dachau

In November 1943, the building that housed DZF was hit by bombs. During this air raid on November 22, the training and apprenticeship workshop fell victim to the flames. The ministry decided to decentralize the work and split the whole company into five independent animation units located in Berlin and Vienna, while the core group was dispatched to Dachau near Munich (Figure 8.1).

FIGURE 8.1 DZF supervising animator Gerhard Fieber. (Courtesy of J. P. Storm.)

DOI: 10.1201/9781003375548-8

Dachau, as is fairly well known, was not only the new home of German animation. Not far away, there was the barbed wire fence of a concentration camp and men driving live-stock wagons.

Moosschwaige, where the cartoonists were now working, was originally a recreation home for artists. The housekeeper was Carola Freiin von Crailsheim-Rügland called Carly:

> German trickfilm had become homeless. How they learned about the large atelier at Moosschwaige remains an unsolved mystery. Anyway, one day Carly was informed that Munich for a certain time would withdraw from the contract at the discretion of the Ministry of Propaganda to make room for Deutsche Zeichenfilm. [...]
> German trickfilm entered with noisy youth. Daily phone calls to Berlin. Many trucks brought animation desks and all the stuff that was needed. Soon architects came to design a studio on a grand scale because the first German cartoon was destined to compete with Walt Disney. [...] I was worried: Would Dr. Goebbels' hosts produce propaganda films at Moosschwaige? No, that was not the case.

In charge of the Dachau cartoon factory was Gerhard Fieber, graphic artist and cartoonist, former assistant to Wolfgang Kaskeline. Fieber had helped to design *Armer Hansi* and, a true opportunist, had become Neumann's ass-kisser:

> *When* Poor Hansi *was finished, I wanted to start a project of my own. It was called* Purzelbaum ins Leben (Somersault into Life), *the story of a dog family which sneezes itself into life. I was supposed to make this film in Dachau because in Berlin we were interrupted in our work by bombs. At first,* Maya the Bee by *[Waldemar] Bonsels was planned. Bonsels lived at Lake Starnberg. But that project was dropped. Maybe he [didn't] like it, and so we began* Purzelbaum ins Leben. *I got about 30 artists, inkers, and colorists to Dachau.*[1]

Fieber put emphasis on receiving screen credit at any price. The finished product of *Poor Hansi* hadn't featured his name. Now, he was striving for something higher.

On May 25, 1944, Karl Neumann responded favorably to Fieber's request (Figure 8.2):

Dear Herr Fieber!

With reference to our conversation yesterday, we confirm the following agreement, subject to the approval of Herr Reich, film intendant, special department Culture Film: In the screen credits of Purzelbaum ins Leben (working title), currently in production at your studio, a full-page title card will record: "Art design by Gerhard Fieber."

If this title card will appear right after the main title or after the other titles will be decided later on.[2]

Fieber, the Dachau department head, got the impression *that all male artists were quite happy, basically fit for active service in times of war, not to be conscripted one way or other. That includes me too.*[3]

Fieber supervised a number of employees who were recruited from foreign or occupied countries for service at Deutsche Zeichenfilm: *Jan Coolen was Dutch, Sergei Sesin was Belarusian, a highly intelligent man who was quite popular with his female in-betweeners, [Robert] Salvagnac, a Frenchman, was in charge of his own working group, but we had to shut that down, because, in spite of the advance praise bestowed on him, he came to grips with us. Otherwise, the foreigners were received very well. I had a relationship with them as with colleagues* [sic!].

FIGURE 8.2   Making a maquette for *Purzelbaum ins Leben*. (Courtesy of J. P. Storm.)

From Wally Feignous, Disney's French representative, the heads of Zeichenfilm GmbH had learned that the Disney Studios allegedly had planned to hire Salvagnac right before German occupation. Even Goebbels was impressed when he heard that: *Exceptionally gifted talent in French film must be hired by us as soon as possible.*[4]
Fieber continues:

In Dachau I had Salvagnac, Mongazon, Fannier, three Frenchmen, to work for me. They were conscripted. Fannier was a man who had some reservations against Hitler and expressed these. Maybe it was foolishness on his part or it was his way, but he used every opportunity to quarrel with a German artist, [Anna-Luise] Subatzus. He always raised trouble, and one day she [Subatzus] turned up in my office and complained about the Frenchman that he would badmouth Hitler and all sort of things and if I wouldn't stop that she would tell her fiancé, an SS officer in the Dachau concentration camp, at least she claimed she was engaged to him, and I certainly would get into trouble. So I asked Fannier to come and see me. *[Laughs]* "Oh brother, can't you shut up, you may have your own thoughts on the matter but if you don't worry about your family, then at least worry about mine. Listen, if you go haywire, we both run into difficulties." And after the next vacation – they got vacation, the French, they were allowed to go home – he didn't return. Instead, he went straight to join the Résistance.[5]

Anna-Luise Subatzus who later lived in Göttingen added:

Fannier belonged, as far as I know, to the underground movement. He always wore the French lily. He always had that. But nobody cared about that. *[sic!]* The other one, Salvagnac, allowed himself a coup. We had a very beautiful, Madonna-like colorist, and he fell in love with her, and then she got a child from him. Her father was a high-ranked SS officer. I guess Neumann intervened so that Salvagnac escaped unscathed. It must have been Neumann who helped him, somehow.[6]

Fieber:

Once we got into trouble concerning an artist. We still were in Berlin, right before I went to Dachau. There was a girl - really a very pretty girl, daughter of an SS officer - and this artist fell head over heels in love with her and got a child from him. That was an affair, like the end of the world. I won't forget it. It was a real sensation. *[Laughs]* Hard to work things out. That was Salvagnac.[7]

Salvagnac got a divorce from his wife who had accompanied him from France so that he could marry the German girl [Sigrid von Weberstedt, the daughter of SS officer Hans von Weberstedt].

They all seemed to be more concerned with their own affairs and hanky-panky than noticing what was going around. In Dachau, they all tried to ignore the existence of a concentration camp as best they could and blinked at the fact, as so many Germans did, who after the war claimed they couldn't remember or didn't know at all.

Anne-Luise Subatzus:

Once, after the bomb raid on Munich, my friend Cecilia and I went to a restaurant where we ate sometimes. Many artists frequented the place, there was an old artist too and one of the people who was in charge of the concentration camp. He said the prisoners had cleared bombs and they were entitled to an extra ration. But that was all that we... [...] All was fenced off you know. There was a meat factory too where some of the prisoners worked and they whistled when they saw us. We didn't consider that dangerous because we didn't realize what was going on. Later when we learned, we couldn't believe. We didn't see anything. Only this encounter with a whole company of prisoners in a dark tunnel, all with clogs, that was horrifying. There were sheepdogs too. It was horrifying, I can tell you. A terrible impression.[8]

Horrifying to whom? To the unlucky prisoners? Or to Ms. Subatzus who was forced to see them?

A female French artist got to know more when in the so-called Black Express from Munich she got in touch with some SS men who let her see what was going on behind the barbed wire fence. None of her colleagues wanted to believe what she reported upon her return. The protected area was actually one of those concentration camps that the Germans tried to ignore at all costs.

Lieber Gott, mach mich stumm, dass ich nicht nach Dachau kumm. – Dear God, make me dumb that I don't come to Dachau.

If the Germans didn't know or didn't want to know anything – they suspected (Figure 8.3).

FIGURE 8.3   Female artist relaxing at DZF Dachau. (Courtesy of J. P. Storm.)

THE SNOW MAN

DZF's ambitious plans soon all turned out to be soap bubbles.

There was one German studio, however, that really delivered a timeless, quality cartoon to "rival" Disney's *Silly Symphonies* of the 1930s, not in quantity or even animation quality, but in content and emotion. This studio was the small Fischerkoesen plant founded by Hans Fischer who was born and raised in Koesen, and therefore had named himself Fischerkoesen (as Fischer was too common a name in Germany). A graduate of the Academy of Arts in Leipzig, Fischerkoesen came to Berlin in the 1920s, joined UFA, and later established his own studio in Potsdam. Before and after the war, he had produced successful animation, mainly advertising films. In the 1940s, Fischerkoesen produced a trio of color animated shorts for *German Newsreel*

that remained unparalleled for their camerawork. In several scenes, instead of a multiplane camera, Fischerkoesen and his cameraman Kurt Schleicher employed Max
Fleischer's three-dimensional "stereo" animation stand, providing a combination of
2D drawings and 3D models (Figure 8.4).

FIGURE 8.4 Hans Fischerkoesen (second from right) and company in Leipzig, 1937.
(Courtesy of J. P. Storm.)

By 1938, there were 5,000 cinemas in greater Germany. The cinema owners
were obliged to run the *German Newsreel* (*Deutsche Wochenschau*) before the
main feature, and they weren't allowed to intersperse some funny shorts at that
time. Audiences who only had in their mind to appear for the main feature were
sent back.

On June 20, 1940, Berlin opened the first cinema devoted entirely to newsreels.
The Nazis planned to build 15–20 special newsreel cinemas in Germany, where audiences could cheaply watch the recent political issues (40 Pfennig: 10:00 a.m. to 4:00
p.m., 60 Pfennig: 4:00 p.m. to 10:00 p.m.). On September 4, 1940, Dr. Goebbels
put the different film departments under a central roof, thus Deutsche Wochenschau
G.m.b.H. was founded under the supervision of Heinrich Roellenbleg.

Newsreel cinemas needed more than the state-controlled propaganda news, so
shorts and cartoons were added. Dr. Goebbels personally cared that there would be
entertaining segments in between the newsreel presentations to please the audience.
On July 7, 1942, the Propaganda Ministry wrote to the propaganda departments of
the supreme military commander in Belgium and northern France re: programming
for newsreel cinemas:

"Currently we are at work, in association with Deutsche Wochenschau G.m.b.H. and in agreement with the Reich Ministry for Enlightenment and Propaganda, compiling programs and will provide, if possible, missing segments (cartoons, trick films, sketches, and films recommended for the youth); particularly, the last-mentioned program segments are vital for comic relief in a program of one-hour length and necessary for attracting the respective audience."

To provide these shorts, Roellenbleg and his associate Dr. Hans Karbe found an ideal studio for their purposes in Fischerkoesen and signed him up for five cartoons. Three of them were finished before the end of the war. Fischerkoesen was happy to get the contract, because at the end of the war there no longer were any orders for advertising films that otherwise would have provided a regular income for the studio (Figure 8.5).

FIGURE 8.5   Fischerkoesen animation studio in Potsdam, early 1940s. (Courtesy of J. P. Storm.)

The first of these Agfacolor shorts, *Verwitterte Melodie* [Weather-Beaten Melody], is truly comparable to a *Silly Symphony* with its music and movement. Only the chubby design of the characters is pure Fischerkoesen: On a sunny summer day a wasp, reminiscent of Waldemar Bonsels' popular *Maya the Bee*,[9] discovers an abandoned phonograph box in a meadow. There is a complicated technical shot of the wasp flying down from the sky and entering the picture through 12 multiplane layers of grass and flowers, and circling around the three-dimensional phonograph box. Accidentally, the wasp touches the record with her stinger and is surprised to hear some chords. Astonished, she checks her stinger, then she runs along the record and produces more sound when she uses her stinger as needle to play the record. The weather-beaten phonograph starts to produce some jazz and swing music, which attracts more insects. Dust makes the wasp come to a standstill and the music sounds distorted. A stately caterpillar curiously watches and comes to the rescue when he cleans the record. On the clean, mirror-like surface the wasp, however, starts to slip and slide. Only with the support of two helpful beetles does she regain her footing. Pairs of beetle dance and sway to the music in the branches (Figure 8.6).

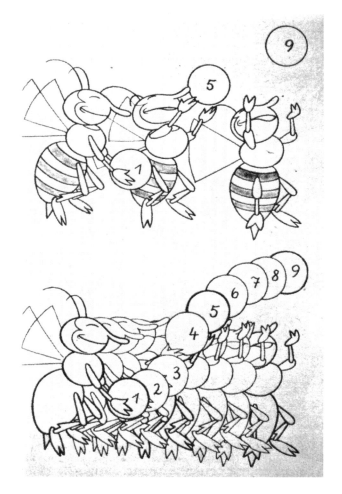

FIGURE 8.6 Animation layout for *Verwitterte Melodie* (*Weather-Beaten Melody*). (Courtesy of J. P. Storm.)

After a while, as a result of intense recording, the wasp's stinger starts to wear down, and beetles refresh her stinger with dewdrops from the cup of a bellflower. A stag beetle whirls the wasp around until she is thrown off the record with a broken stinger. The wasp sharpens her against some rocks, then the show continues.

The late animation historian (and Fischinger biographer) Dr. William Moritz proved to be a good observer and even discovered some subtle "bit[s] of forbidden information" in Fischerkoesen's little cartoon:

> ...the discovery of an abandoned phonograph takes on a new meaning, especially when the record on the turntable is a swing number with lyrics that say, "The week wouldn't be worthwhile without a weekend when we can get away to enjoy nature." Near the phonograph lies an "abandoned" clasp from a woman's garter belt (with a lucky four-leafed clover growing out of it!), which suggests that the interrupted picnic that left behind the musical instrument had also involved erotic play - something also strictly forbidden by the puritanical Nazi codes. So from beneath the charming surface of this cartoon emerges a subversive message: women, far from the unnatural Nazi-designated stereotype of "children, church and kitchen," can escape into Nature to be self-reliant and adventurous, erotic and free - they can discover or revitalize a suppressed world of forbidden joy in music and friendship between diverse creatures who may be brown or white, frog or caterpillar - or even a pair of ladybug beetles who may be a same-sex couple.

According to Moritz *Verwitterte Melodie* is *quite the opposite of the Nazi requirements for a dedicated Aryan citizen* (Figure 8.7).[10]

FIGURE 8.7   Beetle from *Verwitterte Melodie* (*Weather-Beaten Melody*). (Courtesy of J. P. Storm.)

Fischerkoesen transformed the idea with the support of no more than 14 employees in his Potsdam studio. Colorization was outsourced to a studio in The Hague, where another 17 employees were busy colorizing the cels. Horst von Möllendorff, whom we have met as a former staff writer of DZF and who wasn't too happy working there, joined forces with German Newsreel and developed the basic ideas: "Fischerkoesen and his studio worked effectively and very fast on the cartoon. He was in straight competition with Reich-owned Deutsche Zeichenfilm G.m.b.H. which for some time worked on *Hansi*. Based on his many years of experience with advertising films and commercials, Fischerkoesen had developed his own style, and as I was not experienced in manufacturing cartoons, I only submitted the idea for him."[11]

The *Weather-Beaten Melody*, or *Scherzo*, as it was also called, received good reviews from foreign countries too.

Emil Reinegger, head of A.C.E. Paris Film Distributors, reported to UFA Berlin:

> End of November 1943 the aforementioned cartoon film was started at Urban Theatre, Zurich, as supplement to the feature film, *Der weisse Traum* (*The White Dream*).
>
> For me this was a special event because - as is known to you – many years the whole American animation production (Walt Disney - Dave Fleischer) took a prominent place in programming of American films.
>
> At that time, I had the opportunity to participate in the première of *Scherzo* in Zurich. The audience response was surprisingly favorable, and I can say better than the bulk of all American trickfilms. The audience followed enthusiastically and liked the excellent idea, the colors, the score and the supremely funny gags. Particularly surprised were audiences and press by this German work because everybody actually believed that only Americans would be able to produce this kind of film.
>
> While the Americans work with mostly grotesque gags, *Scherzo* caught the eyes particularly for the European view, and the not excessive humor as well as the straightforward narrative made a good impression on the audience. When the movie finished, the audience applauded frenetically as I never experienced with a Walt Disney picture.
>
> During a trip to Berlin, I got the opportunity to see another cartoon, *Der Schneemann*, which I regard on the same level and which should have the same impact as *Scherzo*.
>
> I believe that we cannot render a greater service to German filmmaking than to release these films as soon as possible...[12]

As Reinegger mentioned, German Newsreel had asked Möllendorff immediately for another funny story that could be turned into an animation short. There was one idea he had already offered DZF but was turned down. One evening Möllendorff sat in a Berlin beer garden to concoct a suitable topic for a cartoon and eventually came up with the story of a Snow Man who has a warm spot in his heart. He awakes underneath a full moon in a quiet market place. After some adventures, he creeps into a house to rest on a sofa, where he discovers a calendar. The calendar page for January shows a Snow Man like himself in a winter landscape. He browses through February, March, and stops in July. For the first time, he learns about that loveliest of seasons: summer. He longs to experience the warmer weather, so he "hibernates" in the refrigerator and leaves it with the arrival of summer. Everything looks exactly like the promising picture in the calendar. The snow man is all smiles when he leaves the house. He enjoys the sun tremendously and welcomes "the summer of his lifetime."

The Snow Man picks flowers and spreads them around. He sticks a red rose into his cold breast, and surprises an excited hen with an egg made of ice and snow. The warm July sun begins to burn. Slowly the Snow Man starts to melt, leaving only a top hat and his carrot nose, which is picked up and eaten by a little rabbit. (The snow man's design, by the way, had already been used by Fischerkoesen for a Coca-Cola spot that he did in 1939: *Die erfrischende Pause/The Refreshing Break*.) (Figure 8.8).

FIGURE 8.8 *Der Schneemann* (*The Snow Man*) enjoys summer. (Courtesy of J. P. Storm.)

The Snow Man is a total contradiction of *Poor Hansi*. The canary experiences his trip into freedom as perilous, while the *Snow Man* prefers freedom and death. The Snow Man's tragicomic death, in an odd way, also reflects the millionfold deaths that had become an unyielding part of German society in that era (Figure 8.9).

FIGURE 8.9 The tragic end of the *Snow Man* in the beautiful summer time. (Courtesy of J. P. Storm.)

Karl Neumann of DZF watched Fischerkoesen's rising star with envy. He tried to convince Goebbels to assign Fischerkoesen to the DZF, but Goebbels turned him down:

> Oberregierungsrat [councillor] Neumann whom I have entrusted with the preparation of a cartoon film production makes a report about his previous work. He has tackled with the problem efficiently and has already accomplished notable things. The first cartoon film coming from his production which has been screened to me still shows many weak points; but it is a good beginning. Besides, there is another production from cartoon film producer Fischer-Kösen which Neumann would love to take over with all the bells and whistles and integrate into his own production. I refuse temporarily. As long as a new film production is in its infancy it is good if there is competition.[13]

While Fischerkoesen focused on another short, *Das dumme Gänslein* (*The Foolish Goose/The Silly Goose*), German Newsreel provided even better-paid writing jobs for Möllendorff in the rest of (still Nazi-occupied) Europe, as Germany alone was not able to fulfill the demand of cartoons needed to entertain the troops (Figure 8.10).

FIGURE 8.10   Season's Greetings: *Das dumme Gänslein* (*The Foolish Goose*). (Courtesy of J. P. Storm.)

PRAGUE

Möllendorff:

> In mid-1943, Dr. Karbe showed me a cartoon film made by [Richard] Dillenz in Prague. His *Zauberlehrling* [Sorcerer's Apprentice] in human shape I found too sad. Disney's *Sorcerer's Apprentice* in *Fantasia* with Mickey Mouse was much more flexible, smooth and funnier. Dr. Karbe told me of the problems with Dillenz in Prague.

A mission for Möllendorff, a man who could conceive cartoony stories but certainly not run a cartoon studio! And he didn't want to run it. He didn't need too. He would just provide story ideas and cash the paychecks. Why bother to do the donkeywork? Out of it, *Hochzeit im Korallenmeer* (*Wedding in Coral Sea*) was born. The film's story left enough room for action and imagination: An evil Cossack octopus kidnaps a fish bride and hides her in the wreck of a sunken ship. To please her and win her affections, he performs wild Cherkessian dances (that reveal him as an aggressive Bolshevik type), but this frightens the fish girl who starts to cry. In the meantime, the bridegroom isn't idle. He assembles auxiliaries and frees his beloved with the assistance of other fish, mostly sword and saw fish.

> My activities in Prague were a totally new task for me. Now I was creative director of more than one-hundred artists. They worked, contrary to German animation, on a high, professional level. I always thought that there were some artists with Disney experience involved. To create the optical illusion of underwater life they clamped two panes of glass on top of each other under the camera lens. Between the panes of glass some drops of oil dissolved and, due to the heat and fast photography, left the impression of life in the sea. They had built even some kind of multiplane camera. On the floor there were 10 mtr. (30 feet) tracks and a camera moved towards the different layers to produce depth of focus.[14]

Möllendorff was unaware that he worked with the crème de la crème of the future Czech animation industry: Jiří Brdečka, Eduard Hofman, Stanislav Latal, Josef Kandel, and Jiliš Kalaš.

THE CHAIR FOR HUMOR

The dream of establishing a German animation industry (with the outrageous plan of setting up a European cartoon industry exclusively on Crimea Island[15]) had almost come to an end:

> The animation film companies founded by us or inspired by us, such as Deutsche Zeichenfilm G.m.b.H., are not able to manufacture as many cartoon films as the numerous European cinemas need. Particularly German and foreign newsreel theatres, which due to their concentrated propaganda in a fast-changing program of supporting features and short films reach an extraordinary big number of patrons, need annually about 50 cartoons which will animate audiences – especially the youth – to attend theaters.

As Councillor Neumann failed to deliver sufficient cartoon footage, his administration came up with the plan of usurping the forces of other European studios and slapping the DZF label on them; then it would be a true European animation "studio" competing with Disney.

After all, the animation quality of cartoons in Prague, Rome, and Paris was better than Germany's, and the Germans knew it. This fact is substantiated in a memo by Dr. Karbe:

RE: ANIMATION FILM STUDIO "LES GEMEAUX," PARIS.

> In compliance with the Minister's request to create an efficient animation film production in Europe that under all circumstances must be qualified to compete with transatlantic competitors in quality and to some degree also in quantity, currently smaller

and bigger studios in Berlin, Potsdam, Neubabelsberg, Munich, Vienna, Prague, Zlin, Amsterdam, The Hague, and Copenhagen have been commissioned.

One extraordinarily efficient animation studio stands still aside. This is the group LES GEMEAUX in Paris. About three years ago this studio was assigned by the Ministry of Propaganda through Continental Films to execute a color short Der Notenhändler (The Note Merchand).[16] This film was, regarding artwork and drawings, in each respect remarkable. It reflects a high standard in art, good movements, unusually refined backgrounds, austerity in color and form, limitation and concentration of each frame onto the essential and for the first time in Europe a completely Un-American style of drawing. Unfortunately, scenario-wise the film was misguided. Although the basic idea was excellent, an abundance of (unnecessary!) lacks was admitted, which render the film unintelligible.[17]

In a letter addressed to Mayor Dr. Winkler, Berlin NW 87, Brückenallee 3, re: animation film, Undersecretary Dr. Gast wrote "that after a screening of *The Snow Man* Mr. Roellenbleg has repeated his question if various groups of animation producers should be put under the roof of Deutsche Zeichenfilm G.m.b.H. which would follow the request of Oberregierungsrat Neumann. The Minister, however, expressed that he does NOT wish the subordination of various animation manufacturers under the roof Deutsche Zeichenfilm G.m.b.H. On the contrary, he regards the current state of independent development of these groups far better because it will create a healthy artistic competition." Roellenbleg and Karbe would try to reach their goal without the participation of DZF (and in the long run they had exactly this in mind). Dated February 7, 1944, a paper was compiled with a suggestion to organize an animation film circle throughout Europe, a cluster, now exclusively controlled by German Newsreel. The paper was signed by Heinrich Roellenbleg, and Neumann's name wasn't mentioned in it at all.

Proposal
for a combination of small animation film studios in Europe to raise artistic and economic achievement (efficiency)

A year ago, Deutsche Wochenschau (German Newsreel) got the assignment to organize a German animation film production which should be able to make up for the technical and artistic advance of the Americans in the shortest time. Therefore, concerning qualified commercial film companies in Germany as well as in the occupied countries, appropriate rearrangements have been taken and experts as well as equipment have been supplied. Furthermore, in the occupied countries some companies have been newly established and at last artistic and partly technical supervision of animation departments of the state-controlled companies was taken over. For all units and workgroups, in closest cooperation with the artists and new writers, suitable manuscripts were supplied and submitted to the studios for production.

In no less than 14 studios, spread all over Europe, different animation and puppet film artists are at work. 8 of them have already been signed by German Newsreel, while deals with the rest will soon be closed. (The three units of Deutsche Zeichenfilm G.m.b.H. are not included.) These groups have different prerequisites and craftsmen unevenly distributed, with partly very inadequate technical equipment. All of them, in spite of one-sided experience, have started work. If they have accomplished till today relatively much, nobody can deny that everywhere there are considerable drawbacks. In one group that might be technically superior much is left to be desired regarding artistic discipline while another group that might do splendid animation hasn't much story mind with a nod to the audience. A third group still has problems with color but on the other hand has an exemplary working schedule which saves hundreds of man-hours while another group seems to have found the key to an ideal "Fahrplan" (exposure sheet), which is the heart of any well-organized animation company.

From uneven beginnings the abilities of each respective studio have developed, of course, unequally. One has gained special abilities in this field, another in a different. It is natural that suddenly from all parties comes a desire to cooperate more closely, to exchange experiences, to support each other.

For this reason, it is suggested to establish a

Z in Circle

ZEICHENFILM – RING

(Circle or cluster of animation)

which will enclose all smaller companies with their individual background and ownership left untouched.

This "Zeichenfilm-Ring" shall not transform into a second Deutsche Zeichenfilm G.m.b.H. but shall only and exclusively enhance and promote the artistic and technical development of German animation in Europe and in the interest of all involved parties and in all our interest to streamline methods [of production].

The studios of "Zeichenfilm-Ring"

"Zeichenfilm-Ring" might include the following studios:

1. Fischerkösenfilm, Potsdam and The Hague
2. Bavaria Zeichenfilm, Munich and The Hague
3. Prag Animation, Prague
4. Joop Geesink, Amsterdam
5. Toonder-Bouman, Amsterdam
6. Les Gemeaux, Paris
7. André Rigal, Paris
8. Raymond Jeannin,[18] Paris
9. Dansk Favre ok Tegne Film, Copenhagen
10. Animation department of Descheg, Zlin
11. Philippart, Brussels
12. Former Bassoli Group, Rome

One of the demands was to establish the world's first chair (Professorship) for humor! (Figure 8.11).

The Chair for Humor intends to make animators familiar with the essentials of humor which always should remain sympathetic. It is not intended to train humorists; this task would prove impossible. It has turned out, however, that most humorists and almost all animators lack in mental tools. We must succeed in making them think disciplined and execute their ideas logically. The rules of a punch line et al have to be worked out. But as every gag has to be sympathetic-humorist the element of humor has to be introduced into the drawing itself, i.e., into the line. To contemporary animators these things are only a foggy term if not totally unknown. Suggested as chair holder: Horst von Möllendorff.

FIGURE 8.11   A Chair for Humor and Horst von Möllendorff. (Courtesy of J. P. Storm.)

Controlling would be executed in the offices of Reichsbeauftragter (Reich commis-sioner) for the Deutsche Filmwirtschaft (German film industry) and should include all economic issues of "Zeichenfilm-Ring" as well as Deutsche Zeichenfilm G.m.b.H. and all further advertising or other studios working in the field of 2D and puppet animation.

As in the course of time it has proved unsuitable to execute European animation film matters under the label of Deutsche Wochenschau G.m.b.H. (German Newsreel), they should be summed up in the future under the new label "Zeichenfilm-Ring." The organization of "Zeichenfilm-Ring" remains under the supervision of Sonderreferat Kulturfilm, Reichsfilmintendant.

The implementation of this proposal is possible without high costs and offers an expert way to enhance the efforts of smaller 2D and puppet film studios considerably in quality. Forces, material and equipment will be used better, idle running will be avoided and budgets reduced. Particularly, however, the work of "Zeichenfilm-Ring" will contribute to further development of the characteristics of German animation whose basics have been founded so far and to establish a future, likewise important branch of German film industry with products that will be welcome and seen with joy in all countries as an expression of German character and German nature in a frame-work of European culture.

February 7, 1944.

Signed,

Roellenbleg

The document was received with different reactions.

On March 14, 1944, Karl Julius Fritzsche, Tobis House, answered Friedrich Merten, managing director of UFA Film G.m.b.H.: *"I herewith return the draft by Mr. Roellenbleg re: "Zeichenfilm-Ring". I do not share your opinion that such a*

combination is necessary right now. I think that in free competition the problem will
move faster than it would do in the intended combination. Heil Hitler!"

The heads of UFA Film G.m.b.H. were indeed more sympathetic to the idea of monitoring

European animation and replied to Dr. Karbe that the comments had attracted their interest, but that they would ask to postpone the plan for the time being.

The German Reich never achieved the objective of annually creating 50 cartoons. The Reich had more complex problems than dealing with a fledgling cartoon industry. In certain territories, the Germans were forced to play old Disney cartoons for screenings, and this was tantamount to a bankruptcy declaration.

The Propaganda Ministry's Foreign Department was forced to issue a note:

> Dr. Schmidt vividly insists not to comply with the repeatedly uttered requests to completely withdraw American cartoons from the program of Greek newsreel cinemas.
>
> One cannot object that German short films which would take their place would NOT substitute American shorts in Greece. The screenings of Mickey Mouse films are (as everybody knows) controlled by our Greek branch in accordance with the Propaganda squadron in this place which would exclude any means from here.[19]

Mickey Mouse was still held in high esteem even by German soldiers. We know of fighter pilots who appreciated Disney's mouse as a mascot and painted Mickey Mouse insignia on the fuselage of their fighter planes. One of these was flying ace Adolf Galland:

> We started this in Spain [referring to Legion Condor], and when I painted it [Mickey] on my Me-109E in JG [fighter wing] 26, it was holding a hatchet and smoking a cigar. I loved smoking. But after the war I had to quit cigars.[20]

German fighter pilots, however, had to give up painting mice on their planes in 1943, when the authorities learned that Disney was producing anti-Nazi propaganda.

At that time, leading European animation studios in Italy, France, Belgium, the Netherlands, and Denmark were already preparing for the post-war era, Germany, however, was not.

NOTES

1 Fieber interviewed by J. P. Storm.
2 Bundesarchiv, Letter Deutsche Zeichenfilm G.m.b.H., Kaiserstrasse 29/30, Berlin C 2 dated May 25, 1944, addressed to Herr Gerhard Fieber, Dachau near Munich. Reference: N/Ul. Signed: Neumann.
3 Notes by Gerhard Fieber. Collection of J. P. Storm.
4 Joseph Goebbels, diary entry, May 15, 1942.
5 Gerhard Fieber interviewed by J. P. Storm.
6 Anna-Luise Subatzus interviewed by J. P. Storm, March 11, 1989.
7 Gerhard Fieber interviewed by J. P. Storm.
8 Anna-Luise Subatzus interviewed by J. P. Storm.
9 In the 1950s Bonsels' widow Rose-Marie tried to approach Disney and sell *Maya the Bee* to him.
10 William Moritz, *Resistance and Subversion in Animated Films of the Nazi Era: the Case of Hans Fischerkoesen*. In: Animation Journal, Fall 1992.
11 Horst von Möllendorff interviewed by J. P. Storm.

12 Letter dated January 17, 1944.
13 Goebbels' Diary, September 29, 1943.
14 Horst von Möllendorff interviewed by J. P. Storm.
15 Gerhard Fieber told J. P. Storm about that "project."
16 *Le Marchand de Notes* by Paul Grimault.
17 March 31, 1944.
18 For the Régime de Vichy Jeannin produced the propaganda short *Nimbus Libéré* (1944) in which Mickey Mouse and other American cartoon characters bomb France.
19 July 29, 1944.
20 Interview with World War II *Luftwaffe* General and Ace Pilot Adolf Galland. American History Interviews. World War II. 6/12/2005. www.historynet.com

9 The Denazification of German Trick Film

SMALL, BUT NOT GREAT!

Toward the end, animation in Germany and in the occupied countries unfolded an unexpected dynamic. In the 1944/1945 production plan submitted by the Culture Film Department the following projects were listed in Group B Zeichenfilm[1]: *Das Wetterhäuschen* (*The Weather House*), *Klein, aber oho!* (*Small But Great!*), *Das dumme Gänslein* (*The Stupid Goose*), *Purzelbaum in Leben* (*Somersault into Life*), *Frühlingslied* (*Spring Song*), *Walzermärchen* (*Waltz Fairy Tale*), *Das Steh-Auf-Männchen I* (*The Tumbler Boy I*), *Das törichte Zwerglein* (*The Foolish Little Dwarf*), and *Das verhinderte Klavierkonzert* (*The Prevented Piano Concert*). In addition, they hoped to complete some more films by May 31, 1945:

1. *Two more Fischerkoesen films*
2. *Two to three more Prague films*
3. *At least two more films by Deutsche Zeichenfilm G.m.b.H.*
4. *Probably two films by Bavaria*
5. *Probably two more Steh-Auf-Männchen (Tumbler Boy) films*
6. *Jahrmarkt der Tiere (Fair of Animals, boxing match), Descheg, Zlin*
7. *Puppen-Kabarett (Puppet Cabaret), the next puppet film by Joop Geesink, which we are preparing at the moment, and at least two more puppet films by the dame company.*

Furthermore, the following films might be added:

8. *Vogelschreck (Scarecrow) and more animation films from Les Gemeaux, Paris*
9. *The feature-length animation film Das Feuerzeug (The Tinder Box), Dansk Favre ok Tegne Film [sic!], Copenhagen. (Quality questionable)*

The reason for this industriousness in the final phase of "Grossdeutschland" (Greater Germany) may have been to save artists and administration from being drafted. Most announced projects (1–8) were not finished – and, if so, it would no longer have had any meaning for Nazi Germany as was the case with the *Tinder Box*.

The story of this Danish animated feature titled *Fyrtøjet* (*The Tinder Box*) based on a fairy tale by Hans Christian Andersen began in late 1942. On April 9, 1940, the Germans had occupied Denmark. Their troops stayed there until May 5, 1945.

During the time of occupation, on March 30, 1942, Hans Held, chief artist of the Bavaria animation film department, boarded a plane to Copenhagen. He needed to find some artists who could assist in finishing his color short *Die Abenteuer des Baron*

DOI: 10.1201/9781003375548-9

Münchhausen – Eine Winterreise (*The Adventures of Baron Munchausen: A Winter Journey*). He stayed until April 11 and hired some unemployed Danish artists.

Some months later, Marius Holdt, a producer and cameraman, and artist Bjørn Frank Hensen had the idea to attract the interest of the Germans and adopt their Agfacolor process for Hans Christian Andersen and *Fyrtøjet*. At the same time, they got the Danish artists on board who had worked for Hans Held: Erik Rus, Børge Hamberg, Erik Christensen, Arne "Jømme" Jørgensen, and Otto Jacobsen. Svend Methling (1891–1977), an old-time actor and feature-film director not particularly familiar with animation, was going to direct *Fyrtøjet*. The Germans checked the rushes delivered to the Berlin color film laboratory by Dansk Favre ok Tegne Film routinely:

> The quality of this film is not first-class. The company made the mistake to start with a feature-length movie. But after finishing and experiencing all kind of childhood diseases during the production, they will be able to produce useful films.[2]

In summer 1944, Allan Johnsen, a Danish producer, arrived at the German capital. His mission: to save the negative of the UFA co-financed *Tinder Box* out of the laboratories in Berlin (threatened by permanent air raids) and return it to Copenhagen in a backpack.

The negative was registered as:

> Feature-length animated film commissioned by UFA Foreign Sales Department, produced by Dansk Favre ok Tegne Film (Allan Johnsen), Copenhagen.
> Completion presumably by the end of this year *[1944]*.

When the finished film finally premiered in Copenhagen after the war, on April 21, 1946, the involvement of the Germans was forgotten or suppressed.[3]

JUST GET OUT OF HERE!

On July 25, 1944, Deutsche Zeichenfilm G.m.b.H. had 201 female and 96 male employees on the payroll. Due to the outbreak of total war, it became necessary to close down animation studios and employ the artists in armament factories. A week later on August 4, 1944, the Propaganda Ministry announced that the company would be closed for the war effort: "To keep the useful manpower the company will continue in its own service rooms by order of Rhein-Metall-Borsig trust. The head of Deutsche Zeichenfilm G.m.b.H. is liable that no animation work will continue on the side." In September 1944, UFA stopped payments to Deutsche Zeichenfilm G.m.b.H., "as the company was closed down for matters of total war."

On November 17, 1944, the Court of Auditors of Deutsches Reich complained that in a few years almost six million Reichsmark had been spent on the project, with only one (!) color short finished: *Armer Hansi* (*Poor Hansi*).

In Dachau, the field office of German cartoons, things got dicey for Karl Neumann's protégé Gerhard Fieber (Figure 9.1):

> The film (*Somersault into Life*) wasn't quite finished. There was the infamous downfall. At the end of '44, I was drafted: the so-called Goebbels donation. Then I should come back again since the situation at the front was perhaps a little better. I got a letter from Deutsche Zeichenfilm GmbH, from Neumann, via the High Command, that my

exemption had been requested because they probably had some breathing space and thought they were getting closer to victory again. But it didn't come to that anymore. I was transferred to the High Command for educational films and had to make educational films for the military: anti-tank barriers and so on. Animated. But what I started there, wasn't finished either because the front was getting closer and closer. We knew it was all pointless. We weren't that stupid during this period, so as not to suspect that it was completely hopeless.

FIGURE 9.1   Machine gun training film. (Courtesy of J. P. Storm.)

In 1945 not only Karl Neumann's career came to an abrupt end but also his life.

> Werner Kruse: *Herr Neumann was an enthusiastic National Socialist and honest National Socialist, completely convinced. He committed suicide when the Russians came in 1945. The whole world had collapsed for him.*[4]

> Stefanie Steuer: *When I met him, I greeted him: "Good morning, Herr Neumann." – "Heil Hitler, Ms. Steuer!" And when that was coming to an end, and we were already realizing that the war was lost, we heard our dear Herr Neumann say for the first time: "Good day, Ms. Steuer." I guess, he was sacked by the Russians along with Herr Böhme, our personnel manager.*[5]

> Anna-Luise Subatzus: *I felt sorry for Neumann. He had a family; I think, he had several children. Neumann was keen on me. We had night watches: my friend Cecilia and I and – Neumann. Cecilia and I were in one*

> *room [upstairs], and the two of us had couches. Then Neumann*
> *called from downstairs and asked me to come down to him. That*
> *was fatal to me. I didn't go – and, because I didn't, Neumann had a*
> *soft spot for me. He's never been so nice to me as he was afterwards,*
> *when I didn't go down to him. He had a very nice wife.*[6]

As a result of a denunciation, Neumann was arrested by Soviet soldiers on May 14, 1945, and taken to an internment camp in Weesow near Werneuchen, 25 km outside of Berlin. A month later, the once-powerful chief of Deutsche Zeichenfilm GmbH joined the suicide club of other high-ranked Nazis, Hitler & Co., and committed suicide in captivity.

> Gerhard Fieber: *He lived in Tegel Ort. He is said to have brought a few people*
> *who he might not have liked to a concentration camp. He reported*
> *them. Whether that's true, I can't judge. The Russians picked him*
> *up. And in the cell, he is said to have hanged himself.*[7]

With Karl Neumann's suicide, the Nazis and their followers hadn't vanished from German animation completely, neither the convinced Nazis nor their fellow travelers.

On December 11, 1945, the Magistrate of the City of Berlin, Department of Volksbildung [Popular Education] – Presse Office – informed the Political Examination Committee about a letter they had received in September: "Recently I read in the *Tägliche Rundschau* or *Deutsche Volkszeitung* some articles about Käthe Kollwitz, Heinrich Zille, and Otto Nagel. In this issue I also read reports about the caricaturist Herbert Sandberg, a former concentration camp prisoner,[8] and about the cartoonist Penguin who was a disciple of both, Käthe Kollwitz and Otto Nagel. Now one sees regularly in the *Berliner Zeitung* (which is published by the City) cartoons drawn by one Herr von M ö l l e n d o r f f Pg. [party member] or not. During the Nazi time, this Möllendorff published the most gorgeous drawings of Nazi propaganda in the weekly Saxonian magazine *Lustige Welt*. He glorified Nazism and ridiculed everything that was anti-fascist; he glorified the war and agitated against all enemies of the Nazis. Was this Möllendorff ever a soldier? No, because the Nazis needed him. Just read the old issues of *Lustige Welt*, and you will find Möllendorff again as an extremely active Nazi propagandist. The City of Berlin, however, insists on making this *Mantelträger* [shabby coat] its in-house cartoonist. With this you render the *Antifa* [anti-fascist movement] powerless. Ask M. himself or his colleagues, and you will have my remark confirmed."[9]

Another case was that of Bernhard Huth who had been one of the chief animators at UFA Werbefilm. After the war, he tried to invent excuses and talk his way out:

BERNHARD H u t h.

He explained that he didn't join the Party on his own free will. One day he was told by the works committee that he would receive the [NSDAP] Party membership as a sort of a "gift." He didn't have the courage to refuse as he didn't have the feeling to do something wrong. [...]

Asked again about his Party membership, Herr Huth states that he had come to know in 1937 that he was made a member of NSDAP. He can't exactly remember the exact circumstances of this "gift." He thinks that it must have been in connection with a former membership in the National Socialist Factory Cell Organization. When Party membership was upgraded in 1937, they probably had drawn on old members of that Organization.

Asked if he was a National Socialist, Herr Huth states that this question isn't easy to answer; according to Party doctrine he wasn't. He didn't see himself as genuine National Socialist, otherwise he would have joined NSDAP earlier.

(In fact, Huth was member of the NSDAP not since 1937 but already since 1933!)

He didn't behave like a Nazi because he always thought for himself, contradictory to party discipline.

Herr Huth says that he has remained nonpolitical till today. Nobody could hold it against him that he wants to keep this attitude. Back then he considered National Socialism a worthwhile thing until he realized that this view was wrong. Because he did something politically stupid, he now has to suffer and is forced to dwell with wife and two kids in a room of 10 square meters.[10]

Bavaria animation producer Hans Held (Figure 9.2), on the other hand, talked quite frankly about the role he played in the Third Reich and went so far as to make a disturbing statement about the Holocaust:

Most of the film people were no Nazis. As a schoolboy I joined the SA, although that wasn't actually allowed, that was before [1933] – namely the motor storm. I wouldn't have dared, of course, to go to school in uniform, something like that. And then I had the intention of organizing an aviator squadron with some other fellows who were interested, because there would have been more opportunities. And that was practically the end for me. That's when I realized what was behind the Nazis and I withdrew. There came a gentleman who had served as fighter pilot in World War I. He had meanwhile been fired from a position as controller because he had managed to fill his own pocket. [...] And then he went to the municipal garden center, that was unskilled work and stuff like that. And now he was supposed to become a Sturmführer [storm leader] with us because he was in the party. And that was bad. That's where it ended for me. I was in the SA, but didn't join the party. There was a situation in Marl, there was a vote right after '33: Hitler, yes or no. And then I pushed myself. I played sick. But they got me, the SA. They weren't malicious per se, no, they offered to help me. I had to put on the galoshes and dressing gown, and they drove me to the polling station. ... I don't know if they could check that. Of course, I voted: NO. ... [...] I have never had any difficulties with the Nazis. Probably because I held back. Otherwise, it would have been stupid. What the hell? I had Jewish friends, so I had to be careful about that too. I even took one across the border on a motorbike. He had had problems at home, that was in the 1930s, it was bad then. [...] But it wasn't as bad as they claim nowadays. Except for those who were directly affected, who were having a hard time, including abroad. But if they claim that six million Jews were murdered here, that's a joke. Why do they say that? No, it would have been bad even if it had been a hundred thousand or a hundred, but making six million out of it... so many didn't live here.[11]

FIGURE 9.2   Hans Held. (Courtesy of J. P. Storm.)

ANIMATED CONTINUITY IN EAST AND WEST

When Gerhard Fieber returned from brief war imprisonment, he acted the German wryneck. He didn't come empty handed. In December 1945, he approached the Department of Popular Education of the Berlin Magistrate, introduced himself as estate trustee of Deutsche Zeichenfilm, and offered the funny dog story he had begun in Dachau: *Somersault into Life*.

> This film is in the process of being completed, music as well as color samples are available. Funds still required for completion: approx. 30–40,000 Reichsmark. Duration of work until completion: 3–4 months. Agfacolor film stock available, black and white raw film likewise. Paper and cels: ca. 30,000 sheets available, colors and ink included.

The entire artwork had been transferred to the Zeichenfilm headquarters in Berlin in January 1945 and had suffered war-related fire damage.

At Deutsche Film AG (DEFA), founded on May 17, 1946, in the Soviet sector, people immediately liked Fieber's proposal. It was overlooked that all the previous work had been initiated by Nazis – and that they had animated in Dachau, not far away from the infamous concentration camp, Fieber kept to himself. This is how a Nazi project was turned into the first animated color film of DEFA, which was established by the Soviets and some German artists under progressive auspices:

> After a process that lasted more than six months (sic!), the color cartoon film has now been completed by DEFA's animation department. After the fall of the Hitler regime, *Somersault* is the first animated color film. Up until then only four small black and white cartoons were made. [...] The film [...] treats in a funny way the fate of a dog family. The youngest, "Nies" (Sneeze) "sneezes" away from his mother's breast. While trying to get him back, his mother and his siblings are caught by a dog catcher. In the end, however, they are freed from the hands of the robber with great difficulty by the laziest of the dog family, the "yawner" (Gähner) who yawns constantly.[12]

Himself understood Fieber as apolitical, same as his colleague Bernhard Huth: "Fortunately, we German cartoonists were spared politically and not forced to busy ourselves in any party politics. The evidence: Both of our films, *Armer Hansi* as well as *Purzelbaum ins Leben*, were so-called fairy-tale films, ideally suited for 'big' children, no tendency at all. To the best of my knowledge, except for managing director Neumann and 5 employees (Wöhrle in Munich, Böhme, Blümel, Leberecht, and Preuss in Berlin), there were no other party members employed at Deutsche Zeichenfilm GmbH. Thinking about it today, a lot would strike me. Sure. But I have to tell you, frankly tell you: We were *infatuated* with making cartoon films – *nothing else*."[13]

But while he was building a new career for himself in the ruins of Berlin, ghosts from the past, former colleagues, revealed the truth about Zeichenfilm GmbH, and settled up with the incompetent studio management and Karl Neumann's favorite animation supervisor Gerhard Fieber. In a letter dated August 3, 1946, one of the staff members of Deutsche Zeichenfilm, Bernhard Klein, who was married to a Jewish wife, complained bitterly about his experiences. Klein had a background in theater and painting (the paintings of his older brother, César, were classified *Entartete Kunst* – Degenerate Art and banned) but took an early interest in animated cartoons. He had decided to experiment with animation. In 1938, he came to the conclusion that it would be best for his wife and himself to emigrate, and finally saw a chance to do so in 1941. To raise some money, he tried to sell his finished cartoon film *Sonntagsabenteuer* a.k.a. *Der treulose Wecker* (*Sunday Adventure/The Faithless Alarm Clock*) and found himself trapped in the network of animation under the swastika (Figure 9.3):

> In the meantime, prompted by Disney's success story of *Snow White*, German film industry had become wide-eyed. The Culture Film Department arranged immediately that my film was accepted by Tobis and released successfully. Then, however, they launched their own production and followed my example, initially under the roof of Tobis, where still a certain artistic atmosphere dominated, later under the label Deutsche Zeichenfilm G.mb.H. which was supervised by a scenario-wise completely obstinate chief dramaturge [Frank Leberecht]. At this company happened exactly as I always had feared. Advertising filmmakers and commercial artists were entrusted with the task which was tantamount to assigning poster artists to do a painting.
>
> Under these circumstances I wasn't interested anymore to try to prevent that the Zeichenfilm company would have to make experiences the hard way. Anyway, the people in charge knew better all time with the result that the Zeichenfilm company, with a budget of RM 4.5 million, 100 employees plus 200 trainees, didn't achieve more than I did with a film of the same length but without any assistance.
>
> There was no evidence that any of the five chief animators of Zeichenfilm company was more skilled than others. They were all beginners compared to this artistic

challenge and in some cases not artistically minded at all. If at all, they were appreciated for political reasons and political disposition. Two were foreigners, one a true anti-fascist, the other unpleasant with occasional antisemitic statements. The 5th, however, the artist G. F. fraternized with the National Socialists. He sympathized with the respective ideas of the shop steward, shared deliberately all victory-focused propaganda foolery and spread these delusional ideas. In several copies he made caricatures showing Jews marked with Jewish stars: a street scene populated by Stürmer types, the Yellow Star overemphasized, headline: "Es leuchten die Sterne (The Stars Shine)."[14]

FIGURE 9.3   Antisemitic caricature by Gerhard Fieber. (Courtesy of J. P. Storm.)

All of a sudden, the ground got too hot underfoot. Fieber felt an urgent need to leave Berlin and the Soviet sector straight away. In Bad Sachsa where he rented a spa house at half price, and in Göttingen he undertook a project that would have fulfilled the goals of Deutsche Zeichenfilm G.m.b.H., and would been a just homage to Karl Neumann's ambitions and produced Germany's first feature-length 2D cartoon: *Tobias Knopp, Abenteuer eines Junggesellen* (*Tobias Knopp: Adventures of a Bachelor*) based on Wilhelm Busch. The illustrious actors who loaned their voices to Fieber's Busch cartoon were directed by Wolfgang Liebeneiner, Goebbels' favorite feature-film director and final production chief of Nazi UFA. Fieber must have felt like the righteous Lord Seal Keeper of German Animation (by Goebbels' grace). But critics and audiences didn't like what they saw. If reviews were published at all, they were panned.

As children of Wilhelm Busch, we feel obliged to make the following remarks about the premiere of the film mentioned: As much as it is to be welcomed that the German film industry has invested a great of effort and money in producing a full-length cartoon film for the first time, so must be protested against the way against the working methods in the film studio. In his picture stories, Busch recorded the characteristic scenes of the plot in drawings and words. If the film now inserts further drawings, this can only weaken the overall effect, especially since the patchwork used by the film people is not exactly original and witty. Apparently, the Mickey Mouse films have been thought of far too much. But: Wilhelm Busch served à la Mickey Mouse – that's an impossibility.

There are quite a few individual objections to this film. However, it is sufficient to mention here that Busch's drawings have more verve and movement than the drawings on the screen, that the unity of drawing and word, as it exists with Busch, has been destroyed, and that the figures often are only grimacing faces of their original essence.[15]

Fieber blamed Disney: "Unfortunately the movie was made in black and white, while at the same time Walt Disney's *Snow White* was released in Technicolor. No way. A dwarf against a giant!"[16]

The critics (East and West), however, dealt likewise with the popular Disney and *Snow White* that finally was seen in German cinemas:

This Americanization of a German fairy tale grates on my nerves. […] We will not accept to hear our familiar fairy-tale characters singing with Broadway voices, we don't tolerate a children's revue that is actually made for adults.[17]

The fairy-tale forest of the Grimm Brothers has transformed into a jungle. Trees and bushes reach their ghostly fingers for the king's child. Owl eyes flame. Crocodiles open their jaws…[18]

Ruefully, Fieber returned to advertising films. For his fellow animators and competitors, he didn't have a friendly word. He ridicules them as a "profession of failed existence": "Most of them were fire eaters, sword eaters who were only a bit gifted. Few had a solid art education." Kaskeline he called a *Small like Big* (*Kleiner Gernegross*). Even "friends" like Heinz Tischmeyer weren't spared by Fieber's anger. In 1940, Tischmeyer had produced an emphatically antisemitic color short film for producer Hubert Schonger: *Vom Bäumlein, das andere Blätter hat gewollt*. (*The Little Tree That Longed for Other Leaves*) presented a *Stürmer*-like caricature of a bearded Jew who is after the golden leaves of an innocent little tree. The short was based on a poem by Friedrich Rückert (1813) but replaced Rückert's peasant with a thieving Jew: *…ging der Jude durch den Wald mit grossem Sack und grossem Bart/Der sieht die goldnen Blätter bald;/Er steckt sie ein, geht eilends for/und lässt das leere Bäumlein dort*. […The Jew came through the woods with a big bag and a big beard/Soon he sees the golden leaves/He pockets them and goes away/and leaves the little tree empty.] According to Fieber (Figure 9.4),

Tischmeyer was a man who made excellent individual drawings, but the movements were always fretsaw. There was no dynamic drain. The acting was a bit simple. And that was also a problem with Fischerkoesen. The good things weren't drawn by Fischer either. You always need a staff of people, but he knew what he wanted. He created the basic figure and then said: so and so. And if he then gets such a great idea as Möllendorff's... Möllendorff can tell you novels about it because he hates Fischerkoesen. He claimed to me that Fischer was so indecent that he always put Möllendorff in the credits in small letters.

FIGURE 9.4   Heinz Tischmeyer. (Courtesy of J. P. Storm.)

FISCHERKOESEN'S RENAISSANCE

Fischerkoesen! In Fieber's animated world, it was all hate and envy. Only one person Fieber considered sort of equal. He turned green with envy when he realized the commercial success of his rival Hans Fischerkoesen who had re-entered the field of advertising films:

> Fischer made ten times more money than I. He focused entirely on advertising films, not feature films and such crap I did, works of art. He really made cash.[19]

Fieber didn't know that Fischerkoesen intended very well to produce a longer, almost feature-length animated film based on Wilhelm Busch. According to Dr. Hans Michael Fischerkoesen, that didn't work out for two reasons: "He couldn't find any sponsors, and he didn't simply have the time, because there were orders from the advertising industry, and so he put it aside."[20]

For West Germany's animation producers like him, there was no need to move and change and enter the risky field of feature-length animation as Fieber did. It was better to live off the fat of the land.

Fieber: "Fischerkoesen has dumbly earned it. Alone with advertising. He was incredibly busy. If I had maybe ten customers, he had hundred."

Right after the war, Hans Fischer a.k.a. Fischerkoesen was arrested by the Soviets as suspected Nazi collaborator and producer of Army training films. He was interned in the former concentration camp Sachsenhausen. Dr. Hans Michael Fischerkoesen about the time his father was interned by the Soviets:

> I remember when they came to arrest him. It was a day in December. It was dark out-side. The door-bell rang. There were two men, one in uniform, a Russian, and next to him a little guy in a long black leather coat, with a scar in his face. The guy was Herr Panzerus. Herr Panzerus had complained that my father had made Nazi films. They took him and said: Come with us, we have some questions. My father was going to pack some things. He anticipated what was going on. But they said: No, no, no, tomorrow morning you will be back. This one night transformed into three and a half years. My father didn't get any trial. They were just taken off the streets and were silenced: We don't need them, get rid of them! They weren't forced to labor. They didn't do anything else than hang around and tried to survive, somehow. My father survived because he was artist and able to portray the commanders. He portrayed them as heroes, of course. They gave him colored pencils and paper. And when he was finished with some draw-ing, they threw a slice of bread into the mud.

With Fischerkoesen, in prison was his chief animator Rudolf Bär:

> In Soviet internment, Hans Fischerkösen had the internal prisoner number 99082, Rudolf Bär 99089.[21]
>
> [...] there are a few Russian documents from the camp registration of the Soviet special camp No. 7/No. 1 in Sachsenhausen about Hans Fischerkoesen and Rudolf Bär. First of all, there are short entries about the two in the Camp Journal, in which arrivals and departures, but also the allegations against the prisoners are recorded in brief. They state that Hans Fischer was arrested on December 17, 1945, by NKVD, the Potsdam operative group of the Soviet secrfet police because he was accused of having been a counter-intelligence officer. He was accordingly accused of collaborating with Geheime Staatspolizei (Gestapo), the Secret State Police, an instrument of the "Third Reich" that was used, among other things, to combat political opponents and had been condemned as a criminal organization in the Nuremberg trials. In the case of Rudolf Bär, the accusation is noted that he was deputy counter-intelligence officer. Both were released from the Soviet camp in the course of the first major release action in the sum-mer of 1948, although it is interesting that Fischer and Bär were not released imme-diately. According to the registry documents, they were transferred to the Opeative Sector Brandenburg on July 19 and July 20, 1948.
>
> There is also a transfer list from the operative group of the Potsdam District to the special camp of the NKVD dated December 31, 1945. There are several names men-tioned, including in second place Rudolf Bär:
>
> Beer [sic!], Rudolf, born 1901 in Leipzig, German, medium education [no graduation], NSDAP member since 1933, coming from an employee family, mar-ried, living in Potsdam. From early 1943 to April 1945, he was deputy counter-intelligence officer at Fischer's company where he exposed cases of sabotage and anti-fascist propaganda.

No. 4 on the list is Hans Fischer:

Fischer, Hans, born 1896 in Badkesen [sic! Kösen], German, no party membership, medium education, coming from an employee family, living in Potsdam.

He was owner of the Fischer Company that released films for the navy and the army, where he also was counter-intelligence officer from 1943 to April 1945.[22]

In the meantime, Kurt Schleicher, a tinkerer and inventor, and Leni Fischer, Fischerkoesen's sister, ran the shop: "But there wasn't much, just a few odd commercials."

Dr. Hans Michael Fischerkoesen:

My father was then released because they shut down the camp or were about to close it and they released the people in batches. I was seven years old. My father never spoke to us about it, because you have to understand one thing: the time in the camp the whole Nazi period – they let down a blind, they didn't want to hear anything about it. That's in the past, it was terrible, it was horrible, but now we just want to move forward. You'll get rebuffed once in a while if you ask at all, and then you don't do it. Well, today I really regret that there wasn't much more talk about the time before '45.

When Fischerkoesen was released, the whole family moved to the French occupation zone.

At that time the allies had banned the production of commercials. The only zone that had it more relaxed was the French zone. But where to find a laboratory? Then he came to the town of Remagen, there was IFU, the International Film Union, they had a lab in the Calmuth District, but only for black and white film. Representatives of financial institutions and banks approached him there. My father talked proudly about it: "Fischerkoesen, do you want a credit?" they said. "We will help you." – "I don't want a loan, I don't want money, I want an assignment." And then the assignments came in. The first was for a washing powder called Awalan, maybe a Henkel product, and the film was titled *The Six-Day Racing*. They made small bicyclists from wire and remnants and they organized a cycle race. This symbolized, so to speak: Six days the laundry was collected, and on the seventh it was washed. My father then moved very quickly to Marienfels Castle. We were there for three years. There must have been twenty relatives who took part: they inked, colored. That was from 1949 to 1951, '52. But it quickly became too cramped, and a piece of land was bought in the Mechem District of Bad Godesberg, a former banker's villa, seven or eight hundred square meters of floor space and around it a park of 40,000 square meters. We had bought the back part: 20,000 square meters. The villa had of course been plundered [after the war] by the locals, who had taken out the pipes, everything that was copper. They felled the trees because they needed firewood. The building was run down. He renovated it, still from Marienfels, and then we moved in at the beginning of '52 and added on to the side. My father began with a down payment of 8000 Marks. And after two, three years he had 60 employees who worked 48 hours per week. On Saturdays, work continued until 2 p.m., and then the overtime came. Housewives were allowed to leave earlier – I think on Thursday afternoon –, the shops closed at half past six. It was hard work. Sure. But these were golden years I can tell you.[23]

In the 1950s, Hans Fischerkoesen was the undisputed market leader in German advertising cartoons. He was the only animator who had a cover story devoted to by the renowned German news magazine, DER SPIEGEL.[24] The article

brought to mind that the previous year 160 million German cinemagoers saw
one Fischerkoesen's commercials promoting chocolate and shoe polish, pencils
and bras, cigarettes and toothpaste, dairy butter, and stain remover. It even compared Fischerkoesen with Walt Disney. The old rivalry with the American was
not forgotten. Fischerkoesen seemed to have the finger on the pulse of German
audiences. No, the mood and taste of audiences hadn't changed for the past two
decades. Cinemas still run the old UFA movies – and many of the new ones
looked like the old ones.

A 2-minute film titled *Durch Nacht zum Licht (Through Night to Light)* entertained
moviegoers in several West German cities the last week. [...]

The film begins with a close-up: A girl appears on the screen, tossing and turning
in restless sleep, thick drops of cold sweat stand out on her forehead. Suddenly, the
blonde slides through the headboard of the bed, which opens as a gateway to the realm
of darkness. With her nightgown waving in the air, she floats through space, facing the
terror of hell of a modern Dante.

Bone fingers grasp at the white neck of the sleeping, daggers aim at her breasts. The
girl whirls into a skyscraper canyon, rushes over endless stairs in modern buildings.

There – at the height of the inferno of fear – glistening streaks of lighting break into
the grey-green of the darkness. A voice that sounds redeeming from beyond finally
explains to the cinema-goer why he has been sent into the horrors of a cartoon hell
for two minutes: Nightmares are the result of an upset stomach," thunders the voice.
"Underberg [liquor] helps against an upset stomach.

This advertising film in Eastman-Color is the gem in an assortment of six films, with
which a German commercial film producer wants to do something that no European
animation film producer has ever risked before: the foray into the United States of
America, the citadel of Walt Disney. [...]

Hans Fischerkoesen – that's the name of the stout little gentleman with the imperi-
ous cigar in the corner of his mouth – finally feels strong enough to challenge Walt
Disney in his home country. His economic and artistic supremacy as a commercial
cartoon film manufacturer in Germany is secured. With an annual turnover of six million marks, Fischerkoesen is far at the top of West German advertising cartoon film
producers. [...]

Fischerkoesen's managing director Dr. Ulrich Westerkamp, 70, cites "healthy
humor" which he describes as "folksy" as one of main reasons for the success of
Fischerkoesen's films. In the case of the middle-class cement merchant's son Hans
Fischer, who got the telephone number 12345 for his studio, it is expressed, among
other things, in the fact that he laughs more about his own ideas than is actually appropriate. This humor, which often operates with the banal and self-evident, seems to have
struck a chord with the German public, which [...] still hasn't gotten tired of laughing
at a man who accidentally sits down on a bowl of ice cream. [...]

Measured against today's graphic style, Fischerkoesen's figures are drawn in a surprisingly simple, provincial manner that cannot stand a comparison with, for example,
Walt Disney's urban, strongly contoured and imaginative animation technique. The
characteristics of the figures could have been designed by pupils of a primary school:
red bulbous noses, round apple cheeks, points instead of eyes, potato bellies, and legs
like matches.

Fischerkoesen sticks to this homely typing with the same persistence with which he
wears the same light grey, conservatively cut Glencheck double-breasted suit and the same
tie day for day. Younger artists in his studio try in vain to push a modern graphic style.[25]

NOTES

1 Bundesarchiv/Federal Archive, SONDERREFERAT KULTURFILM Production Planning 1944/45 Group B Zeichenfilm Berlin, May 4, 1944, signed Dr. Karbe.
2 Bundesarchiv/Federal Archive, SONDERREFERAT KULTURFILM: Animation Film Production, Status as of May 15, 1944.
3 *Dansk Tegnefilms Historie: www.tegnefilmhistorie.dk.*
4 Dr. Werner Kruse interviewed by J. P. Storm.
5 Stefanie Steuer interviewed by J. P. Storm.
6 Anna-Luise Subatzus interviewed by J. P. Storm.
7 Gerhard Fieber interviewed by J. P. Storm.
8 Buchenwald.
9 Document found in the collection of J. P. Storm.
10 Document Center/Bundesarchiv: Spruchkammer [Arbitration Board] file Huth, Bernhard. Berlin, May 3, 1948 Gr.
11 Hans Held interviewed by J. P. Storm.
12 *Purzelbaum ins Leben. Erster Zeichenfarbfilm der DEFA,* In: Neues Deutschland No. 175, November 15, 1946.
13 Gerhard Fieber interviewed by J. P. Storm.
14 Collection of J. P. Storm.
15 *Der Traum eines Kritikers. Tobias-Knopp-Film in Hannover.* In: Kölner Rundschau, 5. März 1950.
16 Ibid.
17 R.K., *Disneys* Schneewittchen/*Im Astor.* In: Nachtexpress, Berlin/GDR, March 4, 1950.
18 Barbara Klie, *Schneewittchen und die Disney-Dynastie.* In: Der Kurier, Berlin West, March 4, 1950.
19 Gerhard Fieber interviewed by J. P. Storm.
20 Dr. Hans Michael Fischerkoesen interviewed by J. P. Storm.
21 By email from Dr. Enrico Heitzer, June 28, 2013. Gedenkstätte und Museum Sachsenhausen/Stiftung Brandenburgische Gedenkstätten.
22 Dr. Enrico Heitzer in a mail dated June 19, 2014.
23 Dr. Hans Michael Fischerkoesen interviewed by J. P. Storm.
24 *Minnesang auf Markenartikel.* In: DER SPIEGEL, August 29, 1956.
25 Ibid., pp. 34–36.

10 Comic Strips in Germany (West and East)

YOUTH AHEAD!

In contrast to France and Belgium, comics did not enjoy a particularly good reputation in Germany. This is one of the reasons why cartoon films lagged behind in this country for so long. German graphic artists and draftsmen who worked for the comics were in bad standing. A typical example was Helmut Nickel, born in 1924 in Quohren near Dresden. As a graphic designer, Nickel was self-taught:

> I studied art history and ethnology at the Free University [in Berlin] and received a scholarship of 30 marks 30 pfennigs. I gave my landlady 30 marks. So I had only 30 pfennigs to live on. That's why I wanted to make some money. Before I came here, I was a prisoner of war in Belgium and I was put in a coal mine and that was a job I didn't like. The camp commandant had a father-in-law who owned a cinema and he needed someone to draw posters for him. And because he didn't want to spend any money, he asked around among the camp inmates if anyone could draw. At that time, I had a friend who was lying under me in the double bed and saw himself as an opera singer. I made a drawing of *Tristan and Isolde* for him, which he hung up. During a camp inspection, the commander saw the drawing and asked who made it, and since then I've made cinema posters. Back then, I thought I was born to be an illustrator, and when I returned here and needed to earn some money, I went on to work for an advertising company. A female colleague who also worked for this company had been approached by a comic book publisher. But she was only a signwriter and couldn't draw. So she told them that she knew someone who could draw figures, and that's how I got into it.[1] [...]
>
> *Out in [Berlin] Dahlem there was a small corner publisher who printed his things in the basement. The whole family worked there, on the coloring etc. They took the films themselves and simply wanted to make money. They used different company names that were all camouflage designations for one and the same publisher, because they were always three steps away from bankruptcy. When he went broke, his brother took over, then his father.*[2]

The publisher's name was Gerstmayer, one of many who weren't exactly what you would call trustworthy. He traded, depending on the situation, as Gerstmayer Verlag, Verlag für moderne Literatur, Titanus Verlag, and Druck- und Verlagsanstalt. The old man of the company, Hermann Gerstmayer (1886–1961), had made a name for himself by writing a patriotic series *Mit fliegenden Fahnen* (*With Flying Colors*) during WWI and in the early years of the Third Reich stories for series like *Die Fahne hoch* (*Raise the Flag*) and *Jugend voran!* (*Youth Ahead*). For Gerstmayer and his two sons, Nickel drew *Drei Musketiere* (*Three Musketeers*), *Don Pedro*, and *Robimson* (which he took over from Willi Kohlhoff). He also worked for an even more notorious competitor of Gerstmayer: Walter Lehning.

DOI: 10.1201/9781003375548-10

The business principle of Walter Lehning's publishing house, based in Hanover since 1952, was to bring inexpensively licensed comic stuff in large editions to the market:

> On a vacation trip to Italy, he discovered comic books in strip format at the newspaper stands there. All of a sudden, he sensed a great opportunity and in July 1953 published the first three series licensed from Italy with the subtitle *Piccolo Bilderserie [Piccolo Picture Series]* at a price of 20 pfennigs each.[3]

To save money on licenses, the Italian material was soon replaced by German series like *Akim, Sigurd,* and *Nick der Weltraumfahrer (Nick the Spaceman),* drawn by graphic artists such as Nickel and Hansrudi Wäscher. The artists were paid poorly. Bob (Wilhelm Hermann) Heinz (1923–1984) was one of those who worked for Lehning. He worked on *Pit und Alf* and *Jan Maat*:

> Lehning was actually the super example of the exploitation of graphic artists. He kept ordering and ordering and said to talk about fees later. And then he pushed the fees down so much because he said to himself: "Well, now he's started, then he can't just stop again. And it makes him known." It was almost like we artists should pay him for getting us started. In the time I worked for him, around 1953 to 1958/59, he went bankrupt twice. But he always came out victorious. In bankruptcy he had to commit himself to continue production. But the fees were paid through the bank. If we were entitled to about 30 to 40% of our fees according to the bankruptcy rate, it was pushed down even further. It couldn't get any lower. Since some fees came in only due to the mass of delivered works.[4]

The accumulation of comic books soon became a thorn in the side of German youth protection groups. They used an article published in SPIEGEL magazine titled *Opium in der Kinderstube (Opium in the Children's Room)* as a pretext for a campaign against what they called *Schmutz und Schund* (Dirt and Trash):

> In view of these and similar effects of comics, it is not surprising that psychological warfare makes use of them: American propaganda offices have so far distributed around five million comic books in East Asia in order to use them to combat the communist ideology.
>
> The first attempt in Vietnam was so successful that a large-scale comic book offensive was launched against Red China. U.S. comic books, smuggled in by the thousands from the Hong Kong bridgehead, tell in simple drawings how the communists first came as friends and farmers, but soon seized dictatorial powers. [...]
>
> With the masses of illiterate people, the comic technique seems to have a convincing effect. [...]
>
> However, the opponents of comics in the United States are not happy about the further spread of comics. Leading physicians, pedagogues, psychologists, publicists have condemned the comic book wave. Dr. Frederic Wertham, head of the Lafargue clinic in New York, wrote: "My clinical studies have convinced me that comics poison the well of spontaneous childhood imagination."
>
> The doctor believes that picture books are largely responsible for the rise in adolescent neglect in the United States. Book critic John Mason Brown calls the comics "the opium in the children's room." Gilbert Seldes goes even further. This historian of all forms of popular entertainment is convinced that, over time, picture books will dumb down American people. Because not only the minors, but also the adults will become more and more addicted to comics.[5]

From then on, comics were monitored in Germany and, if necessary, indexed by the *Bundesprüfstelle für jugendgefährdende Schriften*, the Federal Review Board for Publications Harmful to Young Persons, which was set up in 1954:

> The criteria used to review comics give the impression that a desperate attempt has been made to impose the standards of the local, familiar on the imported foreign object. Comics are understood as literature and measured against the "classic" (more precisely: against the traditionally acknowledged). Accordingly, what is foreign and alien appears in the "principles" of the Review Board as actually scandalous: What is fatal about them is the bubble language ("miserable snippets of sentences") and the action principle ("pure presentation of tense, almost incoherently strung together fight scenes"; "any higher context is missing"). The alienation and uncertainty caused by the unfamiliar medium explains the rather simple procedure which served for the Board's decision-making. The authorities decreed that comics are youth literature and are therefore subject to pedagogical standards.[6]

IT CAME FROM ENTENHAUSEN

What was true for the other comics wasn't true for Disney and Ehapa. Ehapa was the German subsidiary of a Danish publishing house founded by Egmont H. Petersen (1860–1914) that secured the Scandinavian and German rights to Disney's comic books. The greatest asset to Ehapa's Disney comics was a woman, Dr. Erika Fuchs, a German philologist. She began by inventing new German names, not for the main protagonists like Mickey, Donald, Goofy, and Pluto, but for the whole ensemble of supporting players – and the names lingered in the memory of the young readers and their families:

> Scrooge McDuck = Dagobert Duck
> Huey, Dewey & Louie = Tick, Trick & Track
> Abigal or Elviry Duck = Dorette Anette Liesette Duck
> Gladstone Gander = Gustav Gans
> Gyro Gearloose = Daniel Düsentrieb
> Gus Goose = Franz Gans
> The Big Bad Wolf = Ede Wolf
> Practical Pig = Schweinchen Schlau
> Chip 'n' Dale = Ahörnchen und Behörnchen
> Pegleg Pete = Kater Karlo
> Beagle Boys = Panzerknacker
> Magica de Spell = Gundel Gaukeley
> Ludwig Von Drake = Primus von Quack

There was even a criminal in Berlin (Arno Funke) whose nickname ran rampant in the German press: Dagobert. Erika Fuchs was far more than a translator. She used her incredible skills to intelligently refine characters' dialogue, and sometimes she improved the original version.

In the United States and other English-speaking countries, the home of Donald Duck, Scrooge McDuck, and their cohorts is Duckburg. However, no German would ever refer to Donald's hometown as Duckburg, because to us it is and will forever be *Entenhausen*.

Erika Fuchs was born Johanna *Theodolinde* (a very, very rare name, so rare that even this writer had not heard it before) Erika Petri on December 7, 1906 in Rostock on the Baltic Sea. She was the second of six children of August Petri and his wife Auguste née Horn. Auguste was a trained singer but worked as elementary school teacher in Augsburg. Her husband became director of the electricity plant for Eastern Pomerania. The family moved to Belgard an der Pesante in 1912. Erika's father was an austere man. She recalled that in her family things wouldn't be discussed or questioned: "There were orders that we had to observe." Due to her studies, she moved around a lot. In the summer of 1926, she began to study art history, archeology, and medieval history in Lausanne, and the following winter 1926/1927 semester, she went to Munich; the third and fourth semesters she studied in London; and in 1928, she returned to Munich, until she was finished in the 1931/1932 winter semester. Erika also spent some months in Florence, Italy, the Netherlands, Britain, and Switzerland. On July 17, 1931, she earned her Ph.D.: *magna cum laude*. Her thesis was devoted to the baroque sculptor Johann Michael Feichtmayr (1709–1772).

In 1932, she married Günter Fuchs, the owner of a small factory that manufactured furnaces: Summa Feuerungen.

Erika Fuchs began to translate after the war, first for the German edition of *Reader's Digest;* then, in 1951, she started work on *Mickey Mouse* comics from the moment Ehapa acquired the rights. She continued to do so until 1988. *Reader's Digest and Mickey Mouse* were both published by Ehapa. When Erika applied for the job to augment her income, she had never read a comic before; but she also never considered that comics were atrocious – a tool that would harm kids as many educators believed in those days.

Fuchs tried hard to introduce quotes from the classics to enhance the quality of her translations and put what would become a winged word into Daniel Düsentrieb's mouth, a variation of the first line of the engineer's song of Heinrich Seidel: *Dem Ingeniör ist nichts zu schwör – Nothing too difficult for the engineer.*

> In addition, Fuchs developed the idea of supplementing the onomatopoeia typical of comics by giving thought processes legible form with "think, think," or a glance of the eye with "blink, blink." These examples set precedents, this principle even became the standard of comic language in Germany, producing strange results at the hands of other texters: "freu, freu," for expressing enthusiasm or "staun, staun," for surprise. Erika Fuchs' admirers introduced the term "Erikativ" to denote this new grammatical form (punning on "genitive," "dative," etc.).[7]

The onomatopoet passed away on April 22, 2005, at age 98 in Munich, and was interred next to her husband who had died in 1984. On August 1, 2015, in Schwarzenbach an der Saale where she had lived since 1933, a museum in her honor was opened: Erika Fuchs Museum – Museum for Comics and Language Art, thanks to the activities of her loyal followers, the so-called "Donaldists."

WALT DISNEY'S MICKEY MAUS GMBH

In the 19560s and 1960s, Disney products and comics were not considered harmful to young people. They were an exception. They were "clean." Right after the war in summer 1946, Disney's brother Roy traveled to various European cities to rearrange financial ties. Before a German Disney branch office was established, all European merchandising activities were controlled from Paris by Armand Bigle (1918–2007). Bigle signed with Disney in 1949 for a commission sales job, opening new territories in Europe; he didn't have a fixed salary but signed for 30% of the gross.

Jimmy Johnson:

> Armand had been with King Features since the war until Kay Kamen had recommended that he run the Paris office. Even at this early stage in his career, Armand seemed to me a real genius in the character merchandising field.
>
> Armand and [his wife] Betty impressed me tremendously. They were bright, cultured, warm, and wonderful. My enthusiasm for them was transmitted to Roy [Disney] and O.B. [Johnston] on my return and shortly thereafter the Bigles did move to Paris.
>
> Of all our many merchandising success stories around the world, none surpasses Armand Bigle's success in France. It isn't just merchandising – his tie-ins with Disney motion picture releases and rereleases are models for the entire world.[8]

By releasing feature-length films and shorts to West Germany, it seemed to be wise to open a branch office in Frankfurt/Main in 1954 that would respond to Bigle. Frankfurt was a serious contender for becoming the government seat of West Germany, but Chancellor Konrad Adenauer, for strictly personal reasons, preferred Bonn in the Rhine Valley. Anyway, concerning banks and money, Frankfurt remained West Germany's secret capital.

Disney's German office was named Walt Disney's Mickey Maus GmbH. Put in charge running the office was a bookkeeper named Kurt Melzer. Melzer's secretary was a Mrs. Schneidermann, but from the late 1950s it was Horst Koblischek who took care of the whole business.

Koblischek was born in Reichenberg, today's Liberec, Czech Republic, and came to Germany in 1948. He was a typical laterant entrant:

> As a young man I dabbled in various things. In 1948, for instance, I worked in the restaurant at Hamburg Fuhlsbüttel Airport as dishwasher to serve the cliché. Then I went to Berlin and worked there until 1958 as sales manager for a textile company. I came to Disney just by accident. I learned from an advertisement in an Ehapa publication that Disney was looking for someone in the licensing department.[9]

He applied for the job. It was just luck – on both sides. In advertisements the small licensing office promised *high sales figures thanks to the popular Disney characters.*

> If you compare it with today business was very modest. The first license I brought in in 1958 was a company named Wallbaum. They manufactured school bags with Disney characters. This company was our licensee steadily from 1958 until ca. 1986. But nobody would beat a path to our door to get a license. We had to find out the respective industry leaders by ourselves and had to present appropriate concepts. We did a few drawings and layouts for products that we considered suitable. Then we approached the respective manufacturer.[10]

The office employed two artists to do all designs and character drawings. These were Wolfgang and Katja Schäfer. Both had studied at the Städel School, the State School for Fine Arts in Frankfurt. Wolfgang studied landscape painting and portrait; Katja did mural painting.

Katja Schäfer recalls:

Sometime the Disney office called, because they needed an illustrator. My husband was recommended, because he already worked for Simplizissimus and Wespennest magazines. The office was located at Weserstrasse in the red-light district of Frankfurt. At that time Paris still had the whip hand. That means that they couldn't work autonomously back then. Everything had to be approved by Disney's branch in Paris. Armand Bigle showed up often to check the projects.

Some products, of course, were taboo: drugs, alcohol, cigarettes, and certain foodstuff.

Koblischek immediately became sales manager, later the chief executive. He was the one to present Walt Disney himself in Burbank in the early 1960s: a toy monorail produced by Schuco, the old-time Disney licensee. The disadvantage: The toy monorail that Walt liked so much wasn't a success, because it could only go around in circles. Nevertheless, Koblischek was the one who built Disney's licensing business systematically to great acclaim in the 1960s and 1970s. Besides France, Scandinavia, and Japan, West Germany became the most important foreign market for Disney products. In the 1980s, Koblischek had reached up to 180 licensees: toys, fashion, textile, stationery supplies, and gift articles.

Mickey Maus GmbH soon moved to larger locations: An der Hauptwache 7–8, above Café Kranzler, then to Taunusstrasse, where most American film distributors had their German branch offices. Finally, they moved to a noble mansion.

Uncle Scrooge McDuck, Donald Duck's grabby relative, would have gotten a real kick out of the company in Frankfurt's Westend: There, in a small villa, resides Walt Disney Productions GmbH, the German offshoot of the Californian Mickey Mouse trust, and shovels millions in money.

Ten employees are used to the full. They collect money from an estimated 130 German and Austrian companies that do business worth 500 million marks annually with Donald Duck and his gang.

Whoever is going to place Donald, Mickey, Practical Pig or Goofy on bibs or foot mats, on t-shirts or watches has to transfer six per cent of his revenues to the licensor in Frankfurt. Even if one attaches only decalcomania pictures of Donald to his product, he has to pay 2.5 per cent. [...]

This year [1984] they will make roughly 30 million marks [in licenses], chief executive Horst Koblischek estimates. The demand for Disney characters is more intense than ever.

"What we experience today," Koblischek explains in a language interspersed with Americanisms, "is the ultimate renaissance of Donald Duck and that worldwide." [...]

Every businessman who is going to use Donald or Mickey, Pluto or Pegleg Pete without permission is issued a warning immediately by a Frankfurt contract attorney. Who is granted the treasured license has to pay the fees for one year in advance, rated to a minimum sale that was fixed by the Frankfurt Disney company.

Generally, German Disney governor Koblischek selects financially strong licensees. He takes – that's his policy – only one leading company per branch of trade.

"Bloss nicht übertreiben - Don't overdo it," Koblischek says, "we don't need to squeeze the copyright to the last."[11]

Koblischek died from cancer on November 11, 2002, at the age of 76. He had been announced a very special honor for a German, a demigod of the Mount Olympus of *Disney Legends* in 1997.

From my own childhood I vividly remember some of the German companies Koblischek had made deals with:

Erdal Rotfrosch released promo trading cards when *Snow White* was distributed to German cinemas for the first time. Kaiser's Kaffee Geschäft offered a *Cinderella* trading card album in 1952. Wilkens produced silverware for kids with Disney characters on forks, spoons, and knives.

Trumpf chocolate had an ensemble of Disney figures on the package.

Graupner offered Disney fretsaw characters.

There were Bause shoes for kids, Böhmer towels, OK chewing gum, and the popular rubber toys as well as Disney calendars produced by Hummelwerk W. Goebel in the predigital days, today all collector's items.

MICKEY MOUSE COMIC BOOKS IN EAST GERMANY

Frank B. Habel, a film historian born and raised in East Germany (and a Mickey Mouse buff), was very kind to share his memories of that time with us.

In the German Democratic Republic (GDR) and East Berlin one couldn't become a Disney fan just like that. And if you were, it seemed to be impossible to live that hobby out. There were first and foremost two reasons. One was economical and had to do with the currency reform in post-war Europe. Currencies of the Eastern bloc were transferable among each other but not with currencies of the Western states. Thanks to trade connections, GDR national economy had Western currency in funds, but these were reserved mainly for primary materials and industry, for cultural goods, however, only to a minor degree. It was not that much a political but an economical question that only a few American films were seen in GDR cinemas. (The first U.S. films released by State distribution company "Progress" were a compilation of Charlie Chaplin silent comedies, *The Charlie Chaplin Festival*, in 1955[12] and a Socialist independent film: *The Salt of the Earth*.)

That doesn't mean that political matters weren't taken seriously. During Cold War the American way of life wasn't the way of life in a system that was completely dependent from the Soviet Union. Notwithstanding, in the 40 years of the existence of the second German state, priorities changed depending on the political and economic situation so that over time, albeit sparingly, American music, films and literature came to GDR.

Living in East Berlin, I came in touch with Walt Disney's Comics in the 1950s, because the situation in Berlin was different from the rest of GDR. Until the wall was built in 1961, Berlin was politically divided but not locally. Berlin citizens could travel without any problem between East and West. The subway lines and S-Bahn connected the whole city. With my parents I often visited my girl cousin and her parents in Westend, and as she was the same age, I could take the Mickey Mouse Comic Books she had finished reading. Actually, it was forbidden to take press products from the West back to East Berlin. There were checks sometimes in the trains, but luckily, we were spared.

Disney products were not generally banned in the Eastern bloc. But comics were regarded, in East as well as in the West, not as a narrative art form but were ill-reputed as being primitive. Added to that, they were afraid in GDR that stories which satirized American everyday life might transport the Western attitude towards life to the young generation.

Nonetheless, Walt Disney's contribution to the art of animation was acknowledged. In popular science specialist books Disney was appreciated – sparsely illustrated with black and white images.

So until the wall was built, Mickey Mouse Comics and some other Disney stuff found its way into the East. From then on, it became difficult. Relatives in the west enclosed Mickey Mouse Comics to the packages they shipped to the East. But such packages were checked randomly, and offset prints that were unwanted and unwelcome were removed – or the packages were confiscated at all. For this reason, relatives weren't going to take the risk to include *Mickey Mouse*. The only chance for us juvenile fans was to exchange the old comic books with other kids after reading them.

SNOW WHITE AND SLEEPING BEAUTY

The first Disney movie of my life I saw four years after the wall had been built in East Berlin's Camera Cinema. This was a cinema that presented in East Berlin, later with branches in a few other GDR cities, films from all over the world in special screenings that were considered important from a film historian's point of view. These screenings were generally admitted from age 14, but I was twelve back then. Luckily, the cashier made an exception for that special picture – and so I could see *Snow White and the Seven Dwarfs* – in color, but dubbed in French language, the only playable print of that picture that existed in GDR archives. For many years, this remained the final time I saw the picture. The particular print wasn't shown publicly anymore for reasons of safety as it was an inflammable nitrate print. As a legacy from the former Reich Film Archive, a German-dubbed version from 1937 was left that was produced with the participation of some Jewish artists (among them the popular comedian Otto Wallburg, who was later murdered in a concentration camp), but from that version we only had a black and white print. This was distributed to film clubs for special screenings all over GDR in the 1970s and 1980s.

The proof that there were no ideological bounds showed when State-controlled DEFA External Trade signed a contract with Disney in 1968/69. So, between 1969 and 1971, five Disney films were released by Progress Distribution to GDR cinemas, including *20000 Leagues Under the Sea* from 1954 that played for many weeks to full houses. The only animated feature film in the package was *Sleeping Beauty* in 70mm and in a Scope version for smaller theaters. That picture was released as a goody three days after the 20th Anniversary of the Republic which was celebrated with pomp and circumstance. The picture played for many months to full houses. The license was purchased for five years so that the movie was often seen in reruns until 1974.

Otherwise, Disney didn't play a role in the daily life of GDR, although the demand was great. Disney characters were occasionally used as a sideshow phenomenon. There were for instance birthday cards for kids in which sometimes Mickey Mice were included. The cards were drawn by artists like Jürgen Kieser, who had created the popular mice couple *Fix and Fax*. Alas, the proportions were not quite right, maybe for copyright reasons. Popular with kids were the decalcomania pictures that were produced by anonymous artists and had characters like mice and ducks drawn in Disney style.

In GDR press Walt Disney and his characters were almost never mentioned. In a corner case an artist like Erich Schmitt would take a Disney character and parody it in an up-to-the-minute caricature, and Hannes Hegen [Johannes Hegenbarth, creator of the *Digedags* comics] would draw dwarfs that looked like the seven from Disney's film.

WALT DISNEY'S DEATH

When Walt Disney died in December 15, 1966, it was immediately reported in GDR media but only as a marginal note. The only transregional newspaper that would run a photo of Disney was *Wochenpost* that had a circulation of millions.

Personally, I remember some very special Disney items, presumably not licensed: little rubber *Mickey Mouse* figures, which sold cheaply. In the 1960s, in West Germany, various Disney characters (Mickey, Minnie, Donald, Bambi, Lady and the Tramp) were offered as plastic reliefs and found their way to the East as gifts. Clever craftsmen filled the hollow molds with plaster. The finished casts were painted then. For a brief time, these products were available in private (not state-controlled) shops. When I left school in the 1970s, my interest in Disney products diminished, so I cannot tell exactly what happened in the 1980s until the fall of GDR.

NOTES

1   Helmut Nickel quoted from Knigge, Andreas C.: *Fortsetzung folgt. Comic Kultur in Deutschland.* Frankfurt/M.; Berlin: Ullstein, 1989. pp. 119–120.
2   Ibid., p. 128.
3   Ibid.
4   Ibid., pp. 146–147.
5   *Opium der Kinderstube.* In: DER SPIEGEL 12/1951, March 21, 1951, pp. 39–40.
6   Ulrike Wiltrud Drechsel/ Jörg Funhoff/Michael Hoffmann, *Massenzeichenware. Die gesellschaftliche und ideologische Funktion der Comics.* Frankfurt am Main: Suhrkamp, 1975, pp. 159–160.
7   Andreas Platthaus, *"Translations Have to Be Better than the Originals!" – Comic Translators and Translations.* www.goethe.de
8   Jimmy Johnson, *Inside the Whimsy Works: My Life with Walt Disney Productions.* Jackson, Mississippi: University of Mississippi Press, 2014, p. 34.
9   Interviewed by Carsten Laqua, *Wie Micky unter die Nazis fiel: Walt Disney und Deutschland.* Reinbek/Hamburg: Rowohlt, 1992, p. 207.
10 Ibid.
11 *Lizenzen nicht wegzudenken.* In: DER SPIEGEL, No. 21/1984, May 21, 1984, p. 60.
12 This was a 1938 compilation of Mutual short films released, with German narration written by Martin Morlock, under the title *Lachen verboten* by Austria Filmverleih in 1954 in West Germany.

11 Go East

THE STRANGE HISTORIA OF DEFA TRICKFILM

Disney or not, trickfilm was very popular in the German Democratic Republic. There were, of course, animated imports from the USSR (including *Nu, Pogodi!,* the popular series with Wolf and Hare), there were animation films from China, Czechoslovakia, and Hungary), and there was a huge, internationally almost unknown output of hand-drawn and puppet animation from DEFA and Deutscher Fernsehfunk, East German TV.

Not only did all of Germany emerge from the ruins of the Third Reich, albeit under democratic or socialist auspices, also the beginnings of East Germany's DEFA animation were unthinkable without the use of leftovers from Deutsche Zeichenfilm GmbH. We have mentioned that DEFA's first official animated short in color, *Purzelbaum ins Leben*, was a project begun in 1944 in Dachau by DZF. Officially (due to lack of funds or assets besides some story rights) Deutsche Zeichenfilm GmbH was dissolved in Berlin West in May 1955. In the report by the auditor, Martin Böttcher, Berlin Charlottenburg, it says:

> At the end of the war, the commercial facilities (equipment, inventories, auxiliary materials and supplies) that were still present in what is now the Eastern sector of Berlin were confiscated by the Soviet occupying forces or taken over by DEFA.[1]

In the early 1950s, the people gathered who were to determine the image of the animation film in the German Democratic Republic, founded on September 15, 1949, in the Soviet occupied sector:

Johannes Hempel, who called himself Jan because of his Sorbian roots, returned from Munich (West) to Bautzen (East) and, at the end of 1950, began to prepare his fist puppet animation film, still under amateurish conditions: *Wolf und Füchsin* (*Wolf and Vixen*).

At the end of July 1950, Kurt Weiler, who originally came from Lower Saxony, returned from exile in London, joined the puppeteer scene, and in 1952 produced his first puppet animation film: *Oskar Kulicke und der Pazifist* (*Oskar Kulicke and the Pacifist*). Kulicke is a bricklayer who is going to promote the ideas of the National Front, an amalgamation of the block parties and mass organizations of the GDR. We see Kulicke in conversation with another pacifist who doesn't understand why the GDR needs to establish national armed forces: *the first animated puppet film that is at the service of our educational work.*[2] Johannes Beutner, a graphic artist, tried to continue Fieber's work at DEFA Trick and Title Department, and establish a studio for 2D animation. The Department moved from Johannisthal to Babelsberg. One of the animators working there was Lothar Barke.

DOI: 10.1201/9781003375548-11

In September 1953, graduates of the Institute for Artistic Work Design Giebichenstein Halle (Saale) joined forces and established a graphics studio. Although they named the studio "We Five," there were actually six: Katja and Klaus Georgi, Otto Sacher, Christl and Hans-Ulrich Wiemer, and Helmut Barkowsky. But they didn't know any technical details of trickfilm making, and were invited to volunteer at the DEFA Trick and Title Department under the roof of DEFA Studio for Popular Scientific Films in Babelsberg and work with Lothar Barke. When Dr. Heino Brandes, who was in charge of DEFA Studio für populärwissenschaftliche Filme, saw their results, he took them on as permanent employees. At the same time, Kurt Weiler and Herbert K. Schulz, another puppet animator, and Bruno J. Böttge, who specialized in Lotte Reiniger's art with the silhouette film *Der Wolf und die sieben Geisslein (The Wolf and the Seven Little Goats)*, came to Babelsberg too. In 1955, the whole Babelsberg group was transferred to Dresden (Figure 11.1):

> With effect from January 1, 1955, the production units for puppet animation, hand puppets, cartoon and silhouette animation are separated from the VEB DEFA Studio for Popular Scientific Films in Babelsberg, and an independent studio is set up in Dresden.[3]

FIGURE 11.1   Silhouette animator Bruno J. Böttge. (©DIAF/Estate Böttge.)

On April 1, 1955, some years after the formation of DEFA-Studio für Spielfilme (DEFA Studio for Feature Films), DEFA-Studio für populärwissenschaftliche Filme (DEFA Studio for Popular Scientific Films) and DEFA-Studio für Wochenschau und Dokumentarfilme (DEFA Studio for Newsreels and Documentary Films), VEB

DEFA-Studio für Trickfilme was officially (retroactively) established in Dresden Korbitz, Kesselsdorfer Str. 208 in the former studios of Fritz Boehner who had produced image, advertising, documentary, and hand puppet films and had left the East Zone to settle in Erlangen, West Germany. The nationally owned (*volkseigen*) studio followed the example of Soyusmultfilm in Moscow and was going to pool all East German animation under one roof – which did not really happen as there was a lot of animation done in East Berlin, Potsdam Babelsberg, and other cities. The DEFA Animation production mostly focused, as politically intended, on children and was an export hit in the 1960s (Figure 11.2).

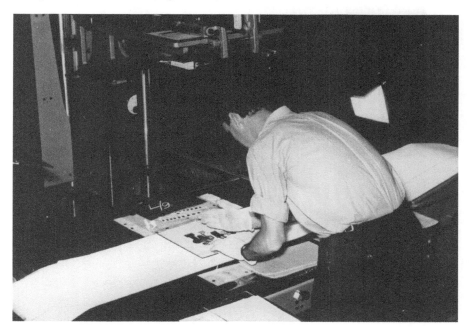

FIGURE 11.2   DEFA cameraman at animation stand. (©DIAF.)

The newly established Dresden studio was headed by Carl Deutschmann, with chief dramaturge Rolf Cichon assisting him. The animators previously working in Babelsberg werde divided into eight units: three units focusing on cartoon animation (Lothar Barke, Klaus Georgi, Otto Sacher), three working on puppet animation (Johannes Hempel, Herbert K. Schulz, Kurt Weiler), the seventh (and most interesting) for silhouette films (Bruno J. Böttge), and the final one for hand puppets (Erich Hammer). In 1957, the company had already 156 employees (Figure 11.3).

FIGURE 11.3   Psaligraph Inge Tapp cuts out silhouettes. (©DIAF/Estate Schulz/Küssner/
Zentralbild.)

The premier entry of the Dresden Trickfilm Studio, however, was neither 2D,
silhouette, nor puppet animation but a hand puppet film by Erich Hammer: *Das
Gespenst im Dorf* (*The Ghost in the Village*) – although a stop-motion short film was
scheduled for release first.

Production in the new studio started in February 1955 with the stop-motion
political satire *Ausgang erlaubt!* (working title: *Liebe Freunde/Dear Friends*) by

Herbert K. Schulz, a satire on the American occupation of West Germany – but the finished film was banned in November 1955 not only for artistic but primarily for ideological reasons. Cold War was already raging. For example, it was criticized that the film allowed "false conclusions that could result in the soldiers in civilian clothes not bothering the German population and tearing themselves to pieces" (Figure 11.4).[4]

FIGURE 11.4 Puppet animator Herbert K. Schulz (l.) and cameraman Erich Günther working on *Der kleine Häwelmann* (*The Little Haverman*, 1956). (©DIAF/Estate Schulz/Küssner.)

The same year, back in Berlin, Ernst Uchrin and Koboldfilm started production of animated advertising films for the East German DEWAG Deutsche Werbe- und Anzeigengesellschaft, a monopoly controlled by the socialist state party SED. Advertisements were made for corn kernel pudding, hairdressing cream, cosmetic products, animal feed, and a lottery (Figure 11.5).

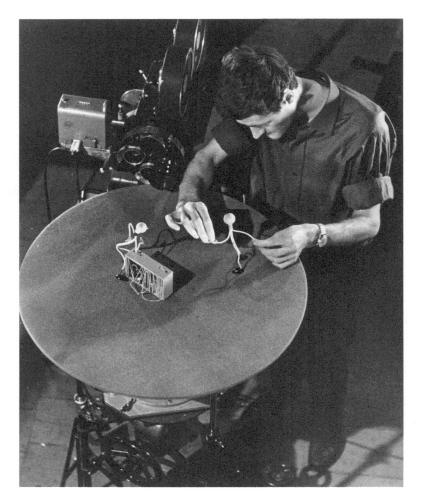

FIGURE 11.5   Jörg Herrmann animates *Der Fachmann* (*The Expert,* 1964) with the wire figures Filopat and Patafil. (© DIAF.)

In spring 1958, Herbert K. Schulz, animator Rosemarie Küssner, and trick cameraman Erich Günther left DEFA Studio für Trickfilme and started a series of animated puppet commercials in a new advertising film studio in Berlin established by DEWAG. Peter Blümel, son of DFZ's background artist Kurt Blümel, created sets and vehicles (Figure 11.6).

FIGURE 11.6   Animator and puppeteer Walter Später. (©DIAF/Estate Schulz/Küssner.)

GDR animators found a special field of activity with Deutscher Fernsehfunk DFF, the state television, which went on the air in December 1952. Most of the GDR animation characters have been forgotten, but there is one that is not: the puppet animation Sandman, which appeared (and still appears) in the evenings and is supposed to lull children to sleep. The character was created as an answer to a project idea of West Berlin TV: Dr. Ilse Obrig, an editor, author, and presenter working for Sender Freies Berlin (SFB), and puppeteer Johanna Schüppel were going to start a series with a hand puppet Sandman on December 1, 1959. In East Berlin, the decision was made to overtake the "class enemy" with a stop-motion *Sandman* created by Gerhard Behrendt in the record time of three weeks. The East Sandman premiered on November 22, 1959, 6:54 p.m.:

> Gerhard Behrendt lovingly gave form to the little sleepbringer, both "childlike and with the mark of wisdom and dignity of old age," as he says himself. The warm and friendly aura makes the puppet almost a real personality whose charm is hard to resist.[5]

While the immediately successful puppet was redesigned and subjected to a necessary facelift for his appearance in hundreds of animates spots, Herbert K. Schulz
and Rosemarie Küssner, who had become his wife, left GDR and founded cinetrick
company in Berlin West. In October 1962, the West *Sandman* became animated and
came flying in the evening on a little cloud, thanks to Schulz and his wife. Schulz
would produce 77 animated intros and 1,500 shorts (cut-outs, silhouettes) for the
Sandman program until he was fired by a new TV editor (Arno Alexander) in the
early 1980s.

NOTES

1 Collection of J. P. Storm.
2 Deutschlands Stimme, No. 39, September 28, 1952.
3 Memo HV Film—Department Film Production dated November 15, 1954. BArch/
   Federal Archive DR 1/4072a.
4 Protocol screening HV Film November 25, 1955. BArch/Federal Archive DR 1-Z.
5 http://www.sandmann.de/.

12 Big Tattoo for Little Men

MUSHROOM PEOPLE AND GARDEN GNOMES

West German TV's demand for animated spots was great. It gave Dr. Werner Kruse a comeback – at least as long as there were cigarette and tobacco ads. After the war, Kruse first ran Trias Film in Berlin Schlachtensee, then founded Kruse Film. Starting in 1958, he produced more than 400 commercials commissioned by Haus Bergmann (British American Tobacco BAT) starring an animated little HB Man, the *HB Männchen* Bruno: *Halt, mein Freund! Wer wird denn gleich in die Luft gehen? Greife lieber zur HB, dann geht alles wie von selbst! – Stop, my friend! Who's getting mad so fast? Better to reach for a HB, then everything goes by itself!* In 1959, the company moved to Munich.

> *Bruno* was a caricature with a messy shock of hair, a huge nose, a very flexible mouth and flexible, stylized limbs. The character always appeared alone, had no partner or opponent, so that the slim, pointed form of the commercial could be preserved. Admittedly, it was precisely in these structures that there was a compulsion for rapid, economical narration, which shortened the films noticeably – with running between ½ and 1 ½ min.[1]

The campaign was planned by Werbe-Gramm, an advertising agency founded by Karl-Heinz Gramm in Düsseldorf in 1953, which in turn commissioned Kruse Film to produce the spots. In the beginning, however, they used a completely different character: a frantic executive seated at a desk, then, in 1957, a bald gnome with horn-rimmed Harold Lloyd glasses. Unfortunately, both turned out to be rather negative figures who did not have the sympathy of the paying audience. Theo Breidenbach, the manager of the agency, also recognized this. He decided to rely on a new concept of a normal, petty bourgeois consumer in the fight of the insidiousness of the object.

> He is one of the best-known and most successful advertising figures in history and is considered the longest-lived character in German advertising. He has been dubbed "the premier commercial television star" and "most popular fictional character" of the Federal Republic. In fact, in the 1960s he achieved a level of awareness of 96 percent among German citizens and thus surpassed even the Federal Chancellor. [...]
>
> Up until 1967, an HB spot consisted of a 45-second introductory sketch in which Bruno was thwarted by an everyday problem, and a 30-second epilogue in which the Little HB King, who was not from this world and was therefore a messenger of the gods, delivered the advertising message to the audience. A single cartoon spot consisted of about 300 keyframes, which marked the cornerstones of the plot, and hundreds of in-betweens. While the first part got by without any cuts, the second part had three cuts. The acoustic identification of the spots was served by the signature tune whistled by Bruno at the beginning and a soothing melody assigned to the Little HB King at the end. Bruno's incomprehensible curses were fragments of words played backwards and faster, borrowed from a washing machine advertisement for Arab countries – and not,

DOI: 10.1201/9781003375548-12

as was sometimes rumored, an excerpt from a speech by Egyptian president Nasser also played backwards. [...]

In every way Bruno was a child of the television age. Like no other television character, he thematized the cultural-historically revolutionary change in everyday life caused by television. From 500,000 TV connections in August 1956 to 1 million in October 1957, the number had already shot up to 3 million by the end of the 1950s. Like the Germans, Bruno also turned his living room towards the television set and bought a television armchair, in which he often spent his far too little time. [...]

From a sociological point of view, Bruno was the single of the time of the economic miracle. His best and only friend was always the HB cigarette. It acted as a social substitute and problem solver. It calmed him down and it made him happy. There were no other humans in his world. As a social monad, Bruno represented the individualizing society of the 1950s and 1960s. [...]

Bruno was an antihero and a narcissist. The noble image that he had of himself and his skills as a hobbyist or sportsman was always shattered by the smallest adversity. Without outside help, he controlled neither himself nor his environment. [...]

Especially in the 1960s, the number of salaried employees increased rapidly and soon outstripped that of manual workers. The spots with Bruno can also be interpreted as a "farewell to proletarianism", to shortage and narrowness, to workload and income insecurity. The differences between blue-collar and white-collar workers tended to converge. The expression of the "leveled middle-class society" arose, with Bruno who possessed all its attributes as its representative. And yet it was by no means as leveled as the formula suggested.

Bruno was a social climber and therefore a role model. [...]

Above all, Bruno was the leisure person of 1,000 hobbies. He embodied modern leisure society as the supposedly new realm of freedom. [...]

In his whole habitus Bruno corresponded to the West German economic miracle man. Just as the average HB smoker Bruno was "the successful, friendly citizen." His world of TV spots matched the living environment and the wishes of most German citizens in terms of personal and economic goals. [...][2]

From 1972, however, there was an advertising ban for cigarettes on television, for Theo Breidenbach a "Lex HB," which was later also transferred to the cinema. When the series was discontinued after 25 years, Kruse was forced to close his company. Roland Töpfer, the actual inventor and animator of the Little HB Man, died a tragic accidental death that could have been a cynical idea for one of his spots. When the brakes of his car came off in September 1999, he was crushed by his own vehicle against a wall.

But there were not only commercials to animate but also commercial separators (*Werbetrenner*). Due to the television contract of the Federal States from 1953, the beginning of the respective commercial had to be clearly marked by an optical signal, an insert, or a wipe. These wipes seemed a little bit boring and so, in 1956, Bayerischer Rundfunk (Bavarian TV) introduced the first animated separator: *Leo the Lion*. This inspired Fischerkoesen, back then still the market leader, who now pushed into the TV business with power. In 1958, he created *Onkel Otto* (*Uncle Otto*) for Hessischer Rundfunk, and from 1959 to 1969 he produced spots with the *Little Seahorse* for Norddeutscher Rundfunk.

In the meantime, Fischerkoesen's rival Gerhard Fieber (actually, they never met), who had "escaped" East-German DEFA (and thus further unpleasant investigations concerning his activities in National Socialist animation), also crept under the lucrative roof of television. In the late 1960s, his company EOS Film merged with Neue Filmproduktion NFP of producer Franz Thies. He packed his equipment and moved from Göttingen to Wiesbaden. There he participated in the production of animated TV spots.

In 1962–1963, Second German Television (Zweites Deutsches Fernsehen ZDF) in Mainz, which had just established itself as Germany's nationwide public television station, was looking for animated identification figures as bumpers/inserts for its commercial screenings. Since the construction team that worked on the property at Lerchenberg in Mainz was nicknamed *Mainzelmännchen* (*Little Mainz Men*) because of their proverbial *Heinzelmännchen* (pixie) diligence, corresponding characters should be created and broadcast under this name.

It was a matter of honor that Fischerkoesen submitted designs that characterized the *Little Mainz Men* as Mushroom People! But Fischerkoesen, who was sure of his cause, had not reckoned on Wolf Gerlach (1928–2012). Gerlach, the in-house stage designer and illustrator of NFP Neue Filmproduktion Franz Thies, was faster. He decided to draw his own designs during the Christmas holidays of 1962.[3] At the beginning of January 1963, he took his drawings and went up to the building ground on Lerchenberg where he found the office of the designated first ZDF director Karl Holzamer open. His idea: a bunch of characters, all 4 in. small, animated against a photographic background. For example, a character should empty a coffee cup with a rubber hose and turn brown in the process.[4]

For Gerlach, "a childhood dream came true, because as a first grader I had wished for tiny little men who would romp in my imagination and help me a bit in school." Gerlach found suitable drawing models in his own portfolio. It was his caricatures of chubby *Centaurs*[5] und *Boy Scouts* that inspired his proposal for the *Little Mainz Men*.

Gerlach knocked twice at Holzamer's door. After some changes, Holzamer agreed and ordered 50 spots of five seconds each (Figures 12.1 and 12.2).[6]

FIGURE 12.1   Die Mainzelmännchen (Little Mainz Men): Samples from recent production. (Courtesy NFP Animation Film GmbH.)

FIGURE 12.2   Die Mainzelmännchen (Little Mainz Men): Samples from recent production. (Courtesy NFP Animation Film GmbH.)

The *Mainzelmännchen* have been modified again and again since they entered TV on April 2, 1963. They received more sophisticated character typifications: Anton the Lazy One, Berti the Hardworking One, Conni the Musical One, Det the Clever One, and Fritzchen the Sporty One. Later they were even equipped with mobile phones and notebooks.

In one respect, however, the odd small group has remained true to its retarded masculinity to this day: Nothing ever happened with women. In terms of relationships, the sixfold Mainz Man is, so to speak, sufficient for himself. This is not to be misinterpreted as an expression of misogyny or a lack of feeling for the signs of the time that have long since become post-feminist, but, as ZDF emphasizes, simply is part of the brand essence of the ultimately asexual sextet.

Gerlach, by the way, had designed some female figures, but they were only brought out once for a Berlin Radio Fair and then disappeared back into the drawer.[7]

At the end of the 1960s, Franz Thies, owner of NFP, brought Gerhard Fieber and his company EOS Film on board. Fieber went to Wiesbaden and was responsible for the production of the spots.

There was not much love lost between Gerlach and Fieber. Gerlach regarded Fieber as an intruder; Fieber critized Gerlach for being ignorant of all things that concerned animation.[8] "Gerlach had no format," Fieber complained.

> My pardner [Franz] Thies, who employed Gerlach, needed a producer. At the time, I was still producing in Göttingen. Eventually we joined forces, because ZDF would have taken *Mainzelmännchen* away from Thies because Gerlach was unable to keep up with the production of the spots.[9] Gerlach was simply not an expert. He didn't come from the movies. He only drew those little sketches. And then I came and threw up the shop, transferred EOS Film so to speak and produced for 16 years. And during that time, Gerlach was no more than a storyboarder, who made the little sketches for my key people. It was I who gave life to the characters. Gerlach wasn't able to give life to the guys.[10]

In the early 1970s, there were capacity problems at EOS. That's how the idea came up to have spots outsourced to Japan, which was still relatively cheap at the time. Fieber and Gerlach traveled to Tokyo and met Isao Takahata, later Hayao Miyazaki's partner at Studio Ghibli. Fieber told this author that Takahata quoted a full poem by Heinrich Heine: in German language! He wanted to show how honored he felt to work with partners from Germany, but the project failed. Fieber: "The Japanese designs of the proto-Germanic Mainz Men were probably considered too Asian for the taste of those responsible at ZDF" (Figures 12.3 and 12.4).[11]

FIGURE 12.3 Mainzelmännchen (Little Mainz Men). (Courtesy of NFP Animation Film GmbH.)

FIGURE 12.4 Mainzelmännchen (Little Mainz Men). (Courtesy of NFP Animation Film GmbH.)

In 1983, "we were finally able to persuade Herr Fieber to give up the management of EOS." A relieved Wolf Gerlach became managing director and 26% shareholder. The chief artist was Jürgen König, to whom the other animators delivered their works of art, which they had made at home according to the specifications of the respective storyboards and exposure sheets:

> Our main animators were spread all over Germany with their small units and shipped part of their films ready to shoot. However, test material and backgrounds, soundtracks and editing meant that our company soon employed more than 50 people, of whom 20 were permanently employed.[12]

The *Mainzelmännchen* were revised again and again in coordination with the respective editorial offices at ZDF:

> Soon there was a demand for longer films, and so an additional series with the title *Kapriolen (Capers)* was created. The *Little Mainz Men* owe this title to Horst Buckwitz, who was head of commercial television at the time. He was also the one who was responsible for our *Mainzelmännchen* from the idea to the storyboard to the editorial approval of the finished spots. [...] In 1975 we had already delivered 10,000 spots and every year around 500 new ones were added. After about 20,000 spots, Horst Buckwitz retired and Wolfgang Köhler took over the advertising TV divison. He gave the *Mainzelmännchen* the opportunity to "refresh" themselves after so many years. The production company in Wiesbaden – which now trades as NFP ANIMATION Film GmbH – formally revised and redefined the characters. Fritzchen blossomed into an athlete, little Conni became even smaller, Edi suddenly returned from the hairdresser with fiery red hair, and Anton turned out to be a victim of his "infatuation" even rounder.[13]

Today *Mainzelmännchen*, in the fourth design generation, are produced digitally. The responsible producer Stefan Thies:

> The long-term development of a brand like *Mainzelmännchen* through television would hardly be possible today. Patience and daily/weekly penetration – i.e., long-term perseverance – are hardly affordable today. The reasons are strong media competition, ratings pressure, risk avoidance and the fast pace of changes by the TV producers, but also by viewers/consumers. The *Mainzelmännchen*, on the other hand, were able to familiarize themselves with people's minds and hearts almost undisturbed for decades. You joined them and grew up with them. They were (and are) part of everyday TV life and are an established classic with a high nostalgia factor.[14]

PAPA'S CINEMA IS DEAD

However, Gerhard Fieber was not the first producer of the *Mainzelmännchen*. In February 1963, when the first spots appeared on TV, there was no studio in Wiesbaden. At that time, production was outsourced to Wolfgang Urchs' small studio in Munich Bogenhausen. Wolf Gerlach moved there with an assistant to oversee the work on site.

Urchs, who was born in Munich in 1922 and was one of the signatories to the Oberhausen Manifesto, was awarded a silver ribbon at the German Film Prize in 1962 for his short film *Die Gartenzwerge* (*The Lawn Gnomes*), a satire about the German garden gnome mentality. Now he was forced to work exactly with the faithful images of these gnomes in the shape of the *Little Mainz Men*:

> In [Urchs'] satirical [anti-*Mainzelmännchen*] parable the garden gnome was chosen as a kitschy icon of German philitinism to illustrate the influence of money and power. Always punctual, always neat and correct, and above all hard-working, is how the German brownie [Heinzelmännchen] of the post-war period presents itself. Figures emerge from the ruins of war, wearing kind of pointed caps on their heads and devote themselves to reconstruction. But what they have in common doesn't last for long: "You have to think about yourself. After all, the chimney has to smoke," says someone and builds a house. The others do the same. First someone has a bicycle, which becomes a

motorcycle, then a car and finally a limousine à la Hollywood. Luxury rules the world and all the others want to achieve exactly the same. The hard-working brownie has transformed into a fat, lazy garden gnome, who resides in a temple with servant and chauffeur. Washing machines and television sets, cars and garden gnomes roll off the assembly line. [...] The prosperous dwarfs get fatter and fatter, they celebrate wild parties with wine, women and song. Well-known paintings hang in their magnificent villas and the price tags are still clearly visible. The fountain in the inner courtyard does not spurt water, but champagne – life in abundance. But humanity falls by the wayside and the fat affluent citizen finally petrifies into what he really is: a garden gnome. As the very last image, Urchs shows drawn rubbish bins.[15]

Wolfgang Urchs:

I grew up in India and was always fascinated by the cartoons that were showing in cinemas at the time. When I was bored with class, I would spend my time making flipbooks with notepads. [...] Because there were no grammar schools in India, we [children] had to go to Germany and lived here in a boarding school. My parents stayed in India. My father was a doctor and was interned throughout the war. Both of us, my brother and I, got a ticket to the reserve corps as soon as we received our diploma. [...] When my brother died a year later, it hit me tremendously. [...]

After the war I discovered my great love for cartoon animation and because there was nothing available, I used to go from hospital to hospital with a handcart to beg for X-ray film sheets. There were heaps of them stored in the archives and they were given to me, the whole handcart full. At home I washed them off with warm water so that the layers came off. I punched the slides with a paper punch and drew on them. And old [Walter] Leckebusch, with whom I was friends and who had already received a license for film production from Eric Pleskow, the U.S. film officer at Bavaria, gave me an old wooden Erneman[n] camera with a single-frame switch. Through him I also got my first assignment. It was a commercial for a shoe polish named "Krellit", and its trademark was a raven. [...]

We were a clique, Haro Senft, Alexander Kluge, Peter Schamoni, Rob Houwer and others, and we always met in the Schwabinger Nest. We have always shown our films at the Westdeutsche Kurzfilmtage, the annual West German Short Film Festival in Oberhausen. At that time, the short filmmakers were the only ones in the entire German film landscape who attracted international attention. [...] Then came the feature film *Das Wunder des Malachias* (*The Miracle of Father Malachia* directed by Bernhard Wicki), this film cost 4 ½ million marks at the time. We were shocked that so much money was wasted on a feature film and we said at a meeting: We can make 10 feature films for the same money, each film between 300,000 and 400,000 marks. Then Detten Schleiermacher came up with the slogan: Papas Kino ist tot – Papa's Cinema is dead.[16]

In Oberhausen, at the West German Short Film Festival, Urchs saw the new animation from Zagreb. 1962 was the year when Vlado Kristl's abstract *Don Kihot* was awarded in Oberhausen. (One year later, Kristl left Yugoslavia and settled in Munich.) The established producers, however, didn't give a damn about what the young were doing. None of the old ones active in West Germany and West Berlin after the war felt cunning (or economic need) to embark on experiments like Urchs did or even venture into the field of animated feature films. The losses that Fieber's

Tobias Knopp had brought in were devastating, and the Diehl Brothers didn't achieve any economic success either with their full-length puppet animation *Immer wieder Glück* (*Always lucky*), which was released in 1950 by Jugendfilm. The Diehls survived mainly by licensing their hedgehog character Mecki to a high-circulation TV program magazine (*HörZu!*) and to a toy manufacturer (Steiff), and by selling millions of postcards with the image of Mecki and his family (photographed by Ferdinand Diehl's son Anton).

Feature-length animation was still left to Disney. And one year after Walt's death, the Burbank animation had its biggest hit, at least in Germany.

TRY TAKING IT EASY

Disney's *The Jungle Book* became the biggest hit Disney ever had in Germany.

The German release of *Das Dschungelbuch* was the first solo effort of Heinrich Riethmüller (1921–2006), who was appointed Disney's new German song and dubbing director. He brilliantly accepted the challenge to write and arrange the German versions of the Sherman Brothers' songs. Riethmüller cast Siegfried Schürenberg, Clark Gable's German voice as Shere Khan, Klaus Havenstein as King Louie, Edgar Ott as Baloo, Joachim Cadenbach as Baghira, and Erich Kestin, a Disney dubbing veteran, as Kaa. Kestin, who also voiced Winnie the Pooh, died in 1969.

Edgar Ott sang *Probier's mal mit Gemütlichkeit* (*Try Taking It Easy* = *The Bare Necessities*). Erich Kestin whispered *Hör auf mich* (*Trust in Me*). Klaus Havenstein did a top job interpreting *Ich wär so gern wie du* (*I Wan'na Be Like You*) (Figure 12.5).

The film's amazing teutonic success story is attributable to talent and lucky timing, and of a group of irreverent German musicians and cabaret artists who freely adapted the original Disney songs to suit their generation. [...]

I don't tend to like dubbed versions, I prefer the originals, but in this case, the German version is better, says Daniel Kothenschulte, film critic for the *Frankfurter Rundschau* and one of the leading experts on animation film in Germany. "Riethmüller makes the song lyrics to *The Jungle Book* better than they actually were."

Take, for example, Baloo's signature song: "The Bare Necessities." Riethmüller's German version, "Probiers mal mit Gemütlichkeit" (or, roughly translated, Try Taking it Easy), changes the original meaning, from "be satisfied with the simple things in life" to "chill out and you'll be happy."

"The original version, by the American folk singer Terry Gilkyson, has a pretty conservative message, when you think of it, of making due with less," says Kothenschulte. "Riethmüller's lyrics are more liberal and positive, they promise both freedom and comfort, the jungle as a sort of boundless utopia." [...]

Before *The Jungle Book*, U.S. films tended to be dubbed into serious high German, with an emphasis on correct, received pronunciation. Riethmüller's translation, and his troupe's voiceover performances, embraced slang and local dialect, as well as irreverent humor. When *The Jungle Book* was released in West Germany on Dec. 13, 1968 (Disney took a full year to do the local version), this style was perfectly in tune with the country's swelling hippie counterculture. A generation of young Germans, many now with young kids of their own, were rejecting their parents' strict authoritarian ways.

FIGURE 12.5   Heinrich Riethmüller. (Courtesy of Dr. Christian Riethmüller.)

Riethmüller had studied liturgical and school music in Berlin. After the war, he was forced out of church music, and began to work for radio shows and films [*Heideschulmeister Uwe Karsten; Der Pfarrer von Kirchfeld* both starring Claus Holm]. Eberhard Cronshagen, originally in charge of Disney dubbing, had met Riethmüller at RIAS Berlin (Radio in the American Sector) and asked him to Germanize *Mary Poppins'* odd coinage *Supercalifragilisticexpialidocious* to *Supercalifragilisticexpialigetisch.*

The Jungle Book *also filled a void in the German theatrical market, which in the late 1960s was dominated by adult fare, including a lot of low-budget, homegrown soft porn. Disney had a virtual monopoly on family-friendly films. In 1968,* The Jungle Book *was just about the only film in German theaters the whole family could enjoy.*[17]

THE CONFERENCE OF ANIMALS

At least the incredible success of *Jungle Book* didn't fail to have an effect on a young copycat from Munich, who made Disney's box-office results a springboard of his own. Budweis-born Curt Linda (1919–2007) was an apologist of stylized, limited animation. Originally, he had nothing to do with animation. He had entered the field quite accidentally working as stage actor and dubbing director at Bavaria Studios. During a production he was involved with in Yugoslavia, he came in touch with Zagreb Animation and decided that animation offered interesting business prospects.

It sounds nonsensical: Linda, the declared anti-Disneyist, was not particularly interested in Erich Kästner's children's book *Die Konferenz der Tiere* (*The Conference of Animals*, which Kästner originally had hoped to sell to Disney animation), but freely rode on the success of Disney's recent release, because without an animal story he wouldn't have interested a distributor:

> To find a distributor for his first feature-length project Linda invested the option money of a German Film Prize in a pilot film. Considering the popularity of author Erich Kästner, he chose as a source the parable *Die Konferenz der Tiere*. Impressed by Linda's work, Munich's Gloria Film *[with Ilse Kubaschewski in charge]* put up some advance money. The distributor's marketing campaign in 1969 was guided by the success of Disney's *The Jungle Book (Das Dschungelbuch*, director: Wolfgang Reitherman). The film's concern of world peace and rapprochement is embezzled in favor of the suggestion of cute animals.[18]

So without Disney's *Jungle Book*, there wouldn't have been the German *Conference of Animals*. Not in Linda's wildest dreams, with the little advance money he got, would he have been able to try something on the level of Disney. As Linda didn't have much spending power, he simply had no other choice than to break away from the costly American style by hiring an artist from Serbia. Boris Šajtinac's art was completely different from Disney's. For a brief time, they were even negotiating to have East-German DEFA Animation Film Studio on board. Eventually the "bourgeois pacifist position" of the project looked as suspicious to the political authorities of GDR as it did for Disney. The reviewers were kind enough when the movie was released, but nobody was really happy with the result.

HIMMLERICK AND HULLBERICK

Linda had definitely no ambition to become a German Walt Disney. Every project he touched thereafter was sparingly calculated. When ZDF canceled a nine-part animated Bible TV series, Linda scaled back the project and produced a single episode, not for TV but for cinema release: the story of Joseph and His Brethren. *Shalom Pharao* premiered at the end of the 87th German Catholic Days in Düsseldorf. Otherwise, Linda relied on the cooperation with Leo Kirch's Beta Film and produced low-cost entries for children, such as *Das kleine Gespenst* (*The Little Ghost*) based on Otfried Preussler's book and *Die kleine Zauberflöte* (*The Little Magic Flute*), Mozart for kids.

Rolf Kauka, another Munich-based entrepreneur, was a different caliber. Kauka's *Wikipedia* entry opens by calling him a "comic artist," but nothing could be farther from the truth. Kauka was no artist, although he tried to convince people that he was the one. Rudolf Paul Alexander Kauka was born on April 9, 1917 in Markranstädt, Saxony, near Leipzig, and until 1951 had absolutely nothing to do with comics. Kauka's father was a blacksmith and cartwright who would change his profession and become a gate tender. During World War II, his son served as career officer. After the war, in 1947, Kauka dabbled in publishing and edited a *Leitfaden für Polizeibeamte* (*Manual for Police Officers*). In 1948/1949, together with his friend Dr. Norbert Pohl, he published textbooks for law students. He founded a short-lived Münchener Verlagsbuchhandlung, followed by Kauka Verlag. Kauka edited *Inventor, Film and Crime Stories: A Magazine for Gentlemen*, another illustrated monthly magazine called *Mix*, and cigarette card books about the Wild West, illustrated by Dutch artist Dorul van der Heide (1903–1994), who also did lots of film posters. Recent evidence revealed by Bodo Hechelhammer, who worked as a historian for Bundesnachrichtendienst (BND), the largest agency of the German Intelligence Community: Rosemie Wessel, the widow of Gerhard Wessel, BND president from 1968 to 1978, told him that her husband and Kauka were friends since the final months of WW2. On top of that, Kauka employed Adolf Hitler's secretary Traudl Junge and Ruth Irene Kalder, the former mistress of Amon Göth, the infamous camp commander of the Kraków-Płaszów.[19]

When Ehapa published the first Disney comics, Kauka realized a market niche for himself. He got a printing house on board, Erich Pabel Verlag in Rastatt, and began to produce comics. His goal was to imitate Disney – however, by using acclaimed German characters: *Till Eulenspiegel* and *Münchhausen*. Van der Heide, although no experienced comic book artist, did the artwork. In issue six of *Till Eulenspiegel*, Kauka introduced two young fox characters and named them Fix and Foxi. Subsequently, the two foxes and their antipode Lupo, a poor man's wolf figure, became the stars of a long-running comic book series. Kauka went on and hired cartoonist and trickfilm artist Walter Neugebauer, his brother Norbert, and other talent from Zagreb to replace van der Heide. Thus, he became interested in animation. His plan was to become a German Disney, but in an opposite manner: he would first produce comic books, then animation. He made commercials for BMW, but his attempts to animate a *Münchhausen* film and make Pauli, a little mole right out of the pages of his comic books, the star of an animated series failed. Werner Hierl, who later headed Bavaria Studios' animation department, began as van der Heide's assistant and in 1959 was asked by Kauka to try puppet film animation.

In an interview, Kauka once claimed that Walt Disney wanted to hire him:

> After the war Disney had granted licenses to various countries. He produced in Milan, Copenhagen, Sao Paulo and Los Angeles and wanted to concentrate everything in the United States to get a clear-cut course. He was looking for somebody [to handle the job]. I rejected although he offered a lot of money [$80,000]. I thought that I could achieve myself on a smaller scale what he had in mind with me. The meeting took place in 1958 in Stuttgart, and we flew together to Copenhagen to see Petersen.[20]

When Kauka finally succeeded in doing a feature-length animated film, *Maria D'Oro und Bello Blue* (*Once Upon a Time*) that was released by Germany's largest distributor, Constantin Film in Munich, he didn't produce it in Germany but at Gamma Film Studios in Milan. When the movie was finished in 1973, Kauka realized that he had forgotten to cast his most popular characters, Fix, Foxi and Lupo, the underdog, and hastily added a short film with the trio as supplement to the feature, but to no avail. The picture was a box-office failure.

Nonetheless, Kauka was important because he was one of the first German comic book editors, even before Ehapa, who purchased, in need for more stories, Franco–Belgian comic material. He acquired *Asterix* (first published in France in 1959) and published the Gaul's adventures in the comic magazine *Lupo Modern*.

Asterix was originally a parody of the Boche, the Nazi troops who had occupied France like Julius Caesar and the Romans. Asterix, the cunning little Gaul who developed super strength thanks to the druid's magic potion, resembled a French Résistance fighter, although artist Albert Uderzo denied this interpretation. Kauka took the incredible step of moving the French story from Gaul to Germania. He not only renamed all the characters: Cunning Asterix became Siggi, strongman Obelix Babarras, Miraculix the druid Konradin, a homage to West Germany's first chancellor Konrad Adenauer – he bastardized all the dialogue too, and went so far as to change content and spirit of the stories.

In the introduction to the story The Golden Sickle, *which opened the Asterix series in the March [1965] issue of* Lupo modern, *it said*

> "At the beginning of the common time, the Germanic tribes had to desperately defend themselves against uninvited guests from all directions. With the exception of the small refuge castle Bonnhalla [i.e., Bonn, back then the Federal capital] all of Germania is occupied." But even in this nest of resistance – as the translation rants – "the thought of reuniting with the brothers and sisters in the rest of Germania has long since been buried under Donar's oak." Instead, Obelix [the local supplier of menhirs] is once asked: "Do you have to carry this guilt complex around with you forever?" – the menhir had become an Auschwitz club.[21]

In their version of the Visigoths and Ostrogoths taken from the story *Asterix and the Goths*, Kauka and his loyal assistant Peter Wiechmann even the more changed the plot into a revanchist parody of West and East Germany and satirized the East-Germans. Cholerik, for instance, the leader of the Ostrogoths, became comrade Hullberick (=Walter Ulbricht) in the new version. Other Ostrogoths, all of them speaking in a Saxon dialect, were named Zimberlick, Genossrick, Volksbetrieberick, Kapitalistrick, and Himmlerick (!). *"Und geht es uns auch noch so schlecht, die Partei hat recht, hat recht."* – *"Despite our miserable life, the [Communist] Party is right, is right."*

After a while, Goscinny and Uderzo caught wind of Kauka's editing practices, and took legal action.

Albert Uderzo: "A friend from Germany advised me to read the magazine *Bravo*. I bought it at a kiosk in France. And it contained an article that spoke of 'my' characters as Siggi and Babarras, the little Germans. I had it translated and was horrified. The article said it was scandalous and harmful to sell such stories with nationalistic overtones to children. [...] We asked the French consul to stop this. He just said he couldn't, because it would be a political intervention. We found that strange. It wasn't legal to falsify our text like this. We then had it banned by a lawyer. I don't know the intentions of Herr Kauka. He insulted me for a long time. He made up stories that I had been a collaborator with the Germans during the war. I was 14 years old during the war [Uderzo was born in 1927]. I think he was a little crazy. But there are people like that in all countries, not just in Germany."[22]

Kauka lost the license, which was in turn sold to Disney's German publishing house Egmont Ehapa.

Editor Adolf Kabatek (1931–1997) liked to tell the story, when Ehapa had decided to publish its own series of *Asterix* comic albums, but the sales weren't initially that promising. Ehapa was on the verge of canceling the series. Kabatek went down to distribution, which was located in the basement of the publishing house, got the new sales numbers, and – lo and behold – they went up. Kabatek's repeatedly used phrase *Die spinnen, die Römer – They're nuts; the Romans* became sort of a dictum.

What *Astérix* and the Franco–Belgian comic books achieved was the rehabilitation of graphic novels among educated citizens in Germany who previously had detested such publications.

One doesn't have to pity Rolf Kauka. He died, a rich man, on September 13, 2000, on his farm in Thomasville, Georgia. In the year of his death, he tried to restart *Fix und Foxi* with his former rival Egmont Ehapa. Yet this attempt didn't work well.

STORIES OF LAUGHTER AND FACTS

In those days, most of the German animation companies, small outfits run by newcomers got on children's TV. No big deal, however, with ZDF. ZDF at that time began to outsource content like *Maya the Bee* to Japanese production companies. So young producers found a niche with First Channel TV (ARD) in TV shows like the West German *Sandmännchen* and *Sendung mit der Maus* (*The Program with the Mouse*), a mix of short child-friendly educational documentaries and animation.

> The [animated] Maus, who always looks a little sleepy, made her first appearance on 7 March 1971, when the WDR (West German Broadcasting) allegedly wanted to create a more serious counterpart to the freshly imported, slightly rowdy *Sesame Street* with *Lach- und Sachgeschichten (Stories of Laughter and Facts)*. One year later, on 23 January 1972, the program was re-named after its hero: *Die Sendung mit der Maus*. [...] The mouse had several mothers and fathers. It owes its appearance to the designer and graphic artist Isolde Schmitt-Menzel, who first drew the orange-brown mouse for a picture story. WDR commissioned the animator Friedrich Streich (1934–2014) to animate the chubby, cosy mouse with the googly eyes. Streich brought the mouse to life, gave it its characteristic facial expressions and gestures. And he gave the lonely mouse a faithful companion: in 1975 the little blue elephant joined the program [...] In 1987, Streich also developed the yellow duck, which has been a regular guest ever since. The mouse does not speak, but communicates through characteristic sounds introduced by Joern Poetzl. The famous eye-blinking sound, for example, is produced with castanets. When the mouse walks, we hear two coconut shells hitting each other.[23]

This author can assure from his own painful experience in the 1980s in Hamburg (*Sandmännchen*) and Cologne (WDR) that the interference of the TV editors in such programs sometimes went very far. Occasionally, they watered down concepts or made them completely impossible.

TWO DISNEY ARTISTS FROM GERMANY

At that time, only two frustrated young artists had ambitions to leave Germany and knock at Disney's door.

Andreas Deja was born on April Fool's Day, 1957, in Gdansk, the former Danzig, and raised in Dinslaken, North Rhine Westphalia, where he saw *The Jungle Book*, which inspired him to become an animator:

> I can only point to one Disney film, *The Jungle Book*. It happened to be the first Disney film I ever saw – in Germany, age 11 – and all of a sudden, my life had a mission. I had to at least try to work for Disney in the future. Of course, living in Germany at that time, my family thought I was nuts and that I would even eventually come to my senses.

I never did. At age 12 I wrote to the studio, asking about what kind of schooling and training might be necessary in order to apply. Disney replied and gave me very valuable information about going to art school and becoming an artist first. I took all that very seriously, and by the late 1970s I contacted Eric Larson, one of Walt's Nine Old Men, who was heading up an animation program for newcomers.[24]

After finishing secondary school, Andreas studied graphic design at the *Folkwang Hochschule* in Essen. His fellow students, who were more interested in abstract art, wrinkled their noses and laughed at him when they learned that Andreas was interested in Disney. Among the students, Disney was considered a "cultural disgrace."

But Andreas found a teacher who was interested in Disney himself and had a great collection of Disney home movies. This was Hans Bacher who was born in 1953. Bacher was trained in graphic design, with an MFA degree at the University of Essen in 1974. Besides teaching, he had established his own little studio madTParty in Düsseldorf. He knew and had worked for Richard Williams and got assignments from WDR television. Bacher was torn between what they used to call "real films," i.e., live action, and his admiration for Disney animation. Luckily for him animation won, but it wouldn't have happened without the support of his student Deja (Figure 12.6).

FIGURE 12.6 The Murks (The Botch) designed by Hans Bacher and Harald Siepermann for an unrealized TV project that was set in the Cologne cathedral. (Author's Collection.)

Deja had done a test for Larson in the meantime. He didn't make a full short film. He made some character animation of a witch who had trouble starting her broomstick. This did it and started his career as a Disney animator in the predigital age:

We most definitely applied ourselves to Walt's process of filmmaking, and we tried to approach our character animation the way some of the Nine Old Men had taught us. For example, a character needs to be animated from the inside out. To deeply understand the emotions and motivations is more important than fancy-looking drawings. At Disney, animation means acting, and you are asked to put a performance on the screen.

Technically, we followed all the steps that were developed by Walt and his crew. Storyboarding, voice recording, pencil layouts showing sceneries, color background paintings, then rough animation followed by clean up animation. *Snow White* was made that way, and so was *The Lion King*. The only category where we differed had to do with coloring the characters. *The Little Mermaid* was the last animated film which used hand painted cels. After that our character drawings could be given color by using the computer, but the end result still looked the same.

One more thing, most of the directing animators were proudly working on vintage animation desks, the ones used by the Nine Old Men. I think secretly we were hoping that some pixie dust would transfer over to us.[25]

Sure enough, Deja was instrumental to bring his teacher Hans Bacher over to Disney too. Bacher had just finished creating an animated series with a duck character for Dutch entertainer Hermann van Veen: *Alfred J. Kwak*, for which he had won a German Golden Camera Award, and was ready to do designs for Disney. As a freelancer he was involved in the production design for *Who Framed Roger Rabbit*, *Beauty and the Beast*, *Aladdin*, and *The Lion King*. In 1994, he moved to Los Angeles and was employed by Disney Feature Animation. Bacher did stylistic designs for *Hercules*, *Fantasia 2000*, and in 1995 designed *Mulan*, the animation feature which Disney intended to please the vast audience in China (although at that time the Chinese wouldn't acknowledge as to them the cartoon characters' faces didn't look Chinese but Korean). In 2003, Bacher moved to the Philippines and taught in Singapore. His advice to young art students who want to be in animation:

Spend time traveling through the World Wide Web and find out what similar artists are doing in other parts of the world. This will help you answer the question: "How good am I?" And more importantly,

"How good should I aim to be?" Don't lose hope if some artists out there seem out of reach. […] everyone starts somewhere.

But at the same time make no mistake about what the competition is and work accordingly. Get a thorough education in the arts and practice drawing at every opportunity you get. Have someone next to you, perhaps a good friend, who is also studying with you and has similar hopes and dreams for the future. This is very important. It's amazing how much easier and more fulfilling it is to grow together than in isolation. Above all, keep alive your love for the medium. For film and animation, you should be so passionate about it, that you are close of being obsessed. I think only when you are obsessed, you have a chance today to survive and be successful.[26]

ASTERIX CONQUERS GERMANY (BUT NOT AMERICA)

So, in the late 1960s, there were some first, however, lukewarm attempts by Curt Linda and Rolf Kauka to change the situation and go for feature-length animation, but the real impetus for a change came from France and was still connected with the success story of *Asterix* in Germany.

Jugendfilm Verleih, a film company founded in 1934 by Willy Wohlrabe, a Quaker who specialized in releasing in children's films and fairy tales, had become the lucky winner of the German distribution rights of the *Asterix* film series that was started by Belvision. Surprisingly, the pictures became more successful in Germany than in the country of their origin. It all began in March 1970 when the company's head, Dr. Friedrich Karl Wohlrabe, who practiced in the morning as dentist and in the afternoon as film distributor, decided to start the German releases with the second, better animated *Asterix and Cleopatra*, not with the first entry *Asterix the Gaul*. The big cinemas at that time had booked a star-spiked German comedy and banned *Asterix* to the smaller houses, but with the totally unexpected success of the animated Gauls, the situation changed and all of a sudden *Asterix* went up to the big cinemas. The success story continued with the release of the third Asterix produced by Studios Idéfix, *The Twelve Labors of Asterix*, in Germany titled *Asterix erobert Rom* (*Asterix Conquers Rome*), which lured more than six million Germans to the box office.

Eventually, Jugendfilm's new head Jürgen Wohlrabe, a presumptuous CDU[27] politician, the grandson of company founder Willy Wohlrabe and nephew of Friedrich Karl Wohlrabe, felt strong enough to negotiate a deal with Les Éditions Albert-René, the copyright owners. His goal was to "outsmart" the former French producers (Gaumont). Gaumont's *Asterix* producer Yannik Piel who had created a fair version of *Asterix in Britain* had a strategy that the Germans (and maybe even Piel himself who began to write scripts under the pseudonym Yannik Voight) didn't understand. He suggested to produce one of the most-liked *Asterix* comic books: *Asterix and the Big Fight* (*Le combat des chefs*) to get German co-production money and, after the money terms were settled, seemingly out of nowhere would take another, less popular *Asterix* book conceived after Goscinny's untimely death, *The Soothsayer* (*Le Devin*) and adapt that. From *Big Fight* Piel took only one single plot element: Druid Miraculix is accidentally hit by Obelix's menhir, thereby losing his memory and with it the formula of the magic potion that made the Gauls so strong and virtually undefeatable. Wohlrabe had a big screen credit reserved for himself in *Big Fight*, but by the time the movie hit the big screen, Wohlrabe had recognized that the French hadn't delivered a *Big Fight* for his state money and so ordered to remove his own credit. He decided to show the French in good Prussian and pull *Asterix* out from under their ass.

After *Big Fight*, Piel and Wohlrabe negotiated a follow-up project and again Piel suggested to link two *Asterix* books, take a boy character from one story that, so he claimed, was liked very much by Uderzo and link him with another plot.

Politely, Wohlrabe listened to the Frenchmen but finally declined. He had ideas of his own. He was going to challenge Disney on his own playground, as Deutsche Zeichenfilm GmbH had attempted, by doing a whole feature-length *Asterix* production outside of France, in Berlin. Working with him for two years, I suggested *Asterix and the* Goths; but he turned me down. As always, he claimed to know better. He had bigger things in mind: *Asterix in America*, based on the comic Book *Asterix and the Great Crossing*, was destined to "conquer" the U.S. market for the Franco–Belgian–German product. I warned him that *Asterix* was virtually unknown in the United States, but he wouldn't listen. Original artwork from *Big Fight* was shipped from France to Hahn's studio, where they tried to copy certain elements.

The expensive result was supervised by Gerhard Hahn, who at that time was mainly a producer of TV series. Unfortunately, that particular *Asterix* lacked the wit of the comic books and turned out to be a pathetic affair. The Germanized *Asterix* fell way behind the undeniable technical qualities of *Big Fight* and failed not only to entertain Americans (most of whom never got to see it) but also German fans. Most reviewers called it well-animated (sic!) but not funny. Wohlrabe died of cancer on October 19, 1995, at age 59, only one year after the release of the picture: "We Wohlrabes are like a lightbulb that shines twice as brightly but only burns for half as long."[28]

GERMAN PRODUCERS GO FEATURE-LENGTH

In the meantime, DEFA Animation production mostly focused, as politically intended, on children and became an export hit in the 1960s. Out of roughly 800 animated productions made for the cinema, however, less than one percent was feature-length, but these few films caused a stir, although for different reasons.

For the film version of *Der arme Müllersbursch und das Kätzchen* (*The Poor Miller's Boy and the Kitten*, 1971) based on a tale by the always reliable and ever-popular Grimm Brothers, DEFA Studio for Animated Films called upon Lothar Barke to direct. He was considered to be an experienced director and brilliant animator whose films were always a guarantor for unanimous and longstanding audience success. Barke, however, refused the directorial commitment, because he wouldn't align himself with the official politics of GDR due to the political unrest in the Prague Spring of 1968. (He returned to the studio in 1969 and stayed there until the end came in 1991.) The Grimm fairy tale was finished by Helmut Barkowsky, but the models weren't lip sync with the audio track. This resulted in a certain artistic breach in the narrative style that is noticeable even today.

As Jürgen Clausen had suggested in the 1940s, East-Germans became successful not so much with 2D but with puppet animation. Produced with great expenditure, *Die seltsame Historia von den Schildbürgern* (*The Strange Historia of the Gothamists*, 1961) tried to tell sort of an "original version" of the well-known German chapbook in stop motion and at the same time indulged itself in innuendos on the (East-German) reality back then. "*In a major effort of three-year production more than 100 puppets had to be built and animated, there were miniatures and sets in great number*," recalled director Johannes (Jan) Hempel later. Yet the finished film wouldn't become the hoped-for artistic and commercial success (Figure 12.7).

FIGURE 12.7   Animator Ina Rarisch working on Die seltsame Historia von den Schiltbürgern (1961). (©DIAF.)

Highly recommended for its animation and "modern child-oriented score" adjacent to "Children Schlager music" was Günter Rätz's *Die Leuchtturminsel* (*The Lighthouse Island*, 1974). Popular bandleader Uve Schikora, who had created the soundtrack, turned his back on GDR shortly after (Figure 12.8).

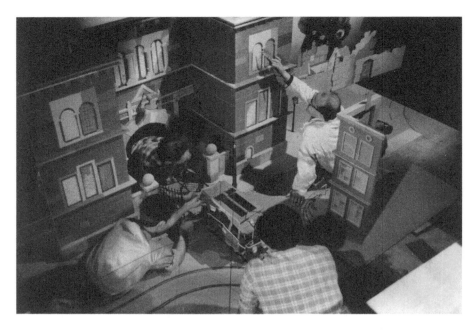

FIGURE 12.8   Der tapfere Strassenbahnwagen (The Brave Tram Car, 1961): Animator Jörg Herrmann (l.), director Günter Rätz (below), set designer Herbert Löchner (r.), technician Ekkehard Wagner (above). (©DIAF.)

Die fliegende Windmühle (*The Flying Windmill*, 1981) written and directed by Günter Rätz was euphorically reviewed by the studio brass: "*We are happy to have this film. We are glad that there is such a director and such a collective.*" Thanks to the bizarre puppets created by Horst Tappert and the pointed dialogue by Rätz, *The Flying Windmill* enjoyed a certain "cult status":

A cheeky young girl named Olli who ran away because of her lousy school certificate, Pinkus the dog and Alexander the horse seek refuge from a storm in an old mill, which happens to be the hidden laboratory of a professor and his crocodile Susi. When Olli inadvertently presses a button, the windmill takes off to outer space.

The end of the GDR also meant the end for the DEFA Studio für Trickfilme. Once again, a final time, the studio reared up. In 1985, Rätz had begun a new puppet film: *Die Spur führt zum Silbersee* (*The Trace Leads to the Silver Lake*), loosely based on the work of the German James Fenimore Cooper: Karl May. When the movie was finished, toward the end of 1989, GDR was too. The picture was released in January 1990. It was not just long but also lengthy (Figures 12.9 and 12.10).

FIGURE 12.9   Günter Rätz shooting Die Spur führt zum Silbersee (The Trace Leads to the Silver Lake, 1989). (©DIAF/Rudolf Uebe.)

FIGURE 12.10   Günter Rätz shooting Die Spur führt zum Silbersee (The Trace Leads to the Silver Lake, 1989). (©DIAF/Rudolf Uebe.)

The political turn hits the studio hard. Safe clients like Progress Film Distribution and GDR Television break away. The same goes for the partners FDGB (Free German Trade Union Federation), Hygiene Museum, the Ministry of the Interior and partners from the industry

The formerly full order books: empty!

The lack of concepts to make the studio compatible with the market economy is painfully noticeable.

There is neither well-founded knowledge about the requirements of the market nor about how the film industry works under market conditions.

However, looking back: If these deficiencies hadn't existed, if the studio had been able to assert itself as an independent economic force, would anyone in charge, i.e. the Trust Agency, have ever been really interested in its continued existence?[29]

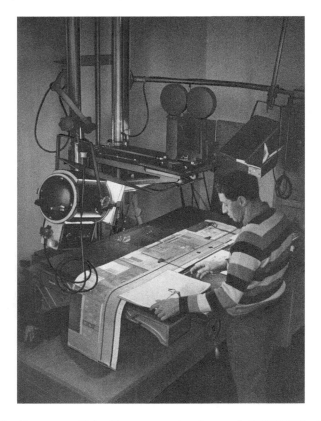

FIGURE 12.11   Cameraman Heinz Unger at an animation stand. (©DIAF/Alfred Paszkowiak.)

On October 3, 1990, East and West German became one. It was the end for DEFA. The DEFA Studio für Trickfilme was dissolved on June 30, 1992 (Figure 12.11).

Only the East *Sandman* survived his counterpart in the West. When he was supposed to disappear from the screen in the autumn of 1990, protests rained down:

Signature lists, resolutions, calls. There were even demonstrations. Hundreds of letters from all parts of the ex-GDR arrived at the contact addresses of the "Interest Group Sandman," several tens of thousands of signatures. In addition to written statements of solidarity, there were dozens of beautiful drawings, collages and handicrafts. To this day they represent unique documents of a broad public love for a little person who had become sort of a folk figure: "We want to keep our Sandman," "Dear Sandman, stay with me, you are so nice," "I like the Sandman a lot and thanks to him I can sleep better," it was said again and again.[30]

The protests caused the radio commissioner of the new Federal States, Rudolf Mühlfenzl from Bavaria, to declare the continued existence of the East *Sandmann* beyond 1991 as a top priority.

Small independent producers meanwhile won the race. At least, it seemed so. In February 1990 *Balance*, an eight-minute stop-motion film by the twin brothers Christoph and Wolfgang Lauenstein won an Academy Award for Best Animation Short, the first ever granted to animation made in Germany.

Five figures on a floating platform. Everyone knows: Balance is only maintained if everyone positions themselves evenly. A game begins in which the balance is more in danger with every step. Suddenly a chest appears and the fatal dependency of the characters becomes obvious. Individual covetousness throws the world off balance.

The figures push each other into the abyss. All that's left is the chest and one who has prevailed. But appearances are deceptive...[31]

NOTES

1 Günter Agde, *Flimmernde Versprechen. Geschichte des deutschen Werbefilms im Kino seit 1897.* Berlin: Das Neue Berlin, 1998.
2 Gerhard Paul, *Das HB-Männchen – Werbefigur des Wirtschaftswunders.* In: Zeithistorische Forschungen/Studies in Contemporary History issue 1–2/2007.
3 Wolf Gerlach, *Autobiographische Notizen/Autobiographical Notes.* Bad Neuenahr. July 2008, pp. 34–35. Handwritten manuscript. Private property of the Gerlach family. Quotes with the kind permission of Wolf's son Dr. Martin Gerlach.
4 Ibid., pp. 35–36.
5 Wolf Gerlach, *Kentaurisches.* Berlin, 1959.
6 Wolf Gerlach, *Autobiographische Notizen.* pp. 36–37.
7 Mathias Zschaler, *Zum Tod von Wolf Gerlach: Der Mainzelmann.* In: SPIEGEL Online Kultur. Tuesday, November 13, 2012.
8 Information by Dr. Martin Gerlach and Stefan Thies (NFP animation film GmbH).
9 According to animator Peter Völker (Email, December 6, 2022), Thies was looking nationwide for an animation supervisor to come to Wiesbaden, Hesse. At the recommendation of Hello Weber, a working lunch was arranged with Völker, Thies and Gerlach: "Thies recommended sole with spinach (the world is dying in posh style, but: delicious! and he also paid for everything), but because of my aversion to the Hessians, was the answer from the start: no."
10 Gerhard Fieber interviewed by J. P. Storm.
11 Gerhard Fieber in a conversation with Rolf Giesen. Colloquium *Der deutsche Zeichentrickfilm vor 1945.* Deutsche Kinemathek Berlin. June 13–14, 2003.
12 Ibid., pp. 69–70.
13 Wolf Gerlach, *Autobiographische Notizen.*

14 Rolf Giesen, *Standardisierte Kinderträume.* In: Frankfurter Allgemeine Zeitung, December 7, 2015.
15 Annika Schoemann, *Der deutsche Animationsfilm Von den Anfängen bis zur Gegenwart 1909–2001.* Sankt Augustin: Gardez! Verlag, 2003, pp. 215–216.
16 *Der Zeichenfilm ist ein modernes Medium. Gespräch mit Wolfgang Urchs.* Interviewers: Christel and Hans Strobel. In: Kinder- und Jugendfilm Korrespondenz. Issue 75-3/1998.
17 *Why Disney's Original "Jungle Book" Is Germany's Biggest Film of All Time.* In: The Hollywood Reporter. April 22, 2016.
18 *CineGraph – Lexikon zum deutschsprachigen Film.* Edited by Hans-Michael Bock. Munich: edition text + kritik, 1984-.
19 Bodo V. Hechelhammer, *Fürst der Füchse. Das Leben des Rolf Kauka.* Munich: Langen Müller Verlag GmbH, 2022.
20 Andreas C. Knigge, *Fortsetzung folgt: Comic-Kultur in Deutschland.* Frankfurt/Main; Berlin: Ullstein, 1986, p. 112.
21 Matthias Heine, *Der Kauka-Effekt.* In: Die Welt, March 22, 2005.
22 *Albert Uderzo: Die Leser haben Asterix am Leben erhalten.* In: Die Welt, October 21, 2013.
23 https://dpma.de/english/our_office/publications/milestones/brandwithhistory/sendung-mitdermaus/index.html.
24 *Bringing the '90s to Life: An Interview with Animator Andreas Deja.* https://ohmy.disney.com.
25 Ibid.
26 *Tete a Tete with Hans Bacher.* August 23, 2012.www.animationxpress.com.
27 Christian Democratic Union of Germany.
28 SPIEGEL Kultur, October 24, 2000.
29 Martha Schumann, *Es war einmal...* In: Trickfilm Brief 1/2018.
30 Volker Petzold, *Das Sandmännchen. Alles über unseren Fernsehstar.* Hamburg: edel EDITION, 2009, p. 292.
31 *Filme für Kinder und Jugendliche.*

13 Bölkstoff for Preschoolers

A TRIP TO THE MOON

With entrepreneurs like Jürgen Wohlrabe pushing down to the grave, at least for a particular period of time, the situation of animated feature film production in Germany changed considerably after reunification. New funding sources made it possible that a number of former TV producers focused on animated feature films.

In the meantime, Wolfgang Urchs, short filmmaker par excellence, decided to go feature-length a second time: *Peterchens Mondfahrt* (*Little Peter's Trip to the Moon/* worldwide: *Peter in Magicland*) was based on a 1912 children's play by Gerdt von Bassewitz (who committed suicide in 1923).

> Children from the age of five will surely enjoy 80 minutes of colorful adventure. The adults, however, will notice that director Wolfgang Urchs couldn't quite make up his mind whether to faithfully stick to the somewhat old-fashioned original or whether he would rather prefer a modern comic strip in speech bubble style. […]
>
> Anyway, the objections of an adult will not spoil the fun on the big screen: flying off to the realm of fantasy with Peter, Anneliese and a beetle [who has lost a leg to the fierce Man in the Moon].[1]

Together with Michael Schoemann—a novice in animation, Urchs had already produced *In der Arche ist der Wurm drin* (*Stowaways on the Ark*) that was released in 1988: A woodworm named Willie who is accused to be responsible for a leak in Noah's Ark unmasks the real culprits – termites. At the end of the production, the relationship between Schoemann, who constantly interfered and claimed to know better, and Urchs were strained. That must be stopped. When Urchs went on his own with *Peterchens Mondfahrt*, Schoemann didn't want to take a back seat to his former partner. Resistant to advice and unimaginative, he again chose a story about a woodworm that was written by his wife, Ute Schoemann-Koll: *Die Abenteuer von Pico und Columbus* (*The Adventures of Pico and Columbus*/U.S.: *The Magic Voyage*): Pico the woodworm convinces Columbus that the Earth is a sphere, and that nothing stands in the way of discovering America. The picture was lavish, no question (14 mill. Marks), and tried to emulate Disney (like the Nazis did), but the box-office result was disastrous. Co-Producer Bavaria Film holed up, the original distributor turned the film down, and only 10,000 cinema-goers appeared to see it on German screens in 1992 when a small Duisburg distribution company (Atlas Film) picked it up from the trashcan.

DOI: 10.1201/9781003375548-13

161

VOMIT LATER!

While Schoemann was squandering other people's money, Gerhard Hahn (Wohlrabe's *Asterix* partner) and Hamburg-based Michael Schaack sensed big business in a comic strip character that was created along the lines of Otto Waalkes—Germany's most stupid but immensely popular bard. *Werner* comics were created by cartoonist Rötger Feldmann ("Brösel") in 1978. Werner is an apprentice plumber who likes two things: beer [Flensburg "Bölkstoff"] and heavily customized motorbikes. The same is true for Feldmann. Werner is his alter ego, with the difference that Feldmann has more business acumen than his comic character. That's about all.

> Werner, the cartoon character with the big nose, the four hinted strands of hair and the two rounded teeth, experienced a meteoric rise in the 1980s, which began with the first Werner comic book in 1981. [...]. German producer *Bernd Eichinger* invested eight million [marks] in the film adaptation of the bulbous-nosed bogey of society [Bürgerschreck] – obviously not enough for a continuous comic story. Thus, the film was provided with a banal background story in which, under the direction of Austrian *Niki List* cartoonist "Brösel" (Rötger Feldmann) as court jester is supposed to make a king laugh and deliver the ordered animation drawings to a film producer. In his desperation, "Brösel" can't think of anything and what comes to his mind are seven animated sequences, all of which, with the exception of two, are taken from existing *Werner* books. Even with the animated sequences standing out in comparison to the stupid frame story, they not only impress with a particularly skillful animation. The simple stick figure technique, with which much is only hinted at in the books, falls victim to the rich colors in the film, which allows the beer philosopher Werner to degenerate into a Disney character.[2]

Werner – Beinhart! (1990 – 5.4 million viewers) and the (fully animated) "dirty language" sequels released between 1996 and 2011 (Das muss kesseln!!!; Volles Rooäää!!!; Gekotzt wird später!; Eiskalt!) were highly successful at the box office in German-speaking territories where they became instant hits.

Michael Schaack gets enthusiastic when he thinks about working with "Brösel":

> Rötger Feldmann regularly came to the shooting. After all, you can't make a *Werner* film without him, that goes without saying. However, Rötger who knows our work has placed so much trust in us that he didn't show up every day. He wrote the screenplay and attended the weekly meetings to check the work. His criticism has flowed into our work. [...] Brösel is a maniac, and such artists are needed when something is created. One who builds his own world and defends it. After all, Werner didn't come about on the drawing board, but from the gut – from Rötger Feldmann's gut. [...] Admittedly, Werner is an anachronism. He has no idea about political correctness and he doesn't like Perrier either. Werner is Werner and will remain so. For every trend there is always a counter-movement. Werner grew up with 'unemployed and having fun' and has been successful with this formula...

Schaack knows that such a character has no chance on foreign markets: "It's generally difficult for Germans to conquer the world market with comedy, whereby our cartoons are still the best suited because the humor used in them is similar to the American one."[3] Schaack doesn't say why: the Nazis drove the best comedy talent out of the country or murdered it.

So the Germans have to be content with *The Little Asshole: Kleines Arschloch* (1997), another cartoon character, this one based on comic strips by Walter Moers, animated under the supervision of Michael Schaack and his TFC Trickompany: a precocious rascal with plenty of morbid humor and a skewed worldview.

> *The Little Asshole* is the title of the film that has been number one in Germany's cinemas in recent weeks. And I can imagine a number of old gentlemen chanting late Roman laments about the decay of moral - o tempora o mores -, because speaking the word "asshole" in public is no longer taboo. But as I estimate the cartoons of Walter Moers that the film is based on, I can't take part in the lamentations. The trailer already had the same drastic comedy as the cartoon: *"The Little Asshole* is coming to the cinema" was, if I remember correctly, the advertising slogan. One could hear corresponding moaning, and then the whitish goo of the ejaculate enveloped the long-nosed, puny figure of the little asshole. Yes, right, disgusting.[4]
>
> Walter Moers was a moderately successful cartoonist in the mid-1980s, whose strange characters always experienced extremely funny things. The [satirical] magazines *Titanic* and *Kowalski* inevitably became aware of the young man from Mönchengladbach. And Moers took advantage of this new, subtly anarchic environment – his favorite bulbous-nosed manikin was increasingly rough with his surroundings in the cartoons. Animals were tortured, the disabled insulted, women were humiliated, stimulant substances were glorified and all sorts of blasphemous things were done. In other words: This kid was a veritable asshole – just a "little asshole" as Moers, anticipating any comedy, cleverly christened his brainchild.[5]

A new market with indefinite chances of independent distribution has, of course, opened up in the internet. Germany's most successful animation, so far, has only been seen in the World Wide Web. Originally, the same Walter Moers who had created the *Little Asshole* was going to be involved in a feature-length animated film about a much bigger asshole: Hitler always welcomed to help German producers and editors earn some money in the "sour grapes phase." But the project ended up as short animation by Felix Gönnert—an alumnus of Film University Babelsberg, today a Professor in the Babelsberg Animation Department: Allegedly inspired by Charles Chaplin (*The Great Dictator*) and director Ernst Lubitsch (*To Be or Not to Be*), the 3D version of Hitler singing in a bathtub inside his bomb-proofed bunker in Berlin drew at least 6–8 million downloads.

Felix Gönnert:

> There were already two essentials for *The Bonker* when they asked me to do the project. On one hand there was a storyboard by Walter Moers himself, on the other hand there was a song by Thomas Pigor. Walter's drawings often consist of cursorily sketched lines. Nevertheless, he puts the expression of the character straight. Therefore, it was quite easy for me to bring the character to life, together with Carla Heinzel. Thomas' song determined the rhythm and creates a catchy tune on the sound level to the rubber ducky theatre on the image level. The main challenge was to translate the charm of Walter's drawings *(sic!)* into the three-dimensional world of computer animation. By the way, the clip remained in the drawer for one year before it was finally published in 2006 and one day later it was uploaded by somebody in the internet. At that time, YouTube and consorts had just started in Germany.

Hitlerian megalomania was also a key factor in Germany's most expensive animation film venture.

SHREK IN GOOD GERMAN

Fortunately for him, Gerhard Hahn, who had accompanied *Asterix* on his Great Crossing and *Werner* into the anal toilet flash, was only slightly involved in the pre-production of *Happily N'Ever After*, maybe the biggest disaster in German animation history, worse than *Pico und Columbus*. Even the story was a mess – as was the whole troubled production. Many cooks spoil the broth, and those involved here didn't even know how to cook but only how to waste money.

Once upon a time in Fairy Tale Land, all is well: Cinderella's at the ball, Rapunzel's letting her hair down, and Sleeping Beauty's about to get a big smooch. But just as it's all headed for *Happily Ever After*, there's a slight hitch. The wise sorcerer who keeps the scales of Good and Evil in balance goes on holiday, and his two dumb-founded apprentices, Munk and Mambo, slip up and let Cinderella's wicked step-mother, Frieda, get hold of his magical staff. Her goal: Nothing less than to take over Fairy Tale Land, let the bad guys win, and turn the ending of all the well-known stories to *Happily <u>Never</u> After*. Now Cinderella (Ella, to her friends) is playing in a whole new ball game. Instead of waiting for her handsome Prince to find her, she's got to wake up from her romantic dream, find a way to stop Frieda, and restore the balance of Good and Evil. With her best friend, Rick, at her side, and an unlikely Army of Dwarves as well as Fairies, Munk and Mambo to back her up, Ella leaps into action. Ninety-two characters appear in 74 minutes, including 11 main charac-ters: a new record.

The Future looks Grimm, and it looked grim for the investors too who put mil-lions into this project and some animated TV series under the label Berlin Animation Film without reading the scripts.

Happily N'Ever After originated from a 1999 2D TV series, *SimsalaGrimm*, Gerhard Hahn's adaptation of German fairy tales starring Yoyo und Doc Croco (in the movie replaced by Munk and Mambo), executed in cheaply set-up Saigon studios by Hahn Film, and sold to 170 countries. The "success" inspired Hahn's partner Nicolaus Weil and his Greenlight Media AG to convince Dresdner Bank to announce an animation fund supervised by Greenlight and the newly-founded BAF Berlin Animation Film GmbH & Co. Produktions KG. In the end, the fund col-lected US $100 mill. from the premium clients. The money went not only into new series concepts but also into that international animated feature film adapted from the original Grimm series, which over the years transformed from 2D to 3D, changed studios (from Hahn Film to BFC Berlin Film Companie), and tried to follow into the big steps of *Shrek*. While all this was going on, the mess of a screenplay was kept.

The first newspaper to blurt out dubious internals from the production and its out-put (outsourced to cheap studios in South East Asia) in spring 2003 was Frankfurter Allgemeine Zeitung (FAZ):

> Once upon a time there was a consulting bank [Dresdner Bank] that sold to its best customers shares in a film fund. The millions collected should be used to finance

the production of high-quality animated films with titles such as *SimsalaGrimm* and *Geschichten aus dem Grossen Wald* (Tales from the Great Forest). Unfortunately, the bank, which had no experience in this field up to that point, chose a production partner who was completely overwhelmed with this project. When the bankers finally noticed that the quality of the cartoons they had started was miserable and that their completion was being delayed for years, they were forced to take matters in their own hands. [...]

But first things first: Between the end of 1999 and mid-2000, Dresdner Bank offered ist premium private customers a payment obligation (minimum deposit: 50,000 Deutsche Mark) to the funding company BAF Berlin Animation Film GmbH & Co. Produktions KG. Approximately 1,600 customers accepted the offer and invested total of 138 million Deutschmark. Investitionsbank Berlin (IBB), which belonged to Bankgesellschaft Berlin, contributed another 30 million Deutschmark. Dabei wurden 70 Prozent durch eine Garantie des Landes Berlin abgesichert. 70 percent were covered by a guarantee from the State of Berlin.

The wealthy private investors were primarily attracted by the fact that they could immediately write off the entire investment amount as a loss for tax purposes. At the same time, Dresdner Bank advertised "the balance between security" and "the open-end profit potential." Specifically, investors were promised a return of 10.9 percent over a period up to 2007; in "good case," according to the emissions prospectus, it could even be 20.2 percent.

Greenlight Media AG acted as guarantor for these – guaranteed unmanageable – forecasts. [...] So the main responsibility for the successful use of the collected 168 million Deutschmark (86 million Euro) rested on them. [...]

In fact, however, Greenlight lacked the skills and experience to handle such extensive animation production. And Dresdner Bank should have known that. [...]

The result was devastating: Not only were there significant delays in production; the quality of most films was so poor that they were not for sale. Admittedly, the Bank only noticed this in mid-2001. The subsequent negotiations with Greenlight brought no improvement whatsoever. The imbalance was so great that Dresdner Bank even considered liquidating the BAF fund company. However, fearing prospectus liability lawsuits that would seriously damage the bank's image and which, according to experts, would have had a good chance of success, the Board of Directors decided on a fallback strategy.[6]

In October 2002, Dresdner Bank exchanged the BAF management and took the 100% subsidiary BFC Berliner Film Companie Beteiligungsgesellschaft mbH completely under its wings. Greenlight Media was off the hook and washed its hands innocent. A certain Rainer Söhnlein was brought in as troubleshooter. He was supposed to supervise and finish the key project of the company: *Happily N'Ever After*. He had some production experience, but in questions of animation was an unwritten sheet. Söhnlein sure was a gifted swagger: With the new management, investors had good chances of realizing financial proceeds, but that's the fine print: There can be no guarantees. The bank cannot be held responsible for losses.

The fairyland on the one hand and the cloud cuckoo land of New Economy on the other, they show remarkable similarities in this fund story: Munk and Mambo and the Dresdner, all of them had no idea what was in store for them. [...]

At this point, the almost 1,600 investors were already unsettled, whose deposits ranged from 25,600 Euros (minimum value) to more than one million. Expert opinions and counter-expert opinions dueled, lawsuits were threatened, rumors circulated. The fear was rampant: that fund money was wasted, that the completion of the series and the cinema film were in danger and the promised return a fairy tale.

A rough calculation went like this: BAF produces seven series with a total of 3,500 minutes of broadcasting, the TV minute costs 8,000 Euros, a total of 28 million; you add another half for marketing and you end up with 42. The calculation for the cinema film: 30 million - officially - for production, plus at least 15 in sales - and the 87 million would already be gone, without a safety margin. According to insiders, but the bank denies this, Dresdner even injected money to keep the fund afloat and its reputation intact.

The 30 million for *Happily N'Ever After* were, shall we say, a strongly fluctuating number. The movie was initially supposed to cost nine million (according to Gerhard Hahn, one of the subcontractors), Rainer Söhnlein (executive producer of the BAF) remembers 21, and after the project had been switched from two-dimensional to 3D, the production company once spoke - Spelling mistake? Confused accounting? Megalomania? - even about an estimated 44 million. Because the horse was swapped in the middle of the river, the standards had also changed: Although located in the district Berlin Mitte, *Happily N'Ever After* was Hollywoodized. The *Shrek*-experienced producer John H. Williams flew in, expensive Mental Ray rendering software was needed, and so the cinema minute price rose and rose: from the usual country-wide 150,000 Euros to 400,000 (at a final price of 30 million) or even 600,000 (at 44). Also Sigourney Weaver and Sarah Michelle Gellar as English voices will not have been easy on the budget. According to the fund plan, investors could have looked forward to a substantial Christmas bonus next month; the issue prospectus promised between 10.9 and 20.2 percent. But before that happens, Little Red Riding Hood and the wolf get married. [...]

Even a BAF spokeswoman considers it "difficult" for the 87 million (or even more) to return to the potty. Nevertheless, private investors are likely to see their deposits again, without interest. Losses are initially at the expense of the Berlin Investment Bank and thus the unsuspecting Berlin taxpayers.[7]

After many years of trial and tribulations, *Happily N'Ever After* finally was released with a special distribution contract thru Lion's Gate in the U.S. For one week in 2006 it was in the U.S. charts, that is, until audiences realized it certainly was not *Shrek* but a poor script concocted from a miserable idea (although the American DVD sales turned out much more promising). In Germany itself, it drew only 20,000 viewers with 200 prints released.

Believe or not, there was a *Happily N'Ever After 2: Snow White Another Bite @ the Apple* in 2009 that basically worsened most of the problems of the original. In the same year BAF was liquidated. The company that had started out so pompously ended up in shame like Goebbels' Deutsche Zeichenfilm GmbH. At about the same time, a favorite idea of Deutsche Zeichenfilm GmbH was revived: *Maya the Bee*.

HITLER'S FAVORITE BEE

In 2013–2014, a computer-animated version of *Maya the Bee* appeared on German TV and finally on the cinema screen, based on an old series concept conceived by Josef Göhlen. Göhlen, who in the 1960s was responsible for the puppet programs of Ausgburger Puppenkiste at Hessischer Rundfunk, had the idea of a TV series adaptation of the 1912 book *Maya the Bee and Her Adventures* by Waldemar Bonsels

(1880–1952) as early as 1968. He saw the cheeky bee as an emancipated female figure of initiation and identification who was to serve as a role model among young audiences, albeit with less anarchic character traits than Astrid Lindgren's rebellious *Pippi Longstocking*. But, contrary to what was planned, it wasn't the Augsburg puppeteers who did the show. Due to Göhlen's move to ZDF, an anime series was created. *Maya* was outsourced in the mid-1970s to Zuiyo Enterprises Japan (today Nippon Animation) where it became *Mitsubachi Maya no boken*.

As a precaution, however, the character designs were commissioned from an American (Hanna-Barbera experienced) draftsman (Marty Murphy), so that they did not look to Far Eastern Anime for the conservative German taste.

When this author pointed out the rather nationalistic, vulgar Darwinistic origin of Waldemar Bonsels' nature fairy tale on Deutschlandradio,[8] a shitstorm arose on social networks. I quote:

Franjo Delic: Hitler ate his soup with a spoon, the spoon should be banned as a nationalist symbol of a brown past!!

Christian Weisweiler: There they are again, our pseudo-submissive virtuosos of consternation who, with the moral self-righteousness of a caste of priests, even see the Antichrist in Maya the Bee.

Ralf Galleisky: So many things are misused for their own purposes; the Nazis and many other atrocity regimes have misused so many things for themselves; Maya can't do anything about that; I grew up with the sweet bee and gay Willi, and had a lot of fun.

But Bonsels was not abused. Rather, he was one of the decidedly creative, anti-Semitic pioneers of the ideology that led to a second world war: a small cog in the gears of a national awareness industry, one that admittedly spread "a lot of fun."

Although some of Bonsels' later, rather frivolous books were on the National Socialist index, Maya the Bee and the 1915 follow-up volume, *Himmelsvolk* (*People in the Sky: Fairy Tale of Flowers, Animals and God*) had circulation records in the Third Reich. In addition, Bonsels was, despite some problems with the Rosenberg office, an outspoken partisan of National Socialism: In the foreword to his novel *Dositos*, which he distributed in 1942 as a private print in an edition of 100 to friends and NS grandees, he paid tribute to the "mighty and violent impetus" that was brought into the world by Adolf Hitler, and that not only shook Judaism "but naturally at the same time everything that suffers from Judaism in the Christian Church."

> There are no Jews in Maya the Bee, but of course the naive and innocent Maya is programmatically alien to all "overheated enlightenment." In the thirteenth chapter [of Bonsels' book], The Adventures of Maya the Bee take an unexpected turn: Maya is captured by the enemy hornets. "My people, my homeland!" she sobs when she learns that the hornets are blowing to attack the bees. But Maya can warn her people – the ex-vagrant rushes home "like a bullet from the barrel of a hunting rifle": the alleged children's book is transformed into a battle painting. Maya is overcome by "a great anger against the enemy and at the same time a blissful will to make sacrifices" - just a vagabond individualist, she now knows what is proper for Bonsels: the bee is nothing, its people are everything.[9]

This principle of looking the other way of ignoring or defusing the historical roots of a template seems to be symptomatic of the commercial German animated film of our day: It likes to use traditional templates and fairy tales, including those collected by the Brothers Grimm, whose cruelty, however, it conceals and played down. The result, the 3D *Maya the Bee*, cleansed and purified for children's view, is uninspired, banal and fussy:

Freshly hatched bee Maya is a little whirlwind and will not follow the rules of the hive. One of these rules is not to trust the hornets that live beyond the meadow. When the Royal Jelly is stolen, the hornets are suspected, and Maya is thought to be their accomplice. No one will stand by her except her good-natured and best friend Willy. After a long and eventful journey to the hornets' hive, Maya and Willy soon discover the true culprit. The picture was produced by Studio 100 (Germany) in association with Buzz Studios (Australia) and awarded a Bavarian Film Prize in 2015.

LAURA'S STAR SHINES BRIGHTLY INTO CHILDREN'S ROOMS

Right after the tragic events of 9/11, Warner Bros. Germany released Thilo Rothkirch's production of *Little Polar Bear* (*Der kleine Eisbär*), which followed the popular children's television series based on the picture books by Dutch writer-illustrator Hans de Beer. The feature had no continuous plot but consisted of three segments, one aboard a Black Ship, sort of an automatic fish factory. Almost three million watched it in German cinemas. This success came as a total surprise. The new German Warner head Willi Geike and Rothkirch who knew each other from their time at the university were that overwhelmed that they gave birth to a wave of animated feature films aimed solely at an audience of children (including their mothers who were supposed to accompany them and buy the tickets). In 2005, another Warner/Rothkirch production adapted from a TV series and books by Klaus Baumgart, *Laura's Star* (*Lauras Stern*), won a German Film Award as Best Children's Film: A little girl befriends a tiny star that has fallen from the night sky. From then on, children's TV became a basic formula for all parties involved in the financing of German animation, including television networks, national film funding institutions, and film distributors. All of a sudden, despite declining birthrates, preschoolers had become a principle, audience, and adaptations of children's picture books the standard rule (Figure 13.1).

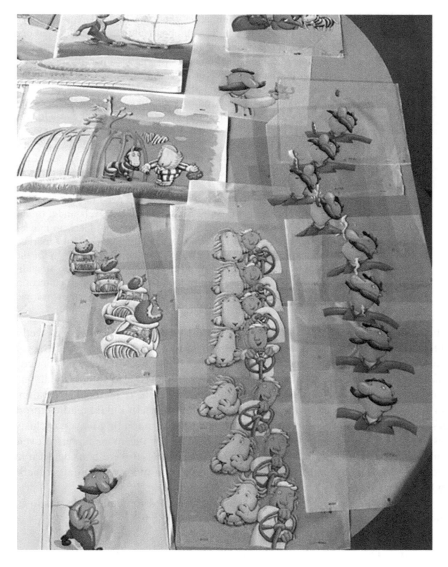

FIGURE 13.1 Artwork for *Tobias Totz und sein Löwe* (*Tobias Totz and His Lion*, 1999) by Thilo Rothirch and Piet De Rycker. (Courtesy Rothkirch Cartoon Film.)

Germans love cartoons, but with preschool fare behind every corner the fun is limited. Belgian animator-turned-director Piet De Rycker belonged to those who decided to join forces with Germany where he was chosen by Rothkirch to co-direct *Little Polar Bear* and *Laura's Star*. He told us:

Unfortunately, under the influence of TV formats, we have split up the audience in all kinds of age groups forgetting that a good story should be able to hold the attention of any spectator, being kid or adult alike.

From my own experience in feature animation, there is a big difference between working for a German project or a British. It is all about culture and about what one thinks entertainment is or should be. I have the impression British culture understands entertainment as a challenge to explore the grandness of a project, not limited by pre-determined ideas if it is of educational value or parent-proof. This state of thinking means that there are a lot of wild, funny, grand ideas on the table that might be hilarious, even over the top which makes the work process hilarious, too. Of course, not all of those ideas make it to the screen. But somehow it influences the way how you look at a project. By trying to be parent-proof, however, as they do in Germany, educationally and politically correct, a lot of potential is cut already out before one starts a project. It means that there is a stop towards high adventure, not only by the false idea of not having the money to visualize it, but just because there is a certain fear to impress, to excel in entertaining filmmaking. This idea of social rightness I see as a self-limitation. In Germany there seems to be an unwritten law that says: we need to protect future generations from crazy irrational behavior. So we will educate them well, and if things would go out of hand nobody can blame us. This doesn't mean that German movies can't be successful. On the contrary, they might be very popular, on the home market. But elsewhere, they will be hard to sell. Maybe because when one doesn't go for the educational, one might go for the burlesque. And that is a style that has also an audience attraction in Germany. As a Belgian, I am in the middle of those two cultures. I understand them both, but the British tongue in cheek, laughing about your own stupid self, holds a charm that we all should embrace in our working life.

The field of commercially more attractive family entertainment was neglected and freely left to the American companies, Pixar, Disney, DreamWorks, Blue Sky, and Illumination, all of them operating on a global level. The Americans flooded the markets with expensive 3D blockbusters that were impossible to compete with on low European budgets. At the same time, the rather small niche of national entertainment for the youngest viewers became occupied by multitudes of kiddie matinee producers. Suddenly, there was too much animation with less marketing power, exclusively reserved for afternoon screenings, but not booked for the more lucrative evening time slots. At that time, half a million viewers (and less) were considered a huge success for German feature animation. The animation quality often left something to be desired.

Here some feature-length examples (some even led to sequels), based in most cases on TV series, chosen by me at random:

FELIX – EIN HASE AUF WELTREISE (FELIX AROUND THE WORLD, 2005)

Cinema compilation of the animated TV series from 2002 starring a rabbit character known to German kids from merchandising products. Produced (and co-written) by Gabriele M. Walther, CEO of production company Caligari Film:

In 1997, I read the first **Felix** book to my nephew. He asked me if I couldn't make **Felix** into a movie. Indeed, I later purchased the media rights from the publisher and produced a TV series. [...] The publisher had initiated the property very cleverly. First there was the stuffed animal manufactured by Spiegelburg followed by the book. And then in the bookstores the books were offered with the stuffed animals. It is rather unusual to introduce a character like *Felix* without a media product. Usually, it is the other way round: first the movie, then the merchandising.[10]

Jasper und das Limonadenkomplott (*Jasper: Journey to the End of the World*, 2008), an animated feature film about two penguin brothers, Jasper and Junior, who, with the help of 9-year-old Emma, retrieve the eggs of a threatened parrot species from the evil Dr. Block.

Mullewapp – Das grosse Kinoabenteuer der Freunde (*Mullewapp: The Big Cinema Adventure of the Friends*, 2009): MotionWorks Halle-animated farmyard tale. The cinema version based on a TV series with characters created by Helme Heine. Unsuccessful entertainer Johnny Mauser ends up in the sleepy village of Mullewapp. On a farm he meets the vain cockerel Franz von Hahn and the ever-hungry pig Waldemar. When the little lamb Cloud is kidnapped, the motley group of friends is chosen to save her from the clutches of the wicked wolf, using all their courage, energy, and astuteness. As they do so, they get to know their strengths and weaknesses, and learn to take responsibility for each other. This should be the start of a wonderful friendship.

Das Sandmännchen – Abenteuer im Traumland (*The Sandman and the Lost Sand of Dreams*, 2010), stop-motion with Germany's TV Sandman set in a live-action frame (with a slight nod to Michael Ende's *NeverEnding Story*): Miko dreams of being a captain. He is an imaginative little boy, but he is just as fearful. Miko is also the only hope the Sandman has to save the dreams of every child in the world. The Sandman's dream-making sand has been stolen by Habumar. Habumar is going to poison the sand and turn people's dreams into nightmares. A mix-up sends Miko into the Sandman's world where all the dreams live on after we wake up. Shot at a special stage at Babelsberg Studios.

Der kleine Rabe Socke (*Raven the Little Rascal*, 2012): Animated animal fable with a raven character from a book by Nele Moost. When cheeky Little Raven accidentally damages the forest dam, the reservoir threatens to flood the woods. Afraid of getting into trouble with Mrs. Badger, Little Raven is determined to fix his mishap. Together with his friends Wooly Sheep and Eddie Bear, Raven makes his way to the beavers to ask them for help. But when he can't bring himself to admit his fault, the beavers refuse any support. Only beaver girl Francie comes to the rescue. Now it's up to Little Raven and his friends to save their beloved forest. Sounds like a lot of action, although it's rather tame.

Ritter Rost – Eisenhart und voll verbeult (2013): 3D-animated fantasy adventures of young *Knight Rusty* who resembles a walking cash register in a land made of scrap metal. In the Kingdom of Scrapland, Rusty is no more than an insignificant knight. Bravery is not one of his outstanding characteristics. He likes it calm and comfortable. Together with Maid Bo and Coke the Fire Dragon, he inhabits the Iron Castle. However, Maid Bo has a completely different image of a true knight's performance. So Rusty must consider whether he wants to live on at a trot. Eventually, he must reclaim his honor after being accused of cheating in a jousting tournament. Based on an idea by Mark Slater and produced by Gabriele M. Walther (Caligari Film)

Der 7bte Zwerg (*The 7th Dwarf*, 2014), the 3D animated Story of the Seven Dwarves, mixing the fairy tales of *Snow White* and *Sleeping Beauty*: The seven dwarves must wake Beauty from her slumber. And fast! Snow White's son has a mysterious illness that only Beauty can heal, if only the dwarves can make it to her birthday in time! The fight against the curse of evil Fairy Dellamorta is a race against time. Literally! Turning back the clock and traveling through time is easy. After all, this is supposed to be a fairy tale.

> Directed by Harald Siepermann (who died mid-production in 2013) and Boris Aljinovic, *The 7th Dwarf* is an animated extension of a franchise that includes two prior live-action features: *7 Dwarfs* (2004), which was one of the most successful Teuton titles of that year, and its lower-grossing sequel, *7 Dwarfs: The Forest Is Not Enough* (2006). Where those pictures freely sampled from the likes of "Snow White," "Little Red Riding Hood" and "Rumpelstiltskin," the new film largely riffs on "Sleeping Beauty" [...] The dwarfs, by contrast, are a pretty inoffensive, forgettable bunch, whose names alone (i.e., Cloudy, Sunny, Cookie, Speedy) serve as a reminder of just how hard it has become to put an original spin on public-domain fairy tales outside the Disney studio auspices.[11]

Ooops! Die Arche ist weg... (Ooops! Noah Is Gone/All Creatures Big and Small, 2015): 3D-animated animal adventures on Noah's Ark with some ugly Nestrians as stowaways: A flood is coming. Luckily for Dave and his son Finney—the two Nestrians, an Ark has been built to save all species of animals. But it turns out, Nestrians are not allowed. Sneaking on board with the involuntary help of two Grymps—Hazel and her daughter Leah, they think they are safe. Until the kids fall off the Ark. Now Finney and Leah struggle to survive the flood and hungry predators. They try to reach the top of a mountain, while their parents Dave and Hazel must put aside their differences, turn the Ark around, and save them. Directed by Toby Genkel and Sean McCormack, and produced by Ulysses Filmproduktion.

Luis & die Aliens (Luis and the Aliens, 2018), an animated feature film developed by Academy Award-winning twin brothers Christoph and Wolfgang Lauenstein, and produced by Ulysses Filmproduktion: a rather Americanized little boy's encounter of the third kind. Luis is 11 years old and a lonely kid. But then he finds real friends in an awesome trio of crazy aliens that has crash-landed on earth. The aliens are going to fix the boy's life in a rather unusual way. However, Luis can't tell his father. Although (or because) his dad is a screwy UFO researcher; he thinks that all aliens are basically dangerous and therefore have to be eliminated. After a while, Luis and the aliens find themselves followed by a growing group of pursuers.

Tabaluga – Der Film (Tabaluga: The Movie, 2018): 3D animation featuring a little green dragon (created by pop singer Peter Maffay) and ice princess Lilli who have to fight an evil wizard and save the world from a terrible snowman named Arktos. Produced by Deutsche Columbia Pictures and Tempest Film.

WORRY EATERS

In the meantime, conditions and production strategies have changed. Gerhard Hahn:

> Depending on the series it's either intended for 4 to 6 years, i.e., preschool, or for 6 to 9 years old. In this age comic strips and their stylings play not that role as they do for the 10 to 12 years old - but for this age group there are no firm time slots on TV. We all

know that kids in this age watch programs wherever they are, that means online. The double-etched formula therefore reads: no time slots, no co-funding from broadcasters, ergo no products.

Regarding the adaptation of approved merchandising characters, we make a point developing, producing and marketing our own intellectual properties. Apart from the distinctively greater creative pleasure in developing own properties, options in financing and re-financing play an important, if not the important part. Considering the funding, let's suppose we have a German broadcaster who contributes to the production of a series. That means that we as producers are forced to put up more than 80 per cent of the budget by ourselves. Therefore, a participation in potential license agreements and merchandise receipts is almost inevitable. We have to keep in mind that the relatively low input of broadcasters makes it necessary that we have to calculate our production budgets as low as possible to obtain funding reliably. This results in the fact that an animation producer today cannot recoup his efforts - which in case of a series might extend over a period of two to three years - solely from producing. A merchandising license deal as early as possible is a relevant factor. We know both extremes from our own work: In the early history of Hahn Film there were successful series like *Benjamin the Elephant (Benjamin Blümchen)* and *Bibi Blocksberg*. This was commissioned work without shares or any additional revenues. 30 years ago, this made sense. Today's situation is different. The other extreme is our series *Worry Eaters*. In order to pitch the series idea, I had presented stuffed dolls some years ago - with the result that the dolls and related products became an instant international sales hit before the first screenplay was written. The relatively absurd or at least untypical effect is that the merchandising recoupments from marketing the dolls now are a significant part of series financing which in turn hopefully will further fuel the merchandising success.

Tony Loeser, retired MotionWorks founder, lamented about the competition from abroad:

In media there is a big problem with globalization: We have program without end. The Americans have succeeded in adapting European content, fairy tales and so on, and have transformed it into a global formula. That kills local content in Europe, in India, everywhere in the world. In France they still have a good cultural policy and reach sufficient quota for French movies. But this is an exception based on a strong national tradition.

GREETINGS FROM CHINA

German and European producers calculate €12,000 per minute of TV animation. A big deal of German production is outsourced to Asia to save money. The first German to regularly go and try working with China was the late Manfred Durniok. Durniok who started with a documentary about China and then, with *Greetings from China*, produced the first big music program for German TV, might be better known for his Academy Award-winning István Szábo film *Mephisto* (1981); but his secret goal was to become the "German Walt Disney." Durniok, a penny pincher, would begin to consequently co-produce cheap animated feature films in the studios of Shanghai. He secured money from German TV, had the scripts prepared, and then commit the projects to the animation filmmakers in Shanghai.

In 1983, he invested some money in *Legend of Sealed Book/Secrets from the Book of Heaven*—one of the classics of Chinese feature animation that he brought to Cannes. Six years later he would continue the cooperation with a 2D *Reynard the Fox*—a project that had been done by Władysław Starewicz long ago with stop-motion puppets. Finally, Durniok would turn to puppets too and establish a series of feature-length Jules Verne stop-motion entries.

Durniok, who became an Honorary Citizen of Beijing, would have carried on if his sudden death in 2003 wouldn't have abruptly ended the relationship between German and Chinese production companies. He had already talked to Wang Borong from the Shanghai Animation Studio about an animated version of Richard Wagner's *The Ring of the Nibelung*.

After Durniok's death the intercultural field was left, until Thilo Rothkirch found a studio in Beijing and announced his first Sino-German co-production: *Laura's Star and the Mysterious Dragon Nian* (originally to be titled *Laura's Star in China*) that was finished in 2009 and two years later was released in China by the Shanghai Media Group.

Set against the background of a rural Mongolian area and the Chinese capital, the picture offers awesome sights of past, present, and future at the time of New Year's Spring Festival. Two girls, Laura born in the West (Germany) and Ling-Ling raised in the East (China), master their initial misunderstandings and with the help of a tiny, miracle-working Star become close friends. But before this is going to happen, there are trials and tribulations to test the seriousness of their friendship. In the Darkest Night of the Year, a whole twilight world of imagination materializes. Although Laura is worried about her Star assuming that it might be blackened, the girls dare to face all dangers and, illuminated by the Star's magic and with the support of a friendly makeshift Nian, overcome their fears to emerge as twin sisters.

Nian, a creature, half dog, half lion, has been awakened by the girls' initial dispute over the ownership of the miraculous Star, although this Nian was only a costume to appear on stage at New Year's Eve. Thanks to the magic of some stardust, Nian comes to life. Riding on the back of the creature, tamed by cookies, the girls travel high above Beijing to defeat the Cloud of Darkness and save the Star from being blackened.

A giant firework celebrating New Year has the Black Cloud retread, and brings the girls back to the reality of their families and to springtime of star-blessed friendship.

It was the first Sino-German co-production in 3D (more than 50% of the footage was produced in Beijing, a small percentage in India, and the rest in Berlin, Germany). Famous Chinese pianist Lang Lang, whose parents were neighbors to a high-ranked supportive Chinese official who once worked in the Chinese Embassy in Berlin, was delighted to take part in the production, as he was started at an early age having seen a Tom & Jerry Cartoon, *Cat Concerto*.

Laura's Star and the Mysterious Dragon Nian won Gold Panda Awards for the Best domestic animated feature film and Best Screenplay in 2011. Rothkirch, however, wouldn't go on. He passed away in 2014 in Berlin.

In 2011, two more animated films from Germany opened in Chinese cinemas: *Animals United* (Hanover-produced 3D animation officially based on Erich Kästner's *Conference of Animals* but more likely a German version of *Madagascar*) became an instant hit, as everywhere else in the world: In the African savannah, all the animals are wondering what happened to the water. It should have been here for a long time ago, streaming down through a valley from the distant mountains. Their increasing thirst turns into real worry, especially as the last remaining water hole is guarded by rivaling buffalo and rhino herds. So brave meerkat Billy and his best buddy, the peaceful lion Socrates, set out in search of water. *Animals United* was produced by Ambient Entertainment (Holger Tappe) and Constantin Film (Reinhard Klooss).

A different case was *Little Big Panda*: High in the majestic mountains the survival of the panda bears is under dire threat as humans (Chinese, not to be seen in the final movie) encroach on their environment, and at the same time the supply of the pandas' cherished sole nutrient, bamboo shoots, is steadily dwindling away. Unfortunately, pandas become extremely apathetic when confronted with change and certainly need a hero to guide them out of misery.

The one they need is Manchu [Chinese version: Pandy]—a little panda known as the "Chosen One," but stupidly he is rejected by his clan due to his hair-brained ideas; but finally gains confidence and leads his community struggling for survival to a better environment—a New Promised Land of Bamboo.

In China, this stereoscopic 2D tale was announced as the most expensive domestic animated feature film up to that time (with a budget of allegedly more than US$50 million). Actually, however, the movie was produced in Europe: in Germany, Spain, and Belgium for less than US$10 million. Xiao Xiong Chen, a wealthy Chinese investor with a network of good connections, bought into the underfinanced project (otherwise it wouldn't have been finished) and released the Chinese dubbing that included well-known voice talent with an outstanding promotional campaign that made the audience think it would be something on the scale of *Kung Fu Panda* but, alas, it wasn't. The German producer, none other than Michael Schoemann, wasn't up to what was internationally expected. Without the financial injection from China, he would not have been able to finish the film that was made with a pretty low budget anyway. Even if he wanted (he didn't), a *Kung Fu Panda* would have been impossible for him.

In between these films, there was a lot of outsourcing: German and European "cooperation" just for the benefit of cheap labor offered by a galaxy of Chinese studios, but that, of course, had nothing to do with upright co-production on an intercultural level. Gerhard Hahn, on the other hand, who had had unpleasant experiences with a studio he had founded in Vietnam, didn't think much of intercultural cooperation with Asia:

> There is a rather mundane, banal reason for the previous and still practiced cooperation between Europe and Asia: the labor costs. This simple fact implicated that our partners in Far East always were service producers. There was no partnership on a creative level which would have led to a coproduction partnership. The situation is changing currently. The artistic potential of companies in Asia begins to grow. Nevertheless, as I see it, the situation will continue for some time that European producers will handle the creative part, from design and script development to animatics, and our Asian partners will do the actual production.
>
> China, on the other hand, rates high alone for the size of the market. But one should not blend oneself by this Klondike-like hype and only have Yuan signs in the eyes. For

some time, we are in touch with Chinese studios but haven't found the likewise artistically and economically compellent case to cooperate necessarily.

The question of chances for intercultural projects can be answered both for and against. Culturally we are looking back at different pictorial and different narrative traditions. Stories and characters that answer a claim of interculturality run the risk of being neither fish nor fowl. When I watch Asian and American series then I am expecting either an Asian or an American series, with all their respective specifics, and nothing else. I think that one shouldn't enforce artificially interculturality and drag it in by the head and shoulders - which will bring us back to the question of European positioning between America and Asia. From my standpoint the specific idiosyncrasies and individualities are significant and this will remain so for some time. The three cultures and particularly these three markets work differently. A comparison of the production terms and budgets in America and Europe alone doesn't place, literally speaking, apples against pears but, considering the sheer volume, melons against lemons. We are well advised [in Europe] to make the best out of lemons and in the most successful case this will be lemonade.

Parts of German shows like *Moonbeam Bear* by Caligari Film (Gabriele M. Walther) were run in China (by a company named Sophie Animation in Dalian) as was *Fritzi: A Revolutionary Tale* (2019), an emotionally told coming-of-age story of an 11-year-old girl who just by accident became part of the Monday demos in Leipzig, East Germany the thrilling days before the Wall fell. The 2D-animated movie was produced by Balance Film Dresden (Ralf Kukula) and TrickStudio Lutterbeck Cologne.

ANIMATION THAT MOVES

In 1987, Richard Lutterbeck founded TrickStudio Lutterbeck in Cologne, joined by Matthias Bruhn in 1998. Besides commercials for TV and cinema, the studio is mainly focusing on TV and cinema animation for kids. To date, numerous short films have been commissioned for the well-known TV show *Sendung with the Mouse*, such as *The Story of the Little Mole Who Knew That It Was None of His Business*, produced in 2006 based on a popular children's book classic, or *The Last Sheep*, a 2020 Christmas movie. TrickStudio employs 12 permanent employees, but depending on the respective production volume, there is also a large number of freelancers. For example, a total of around 200 people were involved in the Studio's first feature film *Molly Monster* (2016) over a period of one and a half years. Instead of paper and foil animations, highly specialized animation software and hardware have long characterized today's animation production and, thus, also the jobs in the TrickStudio. The animated film series *Fritzi & Sophie: Boundless Friendship* (based on the feature *Fritzi*) is being created by using motion capture. In addition to TrickStudio and Balance Film, European partners from Belgium, Luxembourg, and the Czech Republic are involved in the series.

Richard Lutterbeck (Figure 13.2):

Short or feature-length, the critical point of a production is the financing. If a story is to be told as an animated film, it is often more complicated than producing a live-action film. Animation is time consuming and expensive! It hasn't necessarily gotten any easier to close funding, especially for demanding children's films. The German film funding system is very complex and funding is time-consuming and uncertain. Cinema film projects can usually only be realized as European co-productions. Nevertheless, the budget of a European film production is absolutely not comparable with an American blockbuster production, which is in the tens or hundreds of millions. At the box office, however, the films are in competition because the cinema tickets cost the same. So there is a struggle about the placement and the playing times.

FIGURE 13.2 *Ente, Tod und Tulpe* (*Duck, Death and Tulip*). (Courtesy of TrickStudio Lutterbeck.)

The production of short films is and remains an important focus of TrickStudio. Films such as *Post!* (2008), a poetic plea for the bit of anarchy that rules everyday life, *Duck, Death and Tulip* (*Ente, Tod und Tulpe* 2010), based on the book by Wolf Erlbruch, or *The Story of the Fox Who Lost His Mind* (*Die Geschichte vom Fuchs, der den Verstand verlor,* 2015), a poetic animated film about aging and dementia, were produced with the help of Film- und Medienstiftung NRW (Film and Media Funding North Rhine-Westphalia) and Kuratorium/BKM (Cultural Film Funding), and have been awarded numerous national and international prizes.

The collaboration with the Swiss artist Ted Sieger resulted in the series *Ted Sieger's Molly Monster* (52×5 minutes) and the Christmas special *Molly and the Christmas Monster* (*Molly und das Weihnachtsmonster,* 26 minutes) from 2007 to 2011. The studio's first feature film as an international co-production, 2016's *Molly Monster The Movie* (sold to over 90 countries) as well as series and special were aimed at a preschool audience.

The latest feature film production by TrickStudio is the animated film *The Sirene* (*Die Sirene,* 2022), realized in a European co-production with Les Film d'Ici, Katuh Studio, Bac Cinema, and Lunanime. The 100-minute arthouse film, elaborately designed in 3D and 2D, celebrated its world premiere at the Berlin International Film Festival 2023. *The Sirene* tells a modern Ark story at the time of the beginning of the Iran/Iraq war in 1980. The Iranian oil metropolis Abadan sinks into chaos after a rocket attack. The 14-year-old Omid is a food delivery boy looking for his missing brother and for an escape route from the besieged city (Figure 13.3).

FIGURE 13.3   *The Sirene.* (Courtesy of TrickStudio Lutterbeck.)

Richard Lutterbeck (Figure 13.4):

Unlike most other studios in Germany, TrickStudio employs a permanent creative staff. Both in terms of design and content, the team tries to develop animated films that tell stories at a high level of animation. One focus is on the cinematic adaptation of children's books. An important concern of the studio is to transfer the spirit of a book into the medium of film - with the means of animation. The subjects of the projects are also often unusual: death, dementia, loss, jealousy, but of course also friendship or togetherness. The technical means of implementation are constantly changing - but whether classic 2D animation or 3D motion capture technology, whether short film or cinema film: good stories and good storytelling are at the heart of every production. The TrickStudio team can build on growing experience with each new production. Germany now has a large number of animation schools. The quality of education in this country is very high in an international comparison and is also reflected in award winners. The country has a variety of public and private TV stations looking for good content. The TV market for animation films in Germany is huge and should lead to a thriving landscape in the animation industry. When looking through the linear children's TV programs, however, the majority of the animated series does not come from the domestic branch, but increasingly from other European countries in addition to the American productions. The studio systems in other countries are specially promoted, get recognition and have their quotas on domestic public TV. In Germany, however, such systems are rarely found. A solid basis has been established here with special effects studios, which are gladly booked worldwide. In German cinemas, as sort of reinsurance, animated feature film productions are based almost exclusively on established brands. There is hardly any space for original stories. Animated films for adults hardly ever take place on the big screen! The marketing budgets of the film distributors are far too small in this country and often fizzle out on the target group: "Animated film? That's just kid stuff (*Kinderkram*)!." Getting the viewer back into the cinema seat is the great challenge of the next few years and should therefore start with film education in preschool. And: Germany needs a national animation film award. Motivation? Every rejection of an institution's application for funding is an incentive to fight even harder for a project and to push through against all obstacles. Standing up for an alternative film culture and producing animation films for adults that go beyond the mainstream and bringing them to the cinema is not always easy, but it is enormously important! And the greatest motivation is: after months or years, sitting in the front row of the cinema and watching the reactions on the faces of the audience. And if the desired emotion can be recognized, that motivates us a lot!.

FIGURE 13.4 *Fritzi: A Revolutionary Tale.* (Courtesy of TrickStudio Lutterbeck.)

The obstacles that motivate Richard Lutterbeck and his team drive many others to despair. Producers often seem to spend more time fighting for national and European funding than focusing on the quality of production. Tony Loeser:

> The biggest barrier for all people who are creative is the increasing administration in the media. It gets more and more complicated to raise funds. Everything is being bureaucratized. Some bloated machinery has been built up. And the more money they spent for this bureaucracy, the less is available for the creative aspects of production. Unproductive work soaks up parts of the budget that doesn't go into production. Decision-making processes are slowed down and delayed over periods of one to a year and a half. This bureaucratic superstructure paralyzes creative animation production and results in unnecessary compromises.

MOONBOUND

In recent times, we have to mention companies like Animationsfabrik in Hamburg (participating in *Another Day of Life,* a Polish–Spanish–Belgian–German co-production set during the Angolian civil war in 1975, as seen through the eyes of the legendary war reporter Richard Kapuscinski) and Little Dream Entertainment in Cologne with *Tehran Taboo* (2017), the mocap debut film of Ali Soozandeh who was born in Iran. His picture focuses on the lives of young Iran people; lives in which breaking taboos is part of personal emancipation. All characters are acting on an awkward level of imprudence that may come as a surprise to western audiences but is part of everyday life.

To peek behind the curtain of Iran's split society, Soozandeh used the stylistic devices of graphic novels, motion capture, and rotoscope: The fascinating imagery started with shooting real actors in a green screen studio. Then, in one year of hard work, backgrounds were generated, and both, characters and backgrounds, were thoroughly sketched and painted. Finally, all layers were assembled, and camera movements were applied in the process of compositing.

One of the most ambitious projects of the same company during Corona pandemic was *Peterchens Mondfahrt (Little Peter's Journey to the Moon* a.k.a. *Moonbound),* based on the classic children's story by Gerdt von Bassewitz that was 2D-animated already by the late Wolfgang Urchs: the tale of two children, Peter (Pete) and his sister Anneli (Anne), who help a May beetle named Mr. Sumsemann to retrieve his missing sixth leg from the cruel Man in the Moon (Figure 13.5).

FIGURE 13.5   *Peterchens Mondfahrt (Moonbound).* (Courtesy of Little Dream Entertainment.)

With the modern film version in full CG, the challenge for the artists and technicians at Little Dream Entertainment (working halfway in home office under director Ali Samadi Ahadi) was to transfer the values and role concepts created during the reign of German Emperor Wilhelm II to our days, and even make it acceptable to international viewers who never have heard of Bassewitz. Large parts of this project were done, inevitably, in China.

When the movie was finished in spring 2021, it was withheld by the production company paying tribute to the pandemic (and only screened once at the Golden Sparrow Children's Film Festival in Gera), with a new German cinema release scheduled for March 31, 2022. Earlier the movie was seen, however, out of the country of its origin, in Australia, and the United Kingdom (Figure 13.6).

FIGURE 13.6   *Peterchens Mondfahrt (Moonbound).* (Courtesy of Little Dream Entertainment.)

A British reviewer noticed that

this derivative but adequate animated feature fuses together an assortment of vaguely familiar characters and story tropes. The clever bit is that the film takes ideas from folklore and appears to be inspired by pre-existing intellectual property without infringing it.

For instance, one of the characters that early-adolescent protagonist Pete (voiced by Aleks Le) meets on his way to the moon [...] is the Sandman, a traditional figure in northern European mythology and popularized by ETA Hoffmann in the early 19th century. Later on, our heroes get to ride the backs of giant polar bears, remarkably similar to the ones in Philip Pullman's *His Dark Materials* book series. Meanwhile, the humans' guides also include beetles wistfully looking for abducted loved ones that seem to be mutant descendants of Disney's Jiminy Cricket from *Pinocchio* and the creepy crawlies from *A Bug's Life*.[12]

Armin Hofmann, one of the producers, asked about the situation of German producers concerning the contagious disease:

Regarding the feared set-backs due to the pandemic and the effects it might produce:

FEARS

The biggest fear was and still is receding box-office receipts because cinemas have limited occupancy due to hygiene regulations. This is aggravated by the fact that distributors don't pay substantial minimum guarantees because the situation of the cinemas is unstable.

EFFECTS

1. During production of *Peterchens Mondfahrt (Moonbound)* most employees were forced to work remotely, which necessitated increased technical expenses, and permanent feedback and coordination.
2. World sales didn't work as well as estimated because of the unstable situation in the cinema market.
3. The determination of the German release date was quite difficult due to the jam of top-quality productions (including the animation sector), which resulted in a serious competitive situation. Distributors and booking&billing companies have problems to determine the optimal point for release.

Perhaps not everyone might have liked the modernization of Bassewitz's original to the demands of a contemporary *Star Wars* audience (Figures 13.7 and 13.8).

FIGURE 13.7   Preproduction designs for a new animated feature film project: Angst—the story of a girl who is confronted with occult powers in Nazi Berlin. (Courtesy of brave new work GmbH.)

FIGURE 13.8   Preproduction designs for a new animated feature film project: *Angst*—the story of a girl who is confronted with occult powers in Nazi Berlin. (Courtesy of brave new work GmbH.)

NOTES

1 Jane Faber, *Per Zeichentrick zum Mond*. In: Berliner Morgenpost, November 29, 1990.
2 Loh.: *Filmspiegel "Werner – beinhart!."* In: Neue Zürcher Zeitung, January 25, 1991.
3 *Werner – Das muss kesseln!!!* Pressbook. Munich: Constantin Film, 1996.
4 Michael Rutschky, *Das kleine Arschloch*. In: Der Tagesspiegel, March 26, 1997.
5 Karlheinz Wagner, *Kleines Arschloch*. In: Kölner Stadt-Anzeiger, March 8, 1997.
6 Johannes Ritter, *Die Dresdner Bank dreht ihren eigenen Trickfilm*. In: Frankfurter Allgemeine Zeitung, April29, 2003.
7 Hanns-Georg Rodek, *Schreck statt Shrek für Dresdner-Bank-Anleger*. In: Die Welt, November 27, 2007.
8 Deutschlandradio Kultur, April 24, 2014.
9 Wieland Freund, *Die "Biene Maja" ist eine völkische Germanin*. In: Die Welt, April 17, 2012.
10 Blickpunkt:Film, February 7, 2005.
11 Justin Chang. In: Variety, July 30, 2015.
12 Leslie Felperin, *Moonbound review – a mish-mash of folkloric hijinks as kids take trip to the moon*. In: The Guardian, August 6, 2021.

14 Star Wars Worship

German producers hardly stood a chance against the wave of American blockbusters. The invasion of the U.S. majors didn't even stop at the portals of German churches. Two Protestant vicars, a man and a woman, have been celebrating *Star Wars* in the Zion Church in Berlin since December 20, 2015. Instead of the crucifix, they used toy lightsabers to convey their message from a "just war":

> ...people hardly concern themselves anymore with passages from the Bible in which one can easily recognize Christ. All the more so with pop culture myths like the *Star Wars Saga*, but which first have to be worked out. [...]
>
> Under the title The Awakening of the Force, Ulrike Garve, 29, and Lucas Ludewig, 30, are holding a service that is "also part of an educational program" [...]: "We try to take people's enthusiasm for *Star Wars* seriously and show them at the same time how many elements of our Christian culture are part of it."
>
> As an example, Ulrike Garve cites the conflict between "good" (Luke Skywalker) and "evil" (Darth Vader) in the original film trilogy. The fact that Luke "forgoes the fight in the direct confrontation with Darth Vader at the end of Episode VI," says Garve, is a sign of Luke's willingness to "see the good in the other person and to trust in the good." This coincides "with the Epistle to the Romans, where Paul writes that one should overcome evil by repaying with good."[1]

Star Wars trailers were screened in the church, the organ was blaring John Williams' score, a costumed Darth Vader kid spread a bit of hellish horror, and the vicars' sermon was depicting previously unknown connections between sci-fi fantasy and the reality of faith. Popular mythology and Christian religion actually till the same fields.

But no one in the church mentioned the Fascist elements of the Saga. *Fatal memories*. Throughout the Third Reich there was some opposition in the churches (Martin Niemöller and the Confessing Church), but the clergy also conformed with the regime. In 1939, right before the war, 11 German Protestant regional churches founded a "Dejudaization Institute" in Eisenach. The objective: Everything Jewish should be crossed out, painted over, and removed from Bible, hymnals, and church rooms.

And – to return to our days – what else was *Star Wars* in its original packing than WWII in Outer Space? Many of the X-winged VFX elements we saw in 1977 on the screen were modeled frame by frame copying footage from dogfights taken from newsreels and from *The Dam Busters*, a 1955 British war film that described an air raid of Avro Lancaster Bombers against a dam which contained the Möhnesee (May 16/17, 1943).

> ...one of the key visions I had of the film when I started, *Lucas said*, was of a dogfight in outer space with spaceships – two ships flying through space shooting at each other. That was my original idea.
>
> To a World War II history buff, the iconic Millennium Falcon from *Star Wars* resembles one of the best-known bombers of all time.

DOI: 10.1201/9781003375548-14

The greenhouse cockpit configuration, along with the gun turrets, aboard the ship was lifted straight out of the blueprints for the Boeing B-29 Superfortress.

The Superfortress was a workhorse of the US Army Air Forces that was best known for dropping atomic bombs on the Japanese cities of Hiroshima and Nagasaki.

Star Wars creator George Lucas is known to have studied 20 to 25 hours of footage from World War II dogfights while doing research for the film. [...]

According to a 1997 interview with Willard Huyck, a screenwriter who is a friend of Lucas, footage of World War II dogfights was used as a placeholder before the special effects were edited into the original film.[2]

Eventually, the Saga sanctified in a Berlin church became a billion-dollar property of Disney. Like a vacuum cleaner, this Empire has absorbed all franchises that one could wish for. Besides their own Mouse-eared brands, besides theme parks in the United States, France, Japan and China, and besides *Star Wars*, Disney owns 21st Century Fox and the *Marvel Cinematic Universe*. They old sold their imagery to a Mouse that roared.

Remember Pleasure Island, the cursed amusement park designed to turn mischievous boys into donkeys? Disney himself envisioned it while still alive in his animated adaptation of Carlo Collodi's *Pinocchio*! This forerunner of Disneyland is run by a demonic coachman, the alter ego of Scapinelli.

But the Shadow Devil not only answers to the name of Disney. He has various names. He turns up as Google, YouTube, Facebook, Netflix, with others yet unknown already in the starting gates. His manifestation is global, which means that he is an American data and media kraken. But, Asia comes on strong too, with Europe left out in the cold. And the shadows sacrificed to this Moloch are our most personal data in exchange for our *Avatars'* free ticket to Lalaland. Instead of a bottomless wallet we get, as reward, a surprise bag of apps, access to online banking, Amazon, eBay, and – what else? – the total war of "disneyfied" entertainment.

During the course of the 21st century, cinema will be more and more a relic of a bygone era. Since digitization, cinema is competing with all kinds of streaming portals. And people forget that most traditional cinemas were already forced to shut down half a century ago thanks to TV.

But, in the long run TV lost too, because it is not interactive enough.

Linear plots?

Today there is only transmedial franchise, and its content is obviously nonlinear. Anyway, with blockbuster CGI = *Computer Generated Imagery*, it's not so much the content, not the substance, it's the form or to quote Marshall McLuhan: the medium itself that is the message. The minimalist substance is less important than the fascination with the technological aspects of the medium that sometimes absorbs and "devours" the viewer and even its acolytes, the so-called influencers, the career aspiration of all newcomers.

Digitization is standardizing the range of large multiplexes worldwide. The result is no longer variety, but uniformity. Box-office results are calculated for worldwide release, country by country, at the headquarters of the majors in New York City. The branch manager of an American major was ruthlessly replaced when he did not live up to the New York expectations for one of the blockbusters: Instead of the expected six million visitors, he "only" had four million in Germany.

Georg Struck, a lecturer who also works in animation films and games: "It was the language that allowed U.S. producers to operate in the cinema with higher budgets than the Europeans, who stuck to producing for the fragmented markets of their native language. With the advent of the Internet, this competitive advantage of Hollywood studios suddenly extended to the print and television markets. When Netflix offers its subscribers series with budgets in the hundreds of millions, we have to admit that we have missed the boat in Europe and Germany. Such capital is not available for TV series in Europe and will no longer be able to be collected. The Internet therefore de facto belongs to the Americans as a marketing and distribution channel."[3]

NOTES

1   Matthias Kamann, *In der "Star Wars" – Saga steckt biblische Weisheit.* In: Die Welt, December 19, 2015.
2   Alex Lockie, https://www.businessinsider.com/star-wars-world-war-ii-dogfights-2-ww2–2015-12. December 18, 2015.
3   Rolf Giesen, *Der Angriff der Zukunft auf die Gegenwart.* Cologne: Herbert von Halem Verlag, 2018.

15 The Essence of Animation in Germany

But the global standardization of the industry through digitization also has advantages for the domestic industry the next generation. Hardly any cinematic product, even if it's only commercials for television and the internet, can do without CGI and digital animation.

> "All of our graduates are well accommodated. There is a huge demand on the market," says Sven Pannicke from the animation department at the Film Academy in Ludwigsburg [...] The tasks of the digital artists range from mere retouching and corrections to the creation of artificial visual worlds in computer games or feature films. [...] However, the computer is no more than a tool in this latest variant of animated film. That's why students at the private German Film School for digital production in Elstal near Berlin first practice a very old-fashioned art: drawing. The production of a three-minute classic animated film is intended to familiarize them with movement sequences – even the most complex computer programs cannot replace this later. [...] The students are very enthusiastic about the matter. This is also guaranteed by the high tuition fees: almost 80,000 marks up to the diploma examination. In order to be admitted to the renowned Ludwigsburg Film Academy, on the other hand, you need luck and talent above all: Only ten to twelve students with a focus on animation/digital image design can start here in the winter semester, over a hundred apply. And anyone who exceeds the standard study period of four and a half years will be exmatriculated. [...]
>
> Not much more than basic knowledge of digital image processing is taught at technical colleges in the Communication Design or Visual Communication courses. After such a degree, Ralf Ott continued first as an intern, then as an assistant at the media company Das Werk, the German market leader in the field of digital post-production: "At the time, I saw it as a postgraduate course." Today, Ott heads the Frankfurt office and is responsible for hiring new digital artists. [...] "The TV stations always need food," says Ralf Ott. "And when it comes to simulating the plane crashing into the World Trade Center."[1]

The euphoria seemed justified but came too soon.

The private German Film School for digital production (mentioned in the above article) existed for almost ten years and sadly had to file for bankruptcy in 2007. The founder, Professor Bernd Willim, died of cancer a year later. The highly-acclaimed, CG-focused Das Werk struck sail already in 2002.

THE SOBERING REALITY BEYOND FLICKERING DREAMS

In 2016, AG Animationsfilm Leizpig published the results of an industry survey on the situation of animation filmmaking in Germany:

The online survey took place from February 25 to March 31, 2015. 432 people participated, 299 of them filled out the questionnaires completely. The average age

DOI: 10.1201/9781003375548-15

of the respondents (64.5% male, 35.5% female) was 38 years. 71 people worked as producers, 344 were employed or freelancers. 63% mentioned the "love of film" as a reason for choosing the career, 61% felt artistically capable, 49% felt a passion for telling stories, and 35% were fascinated by cinema and technology.

Of the freelancers, 31% could not make a living from their work. They earned annually less than €16,500 on an hourly fee of less than €10. Only 13% earned more than €50,000. 37% of the respondents were dissatisfied with their income, but only 25% were satisfied. 42% stated that they did not make provisions for old age. 45% did not know the artists' social security fund. 52% were not satisfied with their social security or old-age provision.

23% saw good or very good job prospects, but only 20% good or very good financial prospects. 45% had a negative view of their financial future. 68% of those questioned had at least sometimes thought about giving up the profession and leaving the field.[2]

Nonetheless, the animation students are not discouraged, even if a lady working at Film University confessed that they release most of their graduates into unemployment.

EDUCATION IN ANIMATION

FILM UNIVERSITY BABELSBERG "KONRAD WOLF" POTSDAM-BABELSBERG

Located on the lot of the Babelsberg Film and TV Studios, the former UFA and DEFA production ground, the Film University is another important institute of Film and TV education.

The University's B.F.A. program allows students to take responsibility for all steps in the production of an animated film – from the development of the first idea, story and visual style to the creation of storyboards, character design, and artistic/technical implementation as well as sound recording and film playout. Artistic, dramatic, and technical advice is provided primarily in one-to-one sessions to ensure project-specific guidance and the development of an individual artistic style. The emphasis of the program is on practical exercises. Students have access to analog and digital animation studios, 2D and 3D computer animation labs, a render farm, video and audio editing workstations, compositing suites as well as a motion capture system, and student work rooms.

The quality of animation, either 2D or 3D, varies. Usually, students don't find much time to talk about their animation studies. Veronica Solomon did when I asked her some years ago, and what she observed didn't change in the meantime (Figure 15.1):

> I can only tell what I have watched in my own personal surrounding. At the Film University Babelsberg you don't have to finish an own project but there is this tradition and they all want to become filmmakers [auteurs]. Rarely people are pleased to play

a certain supporting part: character designer or background designer or just being an animator for a fellow student. Then you have to do everything yourself: screenwriting, directing, designing, modelling and rigging in case of 3D, animating, compositing, editing and nine times out of ten handling the production chores. So you start very carefully on designs, backgrounds, characters, props and what else – and then you realize that there is no time for extensive animation. You have to finish your degree. In the professional world similar things will happen but these depend on money, I guess.

FIGURE 15.1   *TV City* (2002): Replacement animation set. (Courtesy of Animas Film.)

One of the alumni (he studied from 1995 to 2002) is Alberto Couceiro, today artistic collaborator at the Film University. Together with Alejandra Tomei, he founded a small studio in Berlin, Animas Film, where they do replacement stop-motion animation. Alejandra Tomei (Figure 15.2):

> Our technique allows for more freedom. I have a preference for such techniques because they foster the imagination of the audience. They offer more space for association and one's own thoughts. At the same time, you can establish a kind of own logic without feeling a stranger while watching. There is more space for absurdity and humor which can unfold under these conditions. From a creative point of view, there are no bounds that we are not allowed to overstep. For us animators this is a good feeling.

FIGURE 15.2   Alberto Couceiro and Alejandra Tomei working on *TV City* (2002). (Courtesy of Animas Film.)

THE FILMAKADEMIE BADEN-WÜRTTEMBERG'S ANIMATION INSTITUTE

This institute is part of the Württemberg Animation & VFX Cluster that also includes a leading European Film Festival. The following text was kindly supplied for publication by Animationsinstitut. The institute sees itself as a talent hotspot of Europe's Animation Scene.

Since its founding in 1991, the Filmakademie Baden-Württemberg has had animation and CGI as one of the main pillars of its educational provision. At that time in Germany the unique establishment of a dedicated department of a film school, which later was called Animationsinstitut, would soon become a nationwide leading institution for training talents in animation and VFX appreciated by the worldwide film industry. It also eventually helped turn the Stuttgart–Ludwigsburg region into one of Germany's most prospering regions for animation and effects.

One of the Animationsinstitut's recipes for success, besides aiming at a high artistic level, had always been a strong focus on state-of-the-art technology. This emphasis is based on a prestigious Research and Development department (R&D), where a team of researchers, engineers, and artists explore and work on next-generation tools and equipment.

The research activity at the Animationsinstitut ensures its education quality at the highest standard, while the latest industry development indicates a shift toward an increasing number of Virtual Productions. Its R&D has not only contributed to the technological breakthrough of Virtual Production, but through the research, Virtual Production also found its way into the curriculum of the Animationsinstitut early on. That made the school a major European player in providing experts for the growing demand in the industry.

The New Creative Possibilities of Virtual Production Technology

Currently, the use of Virtual Production brings maybe the most profound change ever seen in film and video production. There are more and more Virtual Production studios around the world that consist of walls and ceilings made of high-resolution LED screens. With them, virtual content can be brought to the set and then combined with live-action content.

New is that Virtual Productions merge live-action footage with CGI in real time. Previously, the combination of digital imagery and live-action required complex post-production processes. In Virtual Production, this happens directly during the production itself.

This is made possible by advances in real-time (gaming) technology and a general price drop for LED panels. The so-called game engines are nowadays so powerful that they enable photorealistic real-time rendering when using LED walls, while sophisticated (volumetric) camera and tracking techniques join virtual and live-action footage.

From a creative point of view, Virtual Production changes production processes in a serious way. For instance, the director has through the instant view better control over the cinematic world. While preproduction is getting more important, the risk of failed shoots gets smaller. Further, production costs are reduced due to the less complex rendering process. In addition to reduced travel expenses, potentially more shots can be realized in a studio. Virtual Production is also boosting the usage of extended reality (XR) applications, as Virtual and Augmented Reality can be used as a substantial part of the production process.

Paving the way to a more sustainable filmmaking

The worldwide boom of Virtual Production technology is partly due to the corona pandemic. When productions around the world were restricted by hygienic measures, the technology was increasingly used as an alternative to shooting at real locations to avoid crew travel.

But, even without any restrictions, the technology continues to be on the rise. This might also be because the film industry is in a period of upheaval with a growing demand for VFX in episodic content for streaming services. While climate change is showing its effects increasingly, the industry is questioning its contribution to global warming. In March 2021, the Sustainable Production Alliance put the average CO_2 emissions of one film production at an exorbitant 3,370 tons. Per shooting day, that is about 33 tons.[3]

More and more industry players now want to get a grip on this problem. In Germany, the joint "Green Shooting" working group, an alliance of industry representatives from the German film, TV, and VoD market developed uniform minimum ecological standards for sustainable productions. They committed to complying with them in a sustainability initiative from January 1,

2022. Filmakademie Baden-Württemberg with its Animationsinstitut will also take on the implementation of these standards.

These efforts will generally increase the importance of Virtual Production. In 2022, the R&D published a report that demonstrated Virtual Production can significantly contribute to reducing energy demands in film productions with VFX components.[4] Researchers took a closer look at two comparable student productions: one using traditional offline rendering and post-production, and the other using an LED wall and In-Camera Visual Effects (ICVFX) where visual effects are captured in the camera instead of the traditional post-production process. It showed that Virtual Production had more than a third less in total power consumption.

Although Virtual Production is not a solution for all aspects of film production, it should be considered as a fantastic opportunity in times of need for environmentally friendly and sustainable solutions. This comes with an increased demand for technical understanding in all departments, and a willingness to adapt to new procedures and methodologies. The Animationsinstitut is keen on addressing these challenges in its global curriculum, by its internal R&D department, and engagement in industry and academic research projects.[5]

The Animationsinstitut offers renowned study programs in Animation, Visual Effects, Technical Directing, Animation/Effects Producing, and Interactive Media. The industry's demand for directors, artists, producers, and technical directors who were trained at the Animationsinstitut has always been high. Usually, its students start successful careers after their studies.

As Virtual Production technologies become common practice, this demand will only increase, since the Animationsinstitut has established training capacities in Virtual Production for some years already. For instance, a LED wall studio has been available for students at the Set Extension Workshop (SEW) since 2020. The SEW is part of the curriculum of the Filmakademie and has participants studying Cinematography, Production Design, as well as Animation and VFX. Student film productions of the Filmakademie have increasingly made use of the school's Virtual Production environment as well.

A strong indicator of the industry's need for new talent is the fact that Animationsinstitut's students with expertise in Virtual Production are already successfully working in the industry, even besides their studies. This applies especially to students of the Technical Directing Course that trains filmmaking professionals, who act as a link between art and technology.

Therefore, the Animationsinstitut continues to aim to train the key experts who can lead the European film world toward a new creative era and more sustainable future (Figure 15.3).

FIGURE 15.3   Virtual production at Animationsinstitut. (Courtesy of Filmakademie Baden-Württemberg GmbH.)

Students are being taught and films produced according to the principle of "learning by doing." Students learn how to make films just by making films: they write the screenplays, do animation and visual effects, compose the film score, and work on sound design and editing. The degree course at the institute takes 4.5 years, after which graduates receive a degree from the Baden-Württemberg Film Academy. Whatever their fields of study, students complete a basic 2-year course. Then they begin a 2.5-year project course either in animation (majoring for example in Concept & Art, Animation & Effects, Animation & Effects Producing) or in interactive media as content director or crossmedia/games producer. Technical directing is an additional qualification, otherwise unique in Germany, which allows graduates of computer science to combine their technical ability with artistic design.

Training focuses on idea generation, concept and design, the production of animated short films and visual effects sequences for games, advertising and documentary films, and the study of real-time animation and interactive media. Cartoon animation, live animation, and stop motion are available to students as well as all the common hard and software systems, and the newest equipment for producing stereoscopic 3D films.

Students receive the Film Academy's diploma upon completion of their chosen specialization in Animation or Interactive Media. The following specializations are on offer: Concept Artist Animation/Effects Directing, Character Animation, Effects Artist, Animation/Effects Producing, Technical Directing, Transmedia/Games Directing, Transmedia/Games Producing, and Transmedia/Games Artist.

The Institute of Animation offers facilities equipped with state-of-the-art technology. All students have their own workstations, which are provided with all current tools as well as special project-based solutions. Students are able to make use, among others, of a digital screening room equipped with 3D Stereo, and an Optitrek Motion Capture and NCam System. Furthermore, they access to the Film Academy's entire infrastructure, which includes a digital 4K cinema fitted with a Dolby Atmos sound system.

The institute charges only a service fee.

STUTTGART FESTIVAL OF ANIMATED FILM

What enables short filmmakers to work is the support and funding system that exists in the different states of the Federal Republic of Germany. An animation creator can finance a great deal of his film project from these various public funds and so, not being dependent on commercial success, can keep the personal and experimental character of his/her film.

Unfortunately, the richness of the short film production has not yet reached the conscience of the wider audience, except for some short film series shown on children's TV. The vast majority of animation shorts is still restricted to festivals. The schools maintain own departments that distribute short films through festivals worldwide.

One favorite playground of short filmmakers is the Stuttgart Festival of Animated Film (Internationales Trickfilm Festival Stuttgart, ITFS). The Festival was launched in 1982 and initially held biennially before becoming an annual event in 2005. The festival's importance has increased steadily over the years. In 2010, the festival welcomed already 50,000 visitors who had come to watch an impressive lineup of 600 animated films. During the course of the festival, a number of awards are handed out; among them the "Grand Prix" sponsored by the State of Baden-Württemberg and the City of Stuttgart as well as the "Lotte Reiniger Promotion Award for Animated Film." In addition to the international competition, the festival features several sidebars such as the Young Animation Competition, which shows a selection of the best films submitted by newcomers and students from film and art schools around the world. The Animated Com Award, launched in 2007, is a separate competition for animated commercials, TV trailers, and music videos. The ITFS continues to gain importance each year, through innovations such as outdoor public screenings at the Schlossplatz in Stuttgart, and also thanks to cooperation with the FMX Conference on Animation, Effects, Games, and Interactive Media, which takes place at the same time. The FMX was launched in 1994 and has become the largest European trade event of the animation sector. It attracts American and non-European companies and professionals as the European ones likewise. The self-proclaimed goal is to foster the "convergence of film, TV, computers, game consoles, and mobile devices." In addition to the actual symposium, the FMX offerings include presentations, a trade floor, workshops, company presentations, a recruiting area complete with job market, film school screenings, and various partner events. The organizer of the FMX is the Institute for Animation, Visual Effects, and Digital Post-production at the Film Academy Baden-Württemberg. Among its numerous sponsors are the Association for Computing Machinery's Special Interest Group on Computer Graphics and Interactive Technique (ACM Siggraph), the Visual Effects Society (VES), and the Academy of Interactive Arts and Sciences (AIAS).

TIGHTROPE WALKERS

We have seen that we find what we are looking for while researching the essence of animation in Germany not in the industry, but in individuals who are willing to take risks and don't give a damn about their income and future. The real artists among German animators are like tightrope walkers. Art means to work up own experiences. Biographies help us to understand the motivation of the unflinching artists among the animators.

Rope Dance (*Seiltänzer*) is the title of a 1986 short film by Raimund Krumme. Krumme began as an animation artist in the wild 1970s of West Berlin. "Today," Krumme says,

> I tell my students how crucial it is for an artist to work up his or her own biography. For myself it was always vital to process things that touch me somehow. Money was not important for us then, a byline of the 1968 generation that didn't care about career. Back then West Berlin was like an island. We had a happy time and completely enjoyed ourselves.

But the time came when he had to leave this island: "Would I have stayed in Berlin, wouldn't I have forced to look for an alternative, everything would have burbled and splattered." It was eviction that led to creativity and new experience and – a new life circle." Krumme found a new playground at CalArts in Los Angeles – before he returned to Germany.

In animation, Krumme feels like a *Weltenschöpfer*, like a Creator God, facing no physical resistance. For him, it is like sculpting and modeling in clay, wood, and stone. He prefers the material more than the virtual, ghostly images of the digital media. Although kinetics has become highly important in virtual and computer games, eviction is missed in kinetics and what determines art. Krumme very much dislikes the motion capture technique, the digital type of marionette play. He thinks that alienation is very important for exploring artificial characters on screen. When Krumme speaks of *Verfremdung* (alienation), he is close to Bert Brecht's Epic Theatre (and Kabuki Theatre, of course, which had a strong influence on Japanese Anime).

He advises his students to study their own personality, as he did himself, although only a selected few are prepared to follow his advice. By being personal in his own attitude toward art, by economizing in a minimalist style, Krumme found a different way to express himself in art: *(e)motion*. "The 'minimal' in his work leaves scope for generalisation and alienation effects."[6]

Currently, Krumme recognizes two tendencies: one to keep regional or local, and the other to create universal pictograms and go global. "Once I was in Jakarta," he says

> There they had total access to all type of new media. While kids played in the mud, they nevertheless had their small video recorders with them. Now you get a laptop for a hundred dollars. The regional type is going to become important again. But the World

Wide Web has assumed a separate, independent existence and is no longer a biproduct of Cold War or an extension of the CIA. There is no means to control it.

The education of animators, lessons in free drawing, seminars in locomotion, and colloquiums in *expanimation* present a new challenge nowadays with software so easily available to everybody, including every dilettante, talented or not. Bill Gates and George Lucas have termed this a process of democratization, which obviously opens the digital screens to amateurism too.

Only rarely a German animator tries to cross the border between short film experiment and feature animation. One is Heinrich Sabl, a traditional stop-motion animator and experimental filmmaker. Sabl (born 1961 in Görlitz/GDR) started out as a locksmith. His objective was to work in the theater as a technician. It was then that he became interested in puppetry. He studied puppetry at Ernst Busch Drama School in East Berlin and turned to stop-motion filmmaking, producing animated short films (including *Père Ubu* and *Mère Ubu*), and devoting most of his lifetime, almost 30 (!) years, to finishing a stop-motion feature film titled *Memory Hotel*, a story set among Germans and Russian troops in the ruins of a Berlin hotel in the aftermath of World War II. Long gone is the little funding he got for the project. He virtually survived by – starving! (Figure 15.4).

FIGURE 15.4 Heinrich Sabl animating *Memory Hotel*. (Courtesy of Heinrich Sabl.)

While I was trained as a puppeteer back in the 1980s, the puppet play tried to emancipate and this was underlined by some theoretical work, for instance by [Sofia-born illustrator and puppeteer] Konstanza Kavrakova-Lorenz. Puppetry discovered the adult audience. And we understood "the puppet" as our tool – as a material which, depending on the story, could be replaced through other materials which includes an actor. In the process of work with the material a terminology was established that has since accompanied my work. The lifeless material (it might be an object, or it might be a puppet) becomes a character by means of animation. In this regard, the term puppet doesn't exist for me. It is just material, a tool that transforms by the process of animation/life giving into a character. A figure with regard to screenplay/the literary source, however, that ceases the right to be a character if we, the recipients, won't believe in it.

When I animate, I have to embrace the material. In the material I find all information for the camerawork, the choreography and, related to that, the animation. This approach takes place from different angles as I have been the past 15 years behind the camera (cinematography, direction) and as animator in front of it. Although some of these three working areas overlap, it was helpful to separate and distinguish these three activities very well from each other. The first impulse is the issue what I am going to tell. This is ever an action, for instance if the protagonist will enter a room or something like that. Is the action defined I search for the best-as-possible camera angles. This process is complex. On the one hand, the camera shall capture that action understandably for the spectator, on the other hand the material (the puppet, the object, the prop) doesn't stand any closeness and proximity, any angle, any lens. Then there is the lighting which – at least in my work – subordinates to the scene, to the narrative. The final decision is about aperture and focus.

Then it needs free ways to be able to animate and the adventure can begin. Similar to instrumentalists whose play we hear and recognize from their own style during a music recording, I am looking for my own style. I always felt the requirement to create strong characters. These I inflict with my own handwriting and this must be strong. For this I need space. This space I grant to my figures, this is why they become characters. In the moment of shooting, of animating I give all to them. This mostly is an arduous live performance. It isn't necessary that the animation is perfect but the power, the motivation and the impulse must be right.

In the moment of animation, I am interested solely in the action that has to be told. Everything else is craftsmanship. If a material/puppet stands safely, the difficulty of a certain movement etc. – all this doesn't count because in the end it's a mixture of craftsmanship, intuition and experience. You can rely on these abilities. More important is what's under the surface, how my protagonist moves from A to B, what does he have in his luggage. In actor's school we called that subtext. This is what really interests me. I never animate original text/dialogue but always so-called subtext. In the forefront I don't time any movement, not even camera movement which has to be segmented into single frames too.

If I type the term "Stop Motion" in the search field of YouTube, I encounter Lego films, Tutorials … etc. I do not want to call the creative efforts of the makers into question as these trials are well-meant. Software easily accessible and approachable for anybody besides camera technique makes it possible. The line of demarcation between hobby and professional aspiration seems to be fluent or seems to disintegrate. A determination of the position is difficult. This is not meant derogatorily, but what is needed is delimitation and differentiation. Anybody can do it, – and yet, to myself, filmmaking is breadwinning and art production at the same time.

I myself can bucket my living only out of the material. Out of the stories that I hopefully will be able to tell in the future, out of my own stylistics, out of my way of animation which, so I hope, I will be able and will be allowed to develop further. These abilities are completely independent from questions of technology. These are questions of physical nature and afford my presence, my senses and my abilities.

FIGURE 15.5 A young Thomas Stellmach prepares stop-motion puppets for *Quest*. (Courtesy of Thomas Stellmach.)

Thomas Stellmach (born on July 21, 1965 in Straubing, East Bavaria), a graduate of the Kassel Academy of Arts where he studied with Paul Driessen, has produced a number of short films after the release of his Academy Award-winning stop-motion film *Quest* (1996) (Figures 15.5–15.10).

FIGURE 15.6   *Quest*. (Courtesy of Thomas Stellmach.)

It was the science-fiction fairy tale *Star Wars* that sparked my dream of becoming a filmmaker in the early 1990s when I was 15 years old. I started drawing sci-fi pictures, made a one-meter-tall model spaceship, drew a sci-fi comic, and wrote sci-fi stories. My parents gave me first a pocket camera, then SLR camera equipment. Super 8 film equipment followed shortly thereafter. I experimented with the camera, edited the cel-luloid footage with music, and showed the results to my family, who were ecstatic. I was planning my first feature film in 1982. It was supposed to be a funny film about school life. The first weekend of shooting was a lot of fun. My schoolmates volunteered as helpers and extras. But over the following weekends, I found it increasingly difficult to encourage my classmates. My inexperience as a cameraman also resulted in blurry footage. I wasn't satisfied with the course and with the filming. I would have needed more lighting equipment and had to reshoot. Disappointed, I abandoned the project and retired to the basement of my parents' house. There was, among other things, my father's workshop, my own craft room and a huge play cellar with 66 square meters.

Disney's *Twenty Thousand Leagues Under the Sea* (1954) and James Bond's *The Spy Who Loved Me* (1977) were the first films I saw in theaters. I was very impressed by the images and actions in these films. Today I smile about the simple tricks that amazed me so much back then. I was fascinated by the expressive possibilities of the film. I was interested in the methods and film tricks that led to the illusions and got hold of specialist books on the subject of special effects and animation film. I found out about the American Ray Harryhausen, who began his career as a stop-motion animator on *Mighty Joe Young* in the late 1940s. And I recognized my limits in the expressive-ness of my drawn images, the written shorts stories and the handcrafted spaceship. The medium of film seemed to me to have many more possibilities to achieve a high impact on viewers. After I failed with my feature film, making an animated film seemed to be less of a problem. I had enough space in the basement to set up a small movie set with dominoes on a table tennis table. I had discovered a box with hundreds of colorful dominoes and decided to make an animated film out of it. I photographed the dominoes using the single-frame function of my film camera. After each frame, I moved them forward a few millimeters and repeated the recording process, 24 times for just one second of film. When I got the exposed film material sent back by post from the special laboratory, I was delighted with the result. I edited the material into my first 6-minute short film. I really enjoyed being able to determine everything myself when making an animated film. My actors, the dominoes, did what I wanted. This is how my first animated short film *Domino-Play* was created, where I was able to gain my first experi-ence of animation with stop motion.

I showed the finished film, edited to music, to my family. I was able to convince my parents that I was serious about making films. My father made contact with the local amateur film club, which happily accepted me. There I found a lot of film enthusiasts and got a lot of praise for my film work. Motivated, I produced more stop-motion ani-mation films and gained a lot of experience. From project to project, I became more and more professional in the stop-motion technique as an autodidact. I dealt with the cinematic design tools, with the animation technique of my cartoon characters and the construction and painting of the film backgrounds. The same applied to the drama-turgy in the story, the animation of the characters, the camera work with simultaneous single-frame recording, the different lighting moods, the film editing, the soundtrack, the music design and the mix.

At the same time, I continued my education in the optional subjects of photography, film studies and theater at my high school. Ten stop-motion animated films were made in six years. I developed short film stories that were considered so good that, with the help of the film club and my school, I was invited to international amateur film and school film festivals because my films were in competition. During this time, I received an estimated 50 film awards. In 1985 I won the amateur film competition on Bavarian television with *Das grosse Labyrinth* (*The Great Labyrinth*) as the youngest winner (20 years old). In the same year I reached the highest-ranking film festival, the World Amateur Film Festival in Argentina. There I received first place for the best film by a young person for my environmentally critical film *Das letzte Blatt.*

FIGURE 15.7   Thomas Stellmach at work on *Quest.* (Courtesy of Thomas Stellmach.)

I moved from Straubing to Kassel in Hesse to study animation at the Art Academy. During my studies I made six short cartoons in animation, pixilation and stop motion. In 1997, along with fellow college student Tyron Montgomery, I received the Hollywood Oscar for Best Animated Short Film of 1996 for our stop-motion film *Quest.* After graduating, I founded and managed an animation film studio in Kassel with two colleagues, which produced commercials. After eight years I longed for artistic freedom. I left the company to go back to developing my own animated shorts. The music film *Virtuos Virtuell* (2013) and the cartoon *The Sausage Run* (2021) were made. I also developed workshops for various trick techniques. This resulted, for example, in my *Spinning Animation Workshop* together with the audiovisual final presentation *The Spinning Animation Show* I developed. I'm particularly proud of my *Trickfilm Show,* where I present all my films in an unusual way in the form of infotainment.

FIGURE 15.8   *Quest.* (Courtesy of Thomas Stellmach.)

Why am I fascinated by cartoons? It is exciting for me to make my ideas and worlds of imagination visible through an animated film. For this I work on the films until a real-looking world is created. My tireless ambition helps me here. I want to use every means of film design to seduce the viewer into an imaginative alien world, as if I had given them a drug. Why don't I feel lonely at my work? I've been living and working alone in my apartment since 2009. In order to get into a workflow, I need a lot of rest. I immerse myself in a meditative state. During this phase I develop content and visual ideas for a film, for example. I like to be alone to dive into my world of thoughts and to visualize my fantasies in my head first and then put them on paper. I like to listen to music to stimulate different moods in me. In addition to the workflow, there is also a creative flow in which images, worlds, scenes and complex stories are created for a film over a period of many months. As a tinkerer and hobbyist with a lot of patience, I don't mind working on something until I like it. It is important that I am not under any time pressure. Film funding, the equity I have saved and my life partner allow me to pursue my artistic interests. I would certainly feel lonely without my partner. Why do I spend years honing the animation of a film? I wish for the best possible artistic and technical quality in the realization of my films. I want the films to be shown at international film festivals. To do that, they have to be among the best and most unusual films in the world. My invented short film stories have to appear believable. I succeed, for example, when I reach the viewer emotionally. This, in turn, succeeds through a sophisticated animation. For example, I invest a year in the implementation of the animation for a 10-minute cartoon so that the story in the film can be understood by the viewer without dialogue. Especially with the large number of artistic means of expression, which are not easy to understand for everyone, an internationally understandable visual language must be used. This includes well thought-out actions that the cartoon characters tell through clear body language. This creates interesting character traits that contribute to a good story. Expressive animation includes, for example, correctly set pauses between individual movements and meaningful key poses for the figures. The high quality is achieved through many small work steps. For example, when animating a cartoon, the work begins with the creation of animation layouts. Movements and poses of the animated objects or characters are sketched here. In the animation that follows, e.g., the figures first roughly animated, the timing set in the animation, on physical laws z. For example, the weighting was taken into account or the continuity in the appearance of the characters was important. This production section is then completed with the addition of animation, e.g., hatching, shadows, body details, clothing details or accessories. Only when everything moves credibly towards each other, interacts correctly and the story is conveyed in an understandable way are (clean-ups) pure drawings created and colored. It is a high art when the viewer who is used to actors can identify with a cartoon or puppet character. He knows that this character is not alive and is initially reluctant to sympathize with her. In order for this to be achieved, however, the character must behave in such a way that it transmits emotions to the viewer. Their behaviors form a character's character and bring the animated drawing or three-dimensional model of a character to life. I find it fascinating to use animation to breathe life into dead things.

FIGURE 15.9 *Quest.* (Courtesy of Thomas Stellmach.)

It's even more fun with an animation team When making my cartoons, I take on many functions. I write the story, I direct, I handle the financing, I manage the production. I'm responsible for animation, compositing and film editing. This saves me costs, ensures the best possible control over the production of a film and I am less dependent on other employees. Nevertheless, I need discussion partners and collaborators in order to be able to make a good film. I enjoy working with consultants or partners from the early development phase of an animated film. As part of my animation studies, many of my films were made in conversation with my animation professor Paul Driessen or in collaboration with fellow students. For example, I made the Oscar-winning stop-motion film *Quest* with Tyron Montgomery. The pixilation film *Small Talk* was created as a joint project with 15 animation film students. On *Virtuos Virtuell* I worked with the drawing artist and director colleague Maja Oschmann. I developed the idea for *The Sausage Run* with my former professor and produced the film with 13 employees. What do I wish for? For me, the premiere event for a newly created film is very important in order to observe the reactions of the audience. Conversations with individual viewers after a screening sometimes give an even deeper insight into how the film was received. I find it very exciting to get in touch with the audience through the film. The competition juries at film festivals provide further information about the quality of the film with their evaluation. I wish there were more audiences for short films. Most short films can be seen at film festivals in a two-year period. Short films are not shown enough in cinemas or on television. Unfortunately, there is very little interest in short films among German viewers. I therefore wish that short films would receive more attention and that the value of these films would be better recognized and appreciated. For this reason, I developed my cartoon show, which I travel nationwide with. There I show my films, tell how they are made and talk about it with the audience. At the end of the performance, the audience is often impressed by my ambition and the effort that went into creating my cartoons.[7]

FIGURE 15.10 Trick Film Show: Poster by Thomas Stellmach. The animator becomes his own distributor. (Courtesy of Thomas Stellmach.)

Still trying to find the essence, I phoned Stefan Lukschy. Luschky is an author and director. His father was a well-known German actor. He was not in animation, but his "mentor" was. I asked him about Vicco von Bülow. Most Germans know von Bülow by the artist's name *Loriot*. Loriot is the French word for oriole, the coat of arms of the von Bülow family. He was a famous cartoonist and had a studio where he produced short cartoon films and spots for TV. Like Frank Tashlin, he later turned to live-action and became an admired comedy director. After von Bülow's death on August 22, 2011, Lukschy published a book.[8]

THE PUPPETEER

by Stefan Lukschy

> Loriot is well known as the creator of hilarious drawings, legendary TV sketches, blockbuster movies and acclaimed opera productions. He is considered the most important German humorist after the Second World War. His work was examined and analyzed from all angles, from newspaper articles to doctoral theses. I was fortunate to be his closest collaborator, helping him direct and edit the production of the famous six Bremen TV sketch programs, among other things. In my opinion, one aspect of his directorial work has not yet been described: Loriot as a puppeteer. There are film and theater directors who give their actors great freedom, wait for acting offers and choose what suits them in their production. The opposite was the case with Loriot. He specified everything very precisely: rhythm, intonation, gesture. Some of the actors didn't always feel comfortable with it, they felt restricted in their creativity and criticized the director for being too pedantic. Of course, when they saw the finished result, they were without exception enthusiastic.
>
> How did it come about that the admirer of great acting, which Loriot undoubtedly was, was so "overly precise" in his own directorial work? My explanation for this is that he had his first directing experience in a genre that obeyed him utterly: animation. His cartoon characters followed his ideas one hundred percent, they had no life of their own, made neither good nor bad suggestions and were also easy to care for and devoted to their master. If he wanted one of his characters to raise one eyebrow slightly and close the other eye right between two words, he just drew it and that was it. If he asked an actor or an actress for the same precision of facial expressions, he did not always get the desired result unless the shot was repeated until it was right. Loriot was also famous for filming many takes.
>
> When the TV editors suggested Evelyn Hamann for a small part in the sketch *Gran Paradiso*, Loriot got involved with the young actress and was immediately enthusiastic. Evelyn had the fascinating ability to be guided by Loriot like a puppeteer's puppet. Whatever tiny verbal or mimic details he asked of her, she delivered with breathtaking precision, even on repeated takes. Of course, in the many roles she played with him, she always remained versatile and very lively. But it was certainly her ability to follow him so unconditionally and with great joy in his obsession with precision, trained in cartoons – one could also call it a "deformation professionelle" – which ultimately enabled her to accompany his life as a television and film director like nobody else was allowed.[9]

There might be some truth in recognizing that acting and spectacle is caricature. It's only a facet, but every major cartoonist directs his creatures as if they were actors. The final purpose of animation: 3D or 2D, puppet, pencil, or computer, is *good animation*.

THE LOST STATE OF THE ART

Well, there always was and always will be worthwhile animation produced in Germany by individuals and film students. But the industry is in bad shape. The leading film critics and institutions despise animation downright.

> Film criticism should not pretend that animated films – drawn or kneaded and hand-crafted with great skill – are just films as well. If you want to write about them from the point of view of film criticism, you should be ready to break through the narrow-mindedness of the criteria offered and refrain from general praise of the "great" drawing and the "delicate lines" and not kneel down in front of the technology – but yourself rise to the meta level. So also think about what the animation does, why it might just come up. […] Why is it logical for DOK Leipzig to program animation and documentary films side by side? Film criticism should not shy away from naming naivety and regression if they are to be found in the films. The fact that this may also have its own value and appeal – this is also a good thing to think about. However, if knowledge about the films is not actually sufficient to write adequately about them, one's own strangeness and insecurities should also be named. As in this text. Which is why film critics' fear of animated films will not vanish.[10]

Not kneeling down in front of the technology – while in the United States or in China a new type of virtual human is being created: The Amazing Transparent Man? Germany takes no part in this – because, digitally speaking, this country is way behind (even) Finland:

> Schools with outdated computers. Health authorities relying on fax machines. Town offices that offer few or none of their services online […] the response to the coronavirus pandemic exposed how digital shortcomings continue to plague Germany's public sector – perplexing observers around the world.[11]

This country was saved to death through industrial outsourcing, etc. Now everything seems ailing. And, don't forget, if, by chance, you see a new German animation short like Sabine Redlich's *Hit the Road, Egg!* or *Glückspfad* by Thea Sparmeier, Pauline Cremer and Jakob Werner on something like YouTube, it's not a German or European digital platform…

NOTES

1 *Beste Chancen für Digital-Trickser.* In: SPIEGEL Online, October 30, 2001.
2 AG Animationsfilm (ed.), *Branchenumfrage zur Situation des Animationsfilmschaffens in Deutschland 2015.*
3 SPA-Carbon-Emissions-Report, March 2021: www.greenproductionguide.com/wp-content/uploads/2021/04/SPA-Carbon-Emissions-Report.pdf
4 Volker Helzle, Simon Spielmann, and Jonas Trottnow. 2022. Green Screens, Green Pixels and Green Shooting. In ACM SIGGRAPH 2022 Talks (SIGGRAPH '22). Association for Computing Machinery, New York, NY, USA, Article 1, 1–2. https://doi.org/10.1145/3532836.3536235
5 http://max-r.eu, https://emil-xr.eu
6 Jürgen Keuneke, *Raimund Krumme – A Master of Animated, Figural Line in Space.* In: Novum.
7 Thomas Stellmach, January 2, 2023.

8 *Der Glückliche schlägt keine Hunde: Ein Loriot-Porträt.* Berlin: Aufbau-Verlag, 2013.

9 January 2023.

10 Dunja Bialas, *Die Angst der Filmkritik vor dem Animationsfilm. Eine unabschliessbare Polemik.* Das Kurzfilmmagazin SHORTFILM.DE, December 21, 2022.

11 https://www.dw.com/en/germany-and-digitalization-why-cant-europes-richest-country-get-up-to-speed/a-58273979.

Timetable

1896

May 18:
Hans Fischer, born in Kösen. Later he will name himself Fischerkoesen.

1899

June 2:
Lotte (Charlotte) **Reiniger**, born in Berlin Charlottenburg.

1900

Experimental filmmaker **Oskar Fischinger**, born in Gelnhausen.

1901

March 28:
Ferdinand Diehl, born in Unterwössen, Bavaria.

1909

December 31:
Two trickfilm shorts by **Guido Seeber**, who was promoted chief cameraman of Deutsche Bioscop company in Berlin: ***Prosit Neujahr!*** (***Happy New Year***) and ***Geheimnisvolle Streichholzdose*** (***A Match Box Mystery***): A legless seller of matches falls asleep and dreams of (stop-frame animated) matches performing tricks.

1911

January:
First object animation in advertising films produced by **Julius Pinschewer**.

1912

Mathematical animation films (Pythagorean theorem, astronomical picture of the sun's motion according to Copernicus, and more) made by **Professor Ludwig Münch**.

1914

January:
First German military map animation (Battle of Sedan, Franco-German War, September 1, 1870).

1914–1918

WW1: Living war caricatures by **Alexander Klar, Fritz Schoen, Jak (Jacob) Winter**, and **Otto Dely**.

1917

April 9:
Comic book editor **Rolf** (Paul Rudolf) **Kauka**, born in Markranstädt, Saxonia.
December 18:
Germany's leading film company, Universum-Film Aktiengesellschaft (UFA) is founded.

1919

December 19:
Actor Paul Wegener recommends his protégé **Lotte Reiniger** to Dr. Hans Cürlis of the recently established Institut für Kulturforschung e.V. in Berlin. Reiniger's first silhouette short ***Das Ornament des verliebten Herzens*** (***The Ornament of the Lovestruck Heart***) is produced by Cürlis.

1920

John Heartfield and George Grosz try to establish an experimental film studio at UFA, but they quarrel with the management and leave. Only their colleague Svend Noldan remains.

1921

Münchner Filmbilderbogen produced by Louis (Luis) Seel.
April 27:
Walter Ruttmann's abstract animation ***Lichtspiel Opus 1*** consisted of 10,000 frames and was shown in Berlin at the Marmorhaus cinema.

1924

Felix the Cat on German screens.
November 5:
Viking Eggeling's *Symphonie diagonal* (*Diagonal* **Symphony**).

1925

May 3:
A unique matinee of *Der absolute Film* (*Absolute Film*) organized by the artists' association November Group with the culture film division of UFA at U.T. Berlin Kurfürstendamm. Films by **Fernand Léger**, **Viking Eggeling** and **Walter Ruttmann** (*Opus 3* and *Opus 4*).

1926

May 2:
At a matinee at Volksbühne Bülowplatz in Berlin, **Lotte Reiniger's** feature-length silhouette picture *Die Abenteuer des Prinzen Achmed* (*The Adventures of Prince Achmed*) is shown.

1927

July 14:
The first **Disney** cartoon released in Germany: *Trolley Troubles*.

1929

February 27:
The first German sound cartoon, *Die chinesische Nachtigall* (*The Chinese Nightingale*) produced by Julius Pinschewer's advertising film company, with silhouette animation by Rudi Klemm.

1930

February:
Südfilm Distribution Company introduces *Mickey Mouse* to Germany.
April 10:
Disney's Mickey and Minnie Mouse protected by the German Reich Patent Office.

1931

January 17:
Ferdinand Diehl who had served as trickfilm cameraman at the now defunct Emelka in Munich has finished a 20-minute silhouette short film in the tradition of **Lotte Reiniger**: *Kalif Storch* (*Caliph Stork*) adapted from the fairy tale by Wilhelm Hauff.
October 15:
Paul Wittke Jr., a Berlin businessman, and **George Pal** who left UFA recently established Trickfilm-Studio G.m.b.H. Pal & Wittke. Pal (besides trying to launch a 2D cartoon series featuring characters from his *Habakuk* comic strip) turns to dimensional animation, which becomes the basic principle of his later *Puppetoons* replacement series. The studio is commissioned to do an advertising film with marching *Oberst* cigarettes.

1934

April 11:

Oskar Fischinger follows **George Pal's** example with animating cigarettes that dance through an advertising film in Gasparcolor: *Muratti greift ein (Muratti Marches On)*.

December 9:

Bayerische Film GmbH compiles a Walt Disney short film program: *Die lustige Palette – Im Reiche der Micky Maus (The Funny Palette: In the Reich of Mickey Mouse)*.

1935

May 3:

Premiere of **Oskar Fischinger's** experimental Gasparcolor short *Komposition in Blau (Lichtkonzert Nr. 1/Composition in Blue: Light Concert No. 1)* at a special screening. Official release date was June 5, 1935 at Capitol in Berlin.

July 7:

Roy and **Walt Disney** arrive in Munich.

1937

October 3:

Premiere of a sound version of **Władysław Starewicz' *Reineke Fuchs (Le Roman de Renard)*** funded by UFA (production unit: Erich Neusser) in Berlin. The original silent was produced between 1929 and 1931 in France. The commentary of the German version was written by Wilhelm Krug and narrated by Leo Peukert with a score composed by Dr. Julius Kopsch. Starewicz comes to Berlin, hoping that the Germans would finance more of his projects; but this doesn't happen.

1938

June:

Ferdinand Diehl has animated a 14-minute short *Der Wettlauf zwischen dem Hasen und dem Igel (The Race between the Hare and the Hedgehog)* that introduces a stop-frame animated hedgehog character that after the war would be known as *Mecki*.

1939–1945

WW2.

1941

August 7:

Deutsche Zeichenfilm Gesellschaft mit beschränkter Haftung (DZF), the German Animation Film Company, founded by UFA and Cautio Treuhand, backed by

Goebbels' Reich Ministry for Public Enlightenment and Propaganda with the clear intention to compete with Disney.

1942

December 22:
Mars-Film GmbH is going to produce military films that will include map and other types of animation. Contributors are Boehner Film, Fischerkoesen, Nar & Polley, Dr. Stier Prague, Curt Schumann, Ewald Film, and Sigma Film.

1943

October 1:
Fischerkoesen's *Verwitterte Melodie* (*Weather-Beaten Melody*).
October 4:
A few days later, Karl Neumann and the state-controlled Deutsche Zeichenfilm Company present their first (and only) finished cartoon *Armer Hansi* (*Poor Hansi*).

1944

December 19:
Der Schneemann (*The Snowman*) produced by **Fischerkoesen** Film Studio in Potsdam (and The Hague): A snow man longs for the melting experience of summertime.

1945

May:
Karl Neumann, former head of Deutsche Zeichenfilm company, commits suicide in Soviet internship.

1946

November:
Gerhard Fieber's *Purzelbaum ins Leben*, the last (unfinished) production of Zeichenfilm GmbH, released as first color animation of East German DEFA.

1949

May 23:
Federal Republic of Germany founded.
October 7:
German Democratic Republic (GDR) founded.

1950

February 24:
Premiere of the first feature-length German 2D (black-and-white) animation project *Tobias Knopp, Abenteuer eines Junggesellen* (*Tobias Knopp: Adventures of a Bachelor*) based on Wilhelm Busch and directed by **Gerhard Fieber** at the Palast Theater in Hanover.

The same day **Walt Disney's** 1937 *Snow White and the Seven Dwarfs* opens in Cologne.

1951

June:
Walt Disney's *Cinderella* wins Golden Bear at Berlin International Film Festival.

1953

Walt Disney's Micky Maus GmbH opened in Frankfurt/Main controls and grants **Disney** licenses.
October 6:
Rolf Kauka starts *Fix & Foxi* comics.

1955

April 1:
VEB DEFA-Studio für Trickfilme officially (retroactively) established in Dresden in the former studios of Boehner Film.
December 23:
The first *Digedags* comic published in East Germany's Mosaik magazine.

1957

March 15:
Official liquidation of Deutsche Zeichenfilm GmbH.

1958

On commission by **H**aus **B**ergmann (British American Tobacco B.A.T.), Kruse Film is going to produce more than 400 Spots with animated character *HB Männchen* (*Little HB Man*).

1959

November 22, 18:54
First appearance of the East German *Sandmännchen* in the program of Deutscher Fernsehfunk DFF.

1962

February 28:
Eighth Short Film Festival in Oberhausen: 26 young West German filmmakers signed the Oberhausen Manifesto claiming license to create a New German Cinema. The festival screens an animated short film *Die Gartenzwerge* (*The Lawn Gnomes*), which was produced by three of the signatories: written by Boris von Borresholm and Peter Schamoni, and animated by Wolfgang Urchs.

1963

April 2:
The newly established West German Second TV Channel introduces the Little Mainz Men: *Mainzelmännchen* spots designed by **Wolf Gerlach** and in the beginning animated by **Wolfgang Urchs**.

1967

January 31:
Oskar Fischinger dies in Hollywood.
February 5:
For Süddeutscher Rundfunk **Vicco von Bülow** a.k.a. **Loriot** turns into the host of a *Cartoon* TV series.

1968

October 10:
Adam II, feature-length Kafkaesque experimental animation by **Jan Lenica** (produced for 650,000 Deutschmark) by Boris von Borresholm, Lux Film Munich) shown at the International Film Festival in Mannheim. The title figure is a curious but lonely character, a modern Gulliver who encounters people with square heads in the land of Quadratonia. The film expresses the desire to renounce from any notion of control through bureaucracy in the era of technology.
December 13:
Disney's *Jungle Book* opens in Germany.

1969

December 18:
Curt Linda's *Die Konferenz der Tiere* (*The Conference of Animals*) based on a book by **Erich Kästner**.

1970

March 20:
Asterix and Cleopatra released in Germany.

1971

March 7:

Start of children's TV series *Die Sendung mit der Maus* (*The Show with the Mouse*) at WDR Westdeutscher Rundfunk Cologne. The format was developed by **Gert Kaspar Müntefering**, **Siegfried Morhof**, **Monika Paetow**, and **Armin Maiwald**. Over the years, it includes many cartoon characters like the *Little Mole* from Czechoslovakia, *Käpt'n Blaubär*, *Little Polar Bear*, *Petzi*, *Tom und das Erdbeermarmeladebrot mit Honig*, and *Shaun the Sheep*. The titular animation character was designed by **Isolde Schmitt-Menzel** and animated by **Friedrich Streich**.

June 18:

Since 1966, East German animators under the supervision of Lothar Barke and Helmut Barkowsky had worked on the feature-length fairy tale *Der arme Müllersbursch und das Kätzchen* (*The Poor Miller's Boy and the Kitten*).

1973

March:

In Germany ZDF TV cancels American *Schweinchen Dick* (*Porky Pig*) cartoons due to the protests of politicians who claim to be concerned about the very young audience and the graphic violence kids are exposed to.

April 23:

Hans Fischerkoesen dies in Mehlem.

December 12:

Maria d'Oro und Bello Blue (*Once Upon a Time*), the first (and due to disappointing box-office results final) feature-length animation film produced by German comic book editor **Rolf Kauka**, interestingly not done by Kauka's regular artists in Munich but by Italian animation studio Gamma Film (Roberto and Gino Gavioli).

1976

March 8:

Vicco von Bülow has his own TV show: Besides sketches, *Loriot* presents animated spots produced in his own cartoon studio: *Comedian Harmonists*, *The Stone Louse*, *The Breakfast Egg*, and *Two Gentlemen in One Bathtub*.

Also this year on TV (WDR):

Starmaus by Franz and Ursula Winzentsen.

1977

February 4:

Die Leuchtturminsel (*The Lighthouse Island*), feature-length East German puppet animation by **Günter Rätz** (in production since 1974) based on children's book *Jonathan* by Günther Feustel.

1978

February 9:
Star Wars released in Germany.

1981

April 6:
Günter Rätz worked since 1978 on the stop-motion animation of the feature-length East German puppet film *Die fliegende Windmühle* (*The Flying Windmill*) produced at DEFA Studio für Trickfilme in Dresden.
June 19:
Lotte Reiniger dies in Dettenhausen.

1982

January 18:
Start of International Trickfilm Festival in Stuttgart, then called Internationale Stuttgarter Trickfilmtage.
April 2:
Meister Eder und sein Pumuckl (*Master Eder and his Pumuckl*): A cabinet maker (played by Gustl Bayrhammer) begins to see a red-haired goblin who's only visible to him. Live action produced in Munich, 2D animation outsourced to Pannónia Studios in Budapest. Produced by Infafilm **Manfred Korytowski**. Released theatrically and as TV series.

1989

Studio FILM BILDER established in Stuttgart, Germany. The studio's core team consists of several producers and a total of six directors, as well as access to a large pool of freelance animators, designers, and technicians.

1990

January 16:
Die Spur führt zum Silbersee (*The Trace Leads to the Silver Lake*) by **Günter Rätz**: Feature-length stop-motion puppet film inspired by Karl May's western stories. Finished at DEFA Studio für Trickfilme in Dresden in 1989 and released after the fall of the Berlin wall.
March 26:
German stop-motion *Balance* by Brothers **Christoph and Wolfgang Lauenstein** wins an Academy Award for Best Animated Short Film.
October 3:
German reunification.
November 29:

Wolfgang Urchs' 2D animated version of **Gerdt von Bassewitz's** *Peterchens Mondfahrt* (*Little Peter's Journey to the Moon/Peter in Magicland*).

Even more successful in German cinemas is a live action/animation mix based on Brösel's (=**Rötger Feldmann's**) comic strip character **Werner – Beinhart!** Animation sequences by Hahn Film AG Berlin and TFC Trickompany Michael Schaack Hamburg.

1992

February 14:
Die Abenteuer von Pico und Columbus (*The Adventures of Pico and Columbus/* U.S.: *Magic Voyage*) produced by **Michael Schoemann** with disastrous results at the box office.

1994

September 24:
Asterix in Amerika/Astérix et les indiens (*Asterix in America*) produced by Extrafilm/Jugendfilm and Hahnfilm in Berlin.

1997

March 6:
Kleines Arschloch (*The Little Bastard*) by TFC Trickompany Hamburg.

1998

March 24:
Quest, a German stop-motion film by **Thomas Stellmach** and **Tyron Montgomery**, wins the Oscar for Best Short Animation: In quest of water, a little sandman leaves the sand world. Following the dripping water, he crosses worlds full of dangers and obstacles made of paper, stone, and iron. In the end, he reaches the water... in a tragic way.

2000

September 13:
Rolf Kauka dies in Thomasville, Georgia.

2001

October 4:
Der kleine Eisbär: Der Kinofilm (*The Little Polar Bear*), a German children's book and TV animation favorite in his first feature film: Lars, the little Polar Bear cub (*Lars de kleine ijsbeer*) created by Dutch author **Hans de Beer**, co-produced by Cartoon Film (**Thilo Rothkirch**) and Warner Bros. Germany (**Willi Geike**).

2004

March 18:
Holger Tappe, who invested a heritage to establish Ambient Entertainment in Hanover, and his friend Lenard Fritz Krawinkel join forces to create the 3D-animated *Boo, Zino & the Snurks*, the goblin-like stars of a televised animation show, who strand in the reality of our world: *Back to Gaya*. Although it was the first feature-length 3D-animated film produced in Germany, and two American writers (Don McEnery and Bob Shaw who had some Disney and Pixar experience) were hired to polish Jan Berger's script, the result is only mildly successful.

September 19:
Lauras Stern (*Laura's Star*): A little girl makes friendship with a small star that has fallen from the nightly sky. 2D-animated feature Anime-style produced by Rothkirch Cartoon Film and Warner Bros. Germany. Based on the children's books by **Klaus Baumgart** and a TV series.

2005

November 11:
Tom & das Erdbeermarmeladebrot mit Honig (*Tom & the Strawberry Jam Bread with Honey*) by Andreas Hykade starts on the Children's Channel (KiKA):

> One day Tom thought of a delicious strawberry jam sandwich with honey. He went for a walk, but he couldn't get the strawberry jam bread with honey out of his head. In search of that strawberry jam sandwich with honey he quickly meets new acquaintances and experiences exciting adventures. There are many ways to make strawberry jam bread with honey. With the help of his friends, the miller, the strawberry mouse, the busy bees or the poor little girl, Tom tries to get his treat. In the end, however, only half a bread with strawberry jam and honey pops out...[1]

2006

December 16:
Westwood, California premiere of *Happily N'Ever After* (German release title: *Es war k'einmal im Märchenland*), a big-budget 3D-animated fairy-tale spoof produced by Berlin Animation Film, a company funded by investors won over by Dresdner Bank, and made especially for the American market where it is released by Lion's Gate. The movie develops into a total failure.

2009

December 25:
The Gruffalo, an Anglo-German animation short by **Max Lang** and **Jakob Schuh** based on the eponymous children's book on BBC TV.

2010

October 7:
Konferenz der Tiere (*Animals United*), officially based on **Erich Kästner's** book but thanks to 3D animation and Americanized characters more like *Madagascar*.

2013

May 16:
German co-funded *Der Kongress* (*The Congress*) offers a very innovative idea (live action and animation) by Israeli-filmmaker **Ari Folman** loosely based on a book by **Stanisław Lem**: An actress (played by an ageing Robin Wright) sells her likeness to Miramount Nagasaki (originally Paramount Nagasaki) to become an animated image within a polluted world that is covered by visual illusions.

2018

May 24:
Luis & die Aliens (*Luis and the Aliens*), an animated feature film developed by **Christoph and Wolfgang Lauenstein** and produced by Ulysses Filmproduktion: a rather Americanized little boy's encounter of the third kind.

2019

October 9:
Fritzi – Eine Wendewundergeschichte (*Fritzi: A Miraculous Revolutionary Tale*).

2020

March 5:
Die Känguru-Chroniken (*The Kangaroo Chronicles*) based on a radio comedy series and books by **Marc-Uwe Kling**. In the feature film version director **Dani Levy** mixes live action with a 3D-animated kangaroo. Produced by X-Filme Creative Pool in association with ZDF and Trixter (computer-animated elements).

2023

February 9:
Maurice der Kater (The Amazing Maurice) by Toby Genkel and Florian Westermann.

NOTE

1 KiKA advertisement.

Acknowledgments

Grateful thanks to the living
Dr. Günter Agde, Klaus Baumgart, Dirk Beinhold (Akkord Film), Wolfgang M. Biehler, Heinz Busert, Karl-Heinz Christmann, Michael Coldewey, Alberto Couceiro, Piet De Rycker, Katrin Dietrich (Film- und Medienfestival gGmbH), Volker Engel, Robi Engler, Ari Folman, Joseph Garncarz, Frank Geiger (Little Dream Entertainment/brave new work GmbH), Dr. Martin Gerlach, Frank Gessner, Didier Ghez, Felix Gönnert, Jeanpaul Goergen, Whitney Grace, Dr. Till Grahl (DIAF), Gerhard Hahn, Mike Hankin, Jörg Hermann, Heinz Hermanns, Armin Hofmann (Little Dream Entertainment/brave new work GmbH), Andreas Hykade, Matthias Knop, Tanja Kröger (DIAF), Carsten Laqua, Tony Loeser, Stefan Lukschy, Dittmar Lumpp, Richard Lutterbeck, Dr. Volker Petzold, Jörn Radel (Animationsfabrik), Dr. Christian Riethmüller, Maya Rothkirch, Heinrich Sabl, Sinem Sakaoglu, Veronica Solomon, Christina Schindler, Frank Schlegel, Ricarda Schlosshan, Dr. Michael Schoemann, Sabine Scholz, Thomas Stellmach, Ulrich Stoll, Stefan Thies (NFP Animation), Alejandra Tomei, Franziska Ullrich (Animationsinstitut, Filmakademie Baden-Württemberg GmbH), Marc Vandeweyer, Aygün and Peter Völker (Pans Studio), Ulrich Wegenast, Johannes Wolters (INDAC), and to my wife, Anna Khan.

... and to those who have passed away
Carl Barks, Giannalberto Bendazzi, Peter Blümel, Ferdinand Diehl, Hanns Eckelkamp, Gerhard Fieber, Wolf Gerlach, Erich Günther, Ray Harryhausen, Helmut Herbst, Gerhard Huttula, Adolf Kabatek, Manfred Korytowski, Curt Linda, Sébastien Roffat, Thilo Rothkirch, Karl-Ludwig Ruppel, Michael Schmetz, Ralf Schenk, Herbert K. Schulz, H[ugo] O[tto] Schulze, Albert Uderzo, Wolfgang Urchs, Prof. Dr. Bernd Willim, and Jürgen Wohlrabe.

Special thanks to **J. P. Storm,** without whose research we wouldn't know less about *Animation in Germany.* In this book, we quote from interviews he conducted with Horst Alisch (June 17, 1988), Gerhard Fieber (July 25, 1988 and March 10, 1996), Dr. Hans Michael Fischerkoesen (July 29, 2013), Dr. Werner Kruse (August 9, 1988), Horst von Möllendorff (July 30, 1988), André Salvagnac (July 28, 2014), Stephanie Steuer (September 22, 1988 and March 31, 1989), Anna-Luise Subatzus (March 11, 1989), and Sigrid Vogt (January 11, 1989).

PHOTO CREDITS

Animas Film (Alberto Couceiro)
Author's Collection
brave new work GmbH
DIAF Deutsches Institut für Animationsfilm e.V.
Filmakademie Baden-Württemberg, Animationsinstitut
Caroline Hagen Hall, Primrose Film Productions Ltd.

NFP Animation Film GmbH
Dr. Christian Riethmüller
Rothkirch Cartoon Film
Heinrich Sabl
Thomas Stellmach
TrickStudio Lutterbeck GmbH
J. P. Storm

Bibliography

Books, Brochures and Catalogues

Ade, Albrecht (ed.), *Animationsfilm aus Deutschland. Filme, Fotos, Zeichnungen und Malerei, Objekte und Puppen*. Exhibition catalogue. Stuttgart: Institut für Auslandsbeziehungen, 1998.

Adorno, Theodor W., Der wunderliche Realist. In: *Noten zur Literatur III*. Frankfurt am Main: Suhrkamp, 1965.

Agde, Günther, *Flimmernde Versprechen. Geschichte des deutschen Werbefilms im Kino seit 1897*. Berlin: Das Neue, 1998.

Alt, Dirk, *"Der Farbfilm marschiert!": Frühe Farbfilmverfahren und NS-Propaganda 1933–1945*. Munich: Belleville, 2013.

Amsler, André, *"Wer dem Werbefilm verfällt, ist verloren für die Welt." Das Werk von Julius Pinschewer 1883–1961*. Zurich: Chronos Verlag, 1997.

Aping, Norbert, *Charlie Chaplin in Deutschland 1915–1924: Der Tramp kommt ins Kino*. Marburg: Schüren, 2014.

Balázs, Béla, *Der Film. Werden und Wesen einer neuen Kunst*. Vienna: Globus Verlag, 1949.

Barten, Egbert and Peters, Mette, *Meestal in't verbogene: Animatiefilm in Nederland 1940–1945*. Tilburg: Nederlands Instituut voor Animatiefilm, 2000.

Bendazzi, Giannalberto, *Cartoons: One Hundred Years of Cinema Animation*. Bloomington: University of California Press, 1994.

Bendazzi, Giannalberto, *Animation: A World History. Volume I: Foundations – The Golden Age. II: The Birth of a Style – The Three Markets. III: Contemporary Times*. Boca Raton, FL: CRC Press/Taylor & Francis Group, 2016.

Boček, Jaroslav, *Jirí Trnka*. 1st English edition. Prague: Artia, 1964.

Bock, Hans-Michael (ed.), *CineGraph: Lexikon zum deutschsprachigen Film*. Munich: Verlag text + kritik, 1984. Entries on Fritz Boehner, Ferdinand Diehl, Hans Ewald, Leni Fischer, Hans Fischerkoesen, Oskar Fischinger, Gerhard Huttula, Theodor Nischwitz, Svend Noldan, Julius Pinschewer, Herbert Seggelke.

Böhme, Olaf, *Kulturelle und ästhetische Aspekte des deutschen Animationsfilms zwischen 1909 und 1939*. Diploma Project. Berlin: Humboldt University, 1995.

Bundesarchiv-Filmarchiv (ed.), Alles Trick. Deutscher Animationsfilm bis 1945. *Retrospective of the 41st International Leipzig Festival for Documentary and Animation Film*. Leipzig/Berlin: Internationales Leipziger Festival für Dokumentar- und Animationsfilm, 1998.

Cavalier, Stephen, *The World History of Animation*. Foreword by Sylvain Chomet. Berkeley/Los Angeles, CA: University of California Press, 2011.

Chevalier, Denys, *Eintritt frei Zeichentrickfilm*. Edited under the supervision of Jean-Pierre Moulin and Yvan Dalain. Translation: Nino Weinstock. Lausanne: Editions Rencontre, 1963.

Deutsches, Filmmuseum (ed.), *Optische Poesie: Oskar Fischinger, Leben und Werk*. Frankfurt/Main: Deutsches Filmmuseum, 1993.

Deutsches, Filmmuseum (ed.), *Mecki, Märchen und Schnurren. Die Filme der Gebrüder Diehl*. Frankfurt/Main: Deutsches Filmmuseum, 1994.

Dewald, Christian, Groschup, Sabine, Mattuschka, Mara, and Renoldner, Thomas (eds.), Die Kunst des Einzelbilds: Animation in Österreich - 1832 bis heute. *ASIFA Austria*. Vienna: verlag filmarchiv austria, 2010.

Dillmann, Martina, *Oskar Fischinger (1900–1967): Das malerische Werk.* Doctoral Thesis. University Frankfurt/Main, 1996.

Downar, Margit (ed.), *Lotte Reiniger: Silhouettenfilm und Schattentheater.* Puppentheater-museum im Münchner Stadtmuseum. Exhibition Catalogue. Munich: Lipp, 1979.

Drechsel, Wiltrud Ulrike, Funhoff, Jörg, and Hoffmann, Michael, *Massenzeichenware. Die gesell-schaftliche und ideologische Funktion der Comics.* Frankfurt/Main: Suhrkamp, 1975.

Dütsch, Werner (ed.), *Lotte Reiniger. Eine Dokumentation.* Berlin: Deutsche Kinemathek, 1969.

Eckardt, André, *Im Dienst der Werbung. Die Boehner-Film 1926–1967.* Edited by Ralf Forster. Berlin: CineGraph Babelsberg Berlin-Brandenburgisches Centrum für Filmforschung e.V., 2004.

Feige, Marcel, *Das grosse Comic-Lexikon.* Berlin: Schwarzkopf & Schwarzkopf, 2001.

Fischerkoesen, Hans Michael, *Experimentelle Werbeeerfolgsprognose.* Wiesbaden: Dr. Gabler, 1967.

Fleischer, Uwe and Trimpert, Helge (eds.), *Wie haben Sie's gemacht? – Babelsberger Kameramänner öffnen ihre Trickkiste.* Marburg: Schüren, 2004.

Flückiger, Barbara, Visual Effects. Filmbilder aus dem Computer. *Zürcher Filmstudien.* Edited by Christine N. Brinckmann. Marburg: Schüren, 2008.

Forster, Ralf, *Sparkassenwerbefilme im Nationalsozialismus.* (=Europäische Hochschulschriften; Reihe 3, Geschichte und ihre Hilfswissenschaften, 842). Frankfurt/Main et al: Lang, 1999.

Forster, Ralf, *Ufa und Nordmark. Zwei Firmengeschichten und der deutsche Werbefilm 1919–1945.* Trier: WVT Wissenschaftlicher Verlag, 2005.

Forster, Ralf, Goergen, Jeanpaul, *Heimkino auf Ozaphan. Mediengeschichte eines verges-senen Filmmaterials.* Filmblatt-Schriften 11. Berlin: CineGraph Babelsberg Berlin-Brandenburgisches Centrum für Filmforschung e.V., 2021.

Gehr, Herbert (ed.), *Film & Computer. Digital Media Visions.* Schriftenreihe Deutsches Filmmuseum. Frankfurt/M.: Deutsches Filminstitut & Filmmuseum, 1998.

Gehr, Herbert and Ott, Stephan, *Film-Design. Visual Effects für Kino und Fernsehen.* Bergisch Gladbach: Bastei Lübbe, 2000.

Gerlach, Wolf, *Autobiographische Notizen.* Handwritten, unpublished. Bad Zwischenahn: Estate Family Gerlach, July 2008.

Ghez, Didier, *Disney's Grand Tour: Walt and Roy's European Vacation, Summer 1935.* Theme Park Press, 2013.

Giesen, Rolf, Special Effects. King Kong, Orphée und die Reise zum Mond. *Deutsche Kinemathek and Internationale Filmfestspiele Berlin.* Ebersberg: Edition 8 ½, 1985.

Giesen, Rolf, *Mickey Mouse, Asterix & Co. – Die Stars des Zeichentrickfilms.* Exhibition Catalogue. Edited by Hilmar Hoffmann and Walter Schobert. Frankfurt/Main: Deutsches Filmmuseum, 1986.

Giesen, Rolf, *Sagenhafte Welten. Der phantastische Film.* Munich: Heyne, 1990.

Giesen, Rolf, *Lexikon der Special Effects. Von den ersten Filmtricks bis zu den Computeranimationen der Gegenwart.* Berlin: Schwarzkopf & Schwarzkopf, 2001.

Giesen, Rolf, *Lexikon des Trick- und Animationsfilms.* Berlin: Schwarzkopf & Schwarzkopf, 2003.

Giesen, Rolf, *Nazi Propaganda Films: A History and Filmography.* Jefferson, NC; London: McFarland & Company, Inc., 2003.

Giesen, Rolf, *Special Effects Artists: A Worldwide Biographical Dictionary of the Pre-Digital with a Filmography.* Jefferson, NC; London: McFarland & Company, Inc., 2008.

Giesen, Rolf, *Der Angriff der Zukunft auf die Gegenwart: Vergangenheit, Gegenwart und Zukunft der Bewegtbilder – Spekulationen diesseits und jenseits der Digitalisierung.* Cologne: Herbert von Halem Verlag, 2018.

Giesen, Rolf, *Bienenstich und Hakenkreuz. Zeichentrick aus Dachau – die Deutsche Zeichenfilm GmbH.* Frankenthal: Mühlbeyer Filmbuchverlag, 2020.

Giesen, Rolf, *Animation in Europe*. Boca Raton, FL: CRC Press, 2021.

Giesen, Rolf and Khan, Anna, *Acting and Character Animation: The Art of Animated Films, Acting and Visualizing*. Boca Raton, FL; London; New York: CRC Press Taylor & Francis Group, 2018.

Giesen, Rolf and Meglin, Claudia, *Künstliche Welten*. Hamburg: Europa Verlag, 2000.

Giesen, Rolf and Storm, J. P., *Animation Under the Swastika: Trickfilm in Nazi Germany, 1933–1945*. Jefferson, NC; London: McFarland & Company, Inc., 2012.

Girveau, Bruno and Diederen, Roger (eds.), *Walt Disneys wunderbare Welt und ihre Wurzeln in der europäischen Kunst*. [German edition of *It était une tois – Walt Disney. Aux sources de l'art des Studios Disney*.] Munich: Hirmer Verlag, 2009.

Goebbels, Josef, *Die Tagebücher von Joseph Goebbels*. On behalf of Institut für Zeitgeschichte Munich. Edited by Elke Fröhlich. Berlin: De Gruyter Saur, 1998.

Goergen, Jeanpaul, *Walter Ruttmann. Eine Dokumentation*. With essays by Paul Falkenberg, William Uricchio, Barry A. Fulks. Berlin: Freunde der Deutschen Kinemathek, not dated.

Goergen, Jeanpaul, *Bibliografie zum deutschen Animationsfilm*. Edited in cooperation with DEFA Stiftung Berlin. Filmblatt-Schriften: Beiträge zur Filmgeschichte, Vol. I. Berlin: CineGraph Babelsberg, Berlin-Brandenburgisches Centrum für Filmforschung e.V., 2002.

Greiner, Rudolf (ed.), *Arbeitstexte für den Unterricht: Comics*. Stuttgart: Reclam, 1974.

Hackbarth, Doris (ed.), *Bestandsnachweis: Deutsche Trickfilme (1909–1945)*. Compiled by Manfred Lichtenstein. Berlin: Bundesarchiv/Filmarchiv, 1998.

Hagemann, Peter A. and Schulz, Herbert K. (eds.), *Deutsches Trickfilmkaleidoskop*. Berlin: Deutsche Kinemathek/Deutscher Trickfilmverband e.V., 1979.

Häntzsche, Hellmuth, *Der Spiel- und Trickfilm für Kinder in der DDR*. Berlin/DDR: Der Kinderbuchverlag, 1980.

Hanuschek, Sven (ed.), *Waldemar Bonsels – Karrierestrategien eines Erfolgsschriftstellers*. Wiesbaden: Harrassowitz Verlag, 2014.

Harder, Jens, *Slapstick im Gleichschritt. Zeichentrickfilme aus dem ‚Dritten Reich*. Diplom Project. Berlin: Kunsthochschule Berlin-Weissensee, Hochschule für Gestaltung, 2002.

Hechelhammer, Bodo V., *Fürst der Füchse. Das Leben des Rolf Kauka*. Munich: Langen-Müller Verlag GmbH, 2022.

Held, Erika and Schubert, Alfred, *Hans Held-Haid. Lebensmosaik eines Genies*. Munich: Verlag Wort-Bild-Technik, 2009.

Hickman, Gail Morgan, *The Films of George Pal*. South Brunswick, NJ; New York, 1977.

Holtz, Reinhold Johann, *Die Phänomenologie und Psychologie des Trickfilms. Analytische Untersuchungen über die phänomenologischen, psychologischen und künstlerischen Strukturen der Trickfilmgruppe*. Doctoral Thesis. Hamburg: Philosophische Fakultät der Hansischen Universität, 1940.

Horstmann, Johannes (ed.), *Der lange Zeichentrickfilm heute*. Aachen: Bundesarbeitsgemeinschaft für Jugendfilmarbeit und Medienerziehung e.V., 1985.

Jonášová, Aneta, *Der deutsche und tschechische Animationsfilm und seine Entwicklung. Versuch einer vergleichenden Analyse*. Diploma Project. Brünn: Masaryk Universität Pädagogische Fakultät Lehrstuhl für deutsche Sprache und Literatur, 2019.

Keller, Joachim (ed.), *Die besten Kinospots der 50er Jahre. Werbewelten im Zeichentrick. Hans Fischerkoesen zum 100. Geburtstag*. Frankfurt am Main: Deutsches Werbemuseum, 1996.

Kennel, Herma, *Als die Comics laufen lernten. Der Trickfilmpionier Wolfgang Kaskeline zwischen Werbekunst und Propaganda*. Berlin: be.bra wissenschaft verlag, 2020.

Klein, Bernhard, *Das künstlerische Gesamtwerk. Gemälde, Aquarelle, Zeichnungen, Radierungen, Holzschnitte*. Edited by F. Karsch. Introduction by H. W. Grohn. Exhibition Catalogue. Berlin: Galerie Nierendorf, 1979.

Knigge, Andreas C., *Fortsetzung folgt. Comic-Kultur in Deutschland*. Frankfurt/Main; Berlin; Vienna: Ullstein, 1986.

Knigge, Andreas C., *Comic Lexikon*. Frankfurt/Main; Berlin; Vienna: Ullstein, 1988.

Kohlmann, Klaus, *Der computeranimierte Spielfilm: Forschungen zur Inszenierung und Klassifizierung des 3-D-Computer-Trickfilms*. Bielefeld: Transcript Verlag, 2007.

Koop, Volker, *Warum Hitler King Kong liebte, aber den Deutschen Micky Maus verbot. Hitlers geheime Filmleidenschaft*. Berlin: be.bra wissenschaft verlag, 2015.

Koshofer, Gert, *Color: Die Farben des Films*. Berlin: Verlag Volker Spiess, 1988.

Krauss, Dieter, Lumpp, Dittmar, and Wegenast, Ulrich, *Die Trickfilm-Festschrift*. Stuttgart: Film & Medien Festival gGmbH, 2018.

Lange, Horst H., *Comics, Jazz und irre Zeiten*. Gelnhausen: Triga, 2000.

Laqua, Carsten, *Wie Micky unter die Nazis fiel: Walt Disney und Deutschland*. Reinbek/Hamburg: Rowohlt, 1992.

Lotte, Reiniger, *Schattentheater – Schattenpuppen – Schattenfilm*. Tübingen: Stadtmuseum, 1981.

Lukschy, Stefan, *Der Glückliche schlägt keine Hunde – Ein Loriot-Porträt*. Berlin: Aufbau Verlag, 2013.

Moritz, William, Resistance and subversion in animated films of the Nazi era. In: Philling, Jayne (ed.), *A Reader in Animation Studies*. London: John Libbey Publishing, 1998.

Moritz, William, *Optical Poetry: The Life and Work of Oskar Fischinger*. Bloomington, Indianapolis, IN: Indiana University Press, 2004.

Mulack, Thomas and Giesen, Rolf, *Special Effects. Planung und Produktion*. Gerlingen: Bleicher, 2002.

Olof, Carl and Petersen, Elly, *Die Moosschwaige. Ein Buch von jungen Menschen und von Tieren, von Lebenslust, von Blumen und von Sonne*. Munich, not dated.

Opfermann, H[ans] C[arl] and Kramer, Georg, *Die neue Trickfilm-Schule: Ein Lehr- und Nachschlagebuch für Filmamateure, Film- und Fernsehfachleute und den filmtechnischen Nachwuchs*. Seebruck/Chiemsee: Heering Verlag, 1963.

Peters, Mette and Barten, Egbert, *Meestal in't verborgene: Animatiefilm in Nederland*. Tilburg: Nederlands Instituut voor Animatiefilm, 2000.

Petzold, Volker, *Das große Ost-West-Sandmännchenlexikon*. Berlin: Verlag für Berlin-Brandenburg, 2009.

Petzold, Volker, *Das Sandmännchen: Alles über unseren Fernsehstar*. Hamburg: Edel Edition, 2009.

Petzold, Volker, *Von der Hand zur Puppe: Ein Leben für den Animationsfilm. Im Gespräch mit Günter Rätz*. Berlin: Bertz und Fischer, 2022.

Rathmann, Claudia, *Was gibt's denn da zu lachen? Lustige Zeichentrickseriem und ihre Rezeption durch Kinder unter besonderer Berücksichtigung der präsentierten Gewalt*. Munich: Nomos, 2004.

Reff, Werner and Vásárhelyi, István, *Filmtrick, Trickfilm*. Leipzig: Fotokino Verlag, 1980.

Reichow, Joachim, *Plaudereien über den Zeichen-Puppentrickfilm*. Berlin/GDR: Henschel, 1966.

Reiniger, Lotte, *Shadow Theatres and Shadow Films*. London; New York: B. T. Batsford and Watson-Guptill Publications, 1970.

Roffat, Sébastien, *Animation et propaganda: les dessins animés pendant la Seconde Guerre mondiale*. Paris; Budapest; Torino: L'Harmattan, 2005.

Roffat, Sébastien, *Propagandes animées: le dessin animé politique entre 1933 et 1945*. Paris: Bazaar & Co, 2010.

Sackmann, Eckart, *Mecki – Maskottchen und Mythos*. Hamburg: Sackmann und Hörndl, 1984.

Schäfer, Horst (ed.), *Lexikon des Kinder- und Jugendfilms im Kino, im Fernsehen und auf Video*. Meitingen: Corian-Verlag, 1998.

Schenk, Ralf and Scholz, Sabine (eds.), *Die Trick-Fabrik. DEFA-Animationsfilme 1955–1990*. Berlin: DIAF Deutsches Institut für Animationsfilm Dresden, 2003.

Schepp, Ole and Kamphuis, Fred, *George Pal in Holland 1934–1939*. The Hague: Holland Animation, Werkgroep Documentatie, 1983.

Schickel, Richard, *The Disney Version. The Life, Times, Art and Commerce of Walt Disney.* New York: Simon and Schuster, 1968.

Schmidlechner, Florian, Der Jude mit der roten Badehose. In: Eder, Barbara, Klar, Elisabeth and Reichert, Ramón (eds.), *Theorien des Comics. Ein Reader.* Bielefeld: Transcript, 2011.

Schmidt, Hans-Gerd and Wiesener, Bernd (eds.), *Werbefilme: Spiegel der Zeiten. Chronik des Alltags.* Bielefeld: Verlag für Regionalgeschichte, 2002.

Schoemann, Annika, *Der Deutsche Animationsfilm. Von den Anfängen bis zur Gegenwart 1909–2001.* Sankt Augustin: Gardez! Verlag, 2003.

Scholze, Sabine, *Animation in Deutschland.* Dresden: Deutsches Institut für Animationsfilm, 2002.

Schröder, Niels, *"Gute Laune ist ein Kriegsartikel": Deutsche und amerikanische Trickfilme, Comics und Cartoons als Mittel der Propaganda während des Zweiten Weltkrieges.* Berlin: be.bra wissenschaft verlag GmbH, 2020.

Schummer, Rudolf J., *Bewegte Bilder: Deutsche Trickfilme der zwanziger Jahre. Filme im Schatten. Der Trickfilm im Dritten Reich.* Booklet. Munich: Institut für Bild und Film in Wissenschaft und Unterricht, 1977.

Seeber, Guido, *Der Trickfilm in seinen grundsätzlichen Möglichkeiten. Eine praktische und theoretische Darstellung der photographischen Filmtricks.* Nachdruck der Ausgabe vom Verlag der Lichtbildbühne Berlin 1927. Frankfurt/Main: Kommunales Kino, 1979.

Seggelke, Sabine, *Herbert Seggelke.* Düsseldorf: Self-Published Print, 2005.

Sigl, Klaus (ed.), *Von "A" bis "Zip/Zip": Trickfilme aus München 1918–1987.* Munich: Münchner Stadtbibliothek and Kulturreferat der Landeshauptstadt München, 1987.

Skodzik, Peter, *Deutsche Comic-Bibliographie.* Berlin: Comicaze, 1978.

Slansky, Peter C. (ed.), *Digitaler Film – digitales Kino.* Konstanz: UVK Verlagsgesellschaft, 2004.

Storm, J. P. and Dressler, M., *Im Reiche der Micky Maus. Walt Disney in Deutschland 1927– 1945.* Filmmuseum Potsdam. Exhibition Catalogue. Berlin: Henschel, 1991.

Strzyz, Klaus and Knigge, Andreas C., *Disney von innen. Gespräche über das Imperium der Maus.* Foreword by Carl Barks. Frankfurt/M.; Berlin: Ullstein, 1988.

Stüler, Alexander and Hotschewar, Marijan V., *Filmtricks und Trickfilme.* Halle: Wilhelm Knapp, 1937.

Thiel, Reinhold E., *Puppen- und Zeichenfilm oder Walt Disneys aufsässige Erben.* Berlin: Rembrandt Verlag, 1960.

Thiele, Jens, *Trickfilm-Serien im Fernsehen. Eine Untersuchung zur Didaktik der Ästhetischen Erziehung.* Oldenburg: Isensee, 1981.

Thomas, Bob, *Walt Disney Die Kunst des Zeichenfilms.* Hamburg: Blüchert, 1958, 1960.

Traumschmelze. *Der deutsche Zeichenanimationsfilm 1930–1950.* Exhibition Catalogue. Dresden: Deutsches Institut für Animationsfilm e.V., 2013.

Urwand, Ben, *The Collaboration: Hollywood's Pact with Hitler.* Cambridge, MA: Harvard University Press, 2013.

Weiss, Harald, *Der Flug der Biene Maja durch die Welt der Medien. Buch, Film, Hörspiel und Zeichentrickserie.* Wiesbaden: Harrassowitz Verlag, 2012.

Weiss, Harald (ed.), *100 Jahre Biene Maja. Vom Kinderbuch zum Kassenschlager.* Heidelberg: Universitätsverlag Winter, 2014.

Werdegang der Firma Diehl-Film GmbH. *Unpublished Typoscript.* Gräfelfing: Diehl Film, not dated [presumably after 1970].

Wiedemann, Julius (ed.), *Animation Now!* Cologne: Taschen Verlag, 2004.

Wohlrabe, Jürgen (ed.), *60 Jahre Jugendfilm, 1934–1994.* Berlin: Nicolai, 1994.

Zurhake, Monika, *Filmische Realitätsaneignung. Ein Beitrag zur Filmtheorie, mit Analysen von Filmen Viking Eggelings und Hans Richters.* Heidelberg: Winter, 1981.

Magazines and Newspapers

Agde, Günter, Der deutsche Werbefilmregisseur Hans Fischerkösen. In: *epd Film*, No. 9, 1996.

Agde, Günter, Ohne Verfallsdatum – Der deutsche Werbefilmregisseur Hans Fischerkösen. In: *Film*, Frankfurt/Main, Volume 13, No. 9, September 1996, pp. 20–25.

Agde, Günter, Goebbels-Gründung und DEFA-Erbe. Beinahe vergessen: Die Deutsche Zeichenfilm GmbH und ihr Nachlass (1942 bis 1947) mit einem Nachtrag 1950. In: *Film und Fernsehen*, Nos. 3+4, 1998, pp. 36–42.

Albert Uderzo, Die Leser haben Asterix am Leben erhalten. In: *Die Welt*, October 23, 2013.

Aus der Anfangszeit des Trickfilms. Ergänzende Feststellungen eines deutschen Trickfilm-Pioniers, der aus dem Ausland zurückgekehrt ist. In: *Film-Kurier*, October 1, 1940 [Ludwig Seel].

Aus deutschen Werbefilmen. In: *Die deutsche Werbung*, First April Issue 1940, pp. 212–215.

Dr. B.: Die Trickfilmzeichnerin. In: *Germania*, March 5, 1933.

Barten, Egbert and Groeneveld, Gerard, Reynard the Fox and the Jew Animal. 22. *Internationales Trickfilm Festival Stuttgart*.

Basgier, Thomas, Die Teutonen Disneys. In: *tip Magazin Berlin*, 20, 1995, pp. 48–51.

Bendazzi, Giannalberto, The First Italian Animated Feature Film and its Producer: La Rosa di Bagdad and Anton Gino Domeneghini. In: *Animation Journal*, Spring 1995, Tustin, CA, pp. 4–18.

Berlin hat seit gestern ein Wochenschaukino. In: *Film-Kurier*, June 21, 1940.

Besuch bei Hans Held. In: *Berliner Illustrierte Zeitung*, 13, 1941.

Betz, Werner, Micky-Maus und Angst/Die Sichtbarkeit des Unsichtbaren. In: *Berliner Tageblatt*, December 20, 1934.

Bialas, Dunja, *Die Angst der Filmkritik vor dem Animationsfilm. Eine unabschliessbare Polemik*. Das Kurzfilmmagazin Shortfilm.de, December 21, 2022.

Boyer, Erich, *Auf jeder Leinwand – ein Fischerkoesen-Film*. Special print hobby. Das Magazin der Technik, September 1955, Fischerkoesen-Film-Studio/Bad Godesberg-Mehlem.

Cebu, C., Achtung! Mickey Maus, Felix der Kater+Co. In: *Leipziger Abendpost*, August 5, 1931 (Illustrations by Hans Fischerkoesen).

Cürlis, Hans, Der Silhouettenfilm. In: *Film und Bild in Wissenschaft, Erziehung und Volksbildung*. Volume 8, Issue 4/5, Berlin, May 1, 1942, pp. 64–65.

Dahlfeld, Karlheinz, Mickey Mouse wird nun entthront. In: *Der Oberschlesische Wanderer*, June 4, 1939 [Kurt Stordel].

De "Held" van de Teekenfilm. In: *Cinema & Theater*, Volume 23, No. 51, Amsterdam, December 17, 1943.

Der deutsche Zeichenfilm. In: *Film-Kurier*, November 11, 1943.

Deutscher Trickfilm weltmarktfähig. In: *Lichtbild-Bühne*, January 1, 1937.

Diehl, Paul, Der Puppenfilm als Kunstwerk. In: *Film und Bild*, Heft 7, Berlin, 1940, S. 118.

Diehl, Paul, Märchen und Film. In: *Film und Bild*, Volume 7, Issue 1, Berlin, January 15, 1941, pp. 12–13.

Diehl, Paul, Kunstschaffen und Kunsterleben. In: *Film und Bild*, Volume 7, Issue 10, Berlin, October 15, 1941, pp. 159–162.

Diehl, Paul, Vom Wesen des Scherenschnitt-Films. In: *Film und Bild*, Issue 4/5, Berlin, May 1, 1942.

Disney, Walt, Warum ich Schneewittchen verfilmte... In: *Mein Film Volume XVIII*, No. 26, Vienna, June 25, 1948.

Ehrler, S. A., Aus der Werkstatt des Werbefilms. In: *Werben und Verkaufen*, 6, 1935, pp. 215–218.

ej, Vom Armen Hansi und von Schnuff, dem Nieser. Besuch bei der Deutschen Zeichenfilm GmbH. In: *Film-Kurier*, No. 139, November 4, 1943.

Der erste deutsche Film nach dem Krieg ist fertiggestellt: Dob, der Stallhase. In: *Berliner Illustrierte*, 3, 1946, pp. 6/7.

Fiedler, Werner, Abenteuer im Schnee. Zwei Filme im Marmorhaus. In: *DAZ*, December 21, 1944.

Fiedler, A., Die deutschen Werbefilme 1934–1935. Eine Generalreportage. In: *Die deutsche Werbung*, 2nd September Issue, 1935, pp. 1434–1440.

Filme werben für den Rundfunk. In: *LichtBildBühne*, April 17, 1939 [Georg Woelz].

Filmwirtschaft auf neuen Wegen. Drei Neugründungen und ihre Ziele. Der Trickfilm in der Entwicklung. In: *Münchener Neueste Nachrichten No. 303*, October 30, 1941.

Filmzeichner berichten über ihre Arbeit. In: *Film-Kurier*, December 24, 1943.

Firschke, Waldemar, Untersuchungen über den Märchenfilm in der Grundschule. Wie wirken RWU-Märchenfilme auf Kinder? In: *Film und Bild in Wissenschaft, Erziehung und Volksbildung*, Volume 6, Issue 3, Berlin, March 15, 1940, pp. 34–39.

Fräulein Mabel fällt aus dem Rahmen. Alles per Trickfilm. In: *DER SPIEGEL, New Year, 1949*, Hamburg, January 1, 1949, p. 23.

Freund, Wieland, Die "Biene Maja" ist eine völkische Germanin. In: *Die Welt*, April 17, 2012.

Gang durch ein Zeichenfilm-Atelier. Aus dem Arbeitsbereich von Hans Fischerkösen. In: *Film-Kurier*, January 7, 1944.

Gensert, Hans-Hubert, Gang durch ein Zeichenfilm-Atelier. Aus dem Arbeitsbereich von Hans Fischerkoesen. In: *Film-Kurier*, February 11, 1944.

Giesen, Rolf, Der Trickfilm. A Survey of German Special Effects. In: *Cinefex No. 25*, February 1986.

Giesen, Rolf, Special Effects. 6 parts. In: *Fernseh&Kinotechnik. No. 4*, April 1986, No. 10, October 1986.

Giesen, Rolf, *Übermenschen. Schauspieler aus dem Computer.* In: *Der Tagesspiegel*, January 4, 1996.

Giesen, Rolf, Als Disney noch Distler hieß. Wie sich die Donald-Duck-Begeisterung der Nazis ins Gegenteil kehrte. In: *Die Welt*, December 7, 2001.

Giesen, Rolf, Bullys Trickfilm Lissi ist sein erster Flop. In: *Die Welt*, October 31, 2007.

Giesen, Rolf, Eine eurasische Affäre – Animationsfilmgeschichte aus Beijing und Berlin: Lauras Stern und der geheimnisvolle Drache Nian. In: *Film-Dienst*, September 28, 2009.

Giesen, Rolf, World Wide Animation. Eine Exkursion durch die Geschichte des Animationsfilms anlässlich der Kinopremiere von Tim und Struppi. In: *Film-Dienst 22, 2011*, Volume 64, October 27, 2011, pp. 6–15.

Giesen, Rolf, Nazimation! Der Zeichenfilm-Ring. In: *Kino – German Film & International Reports*, No. 104, February 2013.

Giesen, Rolf, Der Regisseur, der jedem Kind selbst die Hand gab. In: *Die Welt*, June 12, 2014 [Obituary Thilo Rothkirch].

Giesen, Rolf, Diese Biene Maja ist eine Zumutung für Vierjährige. In: *Die Welt*, September 11, 2014.

Giesen, Rolf, Was Walt Disney in Hitlerdeutschland wollte. In: *Die Welt*, July 5, 2015.

Giesen, Rolf, Standardisierte Kinderträume. Warum sich die hiesige Trickfilmbranche mit Großproduktionen so schwer tut. In: *Frankfurter Allgemeine Zeitung*, December 7, 2015, p. 13.

Giesen, Rolf, Leuchtende Weltentwürfe. Hommage auf den Animationsfilm-Regisseur Piet De Rycker. In: *Film-Dienst 26, 2015*, Volume 68, December 24, 2015, p. 19.

Goergen, Jeanpaul, Julius Pinschewer. Künstler und Kaufmann. Pionier des Werbefilms. In: *epd Film*, No. 3, 1992.

Goergen, Jeanpaul, Discovering Paul N. Peroff. In: *Animation Journal*, Vol. 6, No. 2, Spring 1998, pp. 53–54.

Goergen, Jeanpaul, Zwischen Märchenfilm und Reklamestreifen. Der Puppentrick in Deutschland bis 1945. In: *Film-Dienst*, No. 1, 1998.

Grandt, Jens, Spurensuche eines Außenseiters. Die Galerie Nierendorf entdeckt den Berliner Maler Bernhard Klein wieder neu. In: *Berliner Morgenpost*, September 7, 2013.

Gressieker, Hermann, Vom Vorprogramm zur Filmkunst. In: *Der Deutsche Film*, June 1937, pp. 349–352.

Gringer, Hans-Erdmann, *Über den Schatten gesprungen*. In: *Mitteldeutsche Zeitung*, August 5, 2005.

Guckes, Emil, *Über die Zusammenarbeit der Betriebswerber mit den Werbefilmherstellern*. In: *Die deutsche Werbung*, 2nd September Issue, 1935, pp. 1422–1431.

Hans Held. Ein Trickfilmzeichner. In: *Film-Kurier*, July 24, 1940.

Heine, Matthias, Der Kauka-Effekt. Wie aus den Galliern Asterix und Obelix im März 1965 national gesinnte Germanen wurden. In: *Die Welt*, March 22, 2005.

Henncke, Friedrich, Die Stadtmaus und die Feldmaus. Einsatz im Unterricht. In: *Film und Bild in Wissenschaft, Erziehung und Volksbildung*, Volume 8, Issue 4/5, Berlin, May 1, 1942, pp. 54–55.

Hubel, Hermann, Der Zeichenfilm. In: *Der Deutsche Film*, 6, 1936, pp. 178–179.

Hürlimann, Dr. Martin, Von Micky Maus zur "Idee." In: *Berliner Tageblatt*, January 20, 1936.

Huth, Bernhard, Im Reich der unbegrenzten Möglichkeiten. In: *Berliner Tageblatt*, April 15, 1934.

Jerosch, Ernst, Hans Fischinger zeigte: Tanz der Farben. Ein neuer Schritt auf dem Wege zur absoluten Filmkunst. In: *Der Film*, March 4, 1939.

Jerosch, Ernst, Neue Kurzfilme vor dem Start. In: *Film-Kurier*, June 20, 1944 [Hochzeit im Korallenmeer].

Jockisch, Hermann, Das Werden eines Farbtrickfilms "Einigkeit macht stark" 28000 Einzelbilder für 400 Meter Film. In: *Film-Kurier*, August 7, 1940.

Joop Geesink's Dollywood: The Tribute Site. www.dutch-vintage-animation.org.

Kaskeline, Wolfgang, Zum Beispiel. Einige Möglichkeiten, welche die Trickfilme dem Werbeleiter bieten, mit besonderem Hinweis auf Ton und Farbe. In: *Die Reklame*, 2nd September Issue, 1930, pp. 563–566.

Kaskeline, Wolfgang, Der Trickfilm heute und morgen. In: *Die deutsche Werbung*, 2nd December Issue, 1933, p. 703.

Kindler, Helmut, Micky Maus – ernst gesehen! Grundsätzliches über Märchen, Trick und Märchenfilm. In: *Der Deutsche Film*, March 1939, pp. 252–255.

Klatt, Oliver, Trickfilmpionier Hans Fischerkoesen. Hitlers Disney. In: *SPIEGEL Online*, April 25, 2013.

Kleine Wespe ganz groß. In: *Berliner Illustrierte Zeitung*, No. 24, 1943 [Verwitterte Melodie].

Klie, Barbara, Schneewittchen und die Disney-Dynastie. In: *Der Kurier*, Berlin, March 4, 1950.

Konkurrenz für Micky Maus? Gespräch mit Kurt Stordel. In: *12 Uhr Blatt*, December 22, 1938.

Langer, Edith, Ich wurde Trickfilm-Zeichnerin. In: *Film und Bild in Wissenschaft, Erziehung und Volksbildung*, Volume 8, Issue 1, Berlin, January 15, 1942, pp. 8–10.

Linda, Curt, Animationsfilm – bitte ohne Illusionen! In: *Medien Concret*, No. 3, 1990.

Lizenzen nicht wegzudenken. In: *DER SPIEGEL*, No. 21, 1984, May 21, 1984.

Die lustige Palette. In: *Film-Kurier*, December 21, 1934 [About a Disney compilation].

Machold, Ulrich and Rosenfelder, Andreas, Die Revolution frisst ihre Bürger. In: *Die Welt*, April 8, 2014.

Mahler, Hugo, *Im Filmstudio Fischerkösen, Bad Godesberg*. Special print, Westermanns Monatshefte, 12, 1954, pp. 67–74.

Maraun, Frank, "Poet am Tricktisch" Besuch bei Starewitsch. In: *Der deutsche Film*, September 1938.

Maresch, Rudolf, *Ohne Körper geht es nicht. Ein Text mit und für Dietmar Kamper*. Freitag, May 19, 1996.

Märchenfilme bei den Soldaten. In: *Film und Bild*, Volume 8, May 1, 1942.

Marsch gegen die Micky-Maus. In: *Dresdner Neueste Nachrichten*, March 4/5, 1939, p. 37 [About Kurt Stordel].

Menter, Leo, Märchenbuch aus Licht und Schatten. In: *Neue Film-Welt Heft 12*, Berlin, 1949.

Meuer, Adolph, Ein Kurzfilm -50000 Einzelzeichnungen. Neuaufbau einer deutschen Zeichenfilmproduktion. In: *Hamburger Fremdenblatt*, No. 312, December 7, 1943.

Meyer, Alfred Richard, Die Stadtmaus und die Feldmaus. Floskeln um eine kleine Bibliographie 1. Teil. In: *Film und Bild*, Volume 6, Issue 4, Berlin, April 15, 1940, pp. 56–57. 2nd part. In: *Film und Bild*, Volume 6, Issue 5, Berlin, May 15, 1940, pp. 72–74.

Minnesang und Markenartikel. In: *Der Spiegel*, 35, 1956, Hamburg, August 29, 1956, pp. 34–40 [Cover story: Hans Fischerkoesen].

Möllendorff, Horst von, Wie ich die Idee fand... In: *Film-Kurier*, December 7, 1943.

Moritz, William, Resistance and Subversion in Animated Films of The Nazi Era: the Case of Hans Fischerkoesen. In: *Animation Journal*, #1, Fall 1992.

Naturfarbiger Pál-Doll-Trick. Verfahren. Apparatur. In: *Kinotechnische Rundschau*, "Film-Kurier," supplement in No. 291, December 12, 1931.

Neue Werbefilme. In: *Die deutsche Werbung*, April 1941, pp. 252–256.

Ein neuer Fisch aus Prag. Der Brautschleierfisch. Bilderschau aus dem Film "Hochzeit im Korallenmeer." In: *Berliner Illustrierte Zeitung*, 6, 1944, February 10, 1944.

Opium der Kinderstube. In: *DER SPIEGEL*, No. 12, 1951, March 21, 1951, p. 39.

Oskar Fischingers Farb-Ton-Spiel "Kreise." In: *Film-Kurier*, October 18, 1934.

Der quäkende Narr – die tönende Micky-Maus. In: *Filmwelt*, July 27, 1930.

Pal, Georg, *De trucfilm*. Meer Baet, April 1934.

Paul, Gerhard, Das HB-Männchen – Werbefigur des Wirtschaftswunders. In: *Zeithistorische Forschungen/Studies in Contemporary History*, Issue 1–2, 2007.

Petzold, Volker, *Grenzgänger des Trickfilms*. Dresden: Deutsches Institut für Animationsfilm e.V., 2006/2007 [Rosemarie and Herbert K. Schulz].

Poppen als film-acteurs. Wereldkroniek, September 11, 1937.

Poppen als film-artisten. De Week in Beeld, April 7, 1939.

Reck, Erwin, Eine Sekunde Zeichentrickfilm. In: *Der Deutsche Film*, February 1943, pp. 13–15.

Riese und Zwerg. Trickfilm-Studios in Amerika und Deutschland. In: *Revue*, January 23, 1947.

Der Ritt ins Wunderland. In: *Mein Film*, Volume XIX, No. 12, Vienna, March 25, 1949.

Ritter, Johannes, Die Dresdner Bank dreht ihren eigenen Trickfilm. In: *Frankfurter Allgemeine Zeitung*, April 29, 2003.

Rodek, Hanns-Georg, Schreck statt Shrek für Dresdner-Bank-Anleger. In: *Die Welt*, November 27, 2007.

Roll, Evelyn, "Wir wollten einen Knalleffekt." In: *Süddeutsche Zeitung*, 17, 5, 2010.

Schacht, Sven, Abenteuer unter dem Dachstuhl. Ein Film stellt sich vor. In: *Berliner Tageblatt*, July 12, 1936.

Schamoni, Victor, Die Anfänge des absoluten Films in Deutschland. In: *Der deutsche Film*, Volume 2, Issue 9, March 1938, pp. 242–246.

Schindelbeck, Dirk, Der deutsche Disney. Hans Fischerkösen, der Erfinder des Werbezeichentrickfilms. In: *Trödler & Sammler Journal*, 11, 2001.

Schirrmacher, Frank, Der Engel fährt zur Hölle – Breloers Film über Albert Speer... In: *Frankfurter Allgemeine Zeitung*, March 18, 2006.

Schneider, Walther, Micky Maus ist geisteskrank. In: *Der Querschnitt*, 10, Berlin, 1931, p. 679.

Schosch, Stefan, "Konferenz der Tiere": Erster deutscher 3-D-Trickfilm kommt aus Hannover. Regisseur Holger Tappe im Interview. In: *Hannoversche Allgemeine*, October 2, 2010.

Schreiber, Leopold, Wolfgang Kaskeline. In: *Gebrauchsgraphik*, 4, 1934, pp. 2–9.

Schreiber, Leopold, Hans Fischerkoesen. In: *Gebrauchsgraphik*, 12, 1934. pp. 46–52.

Schuhmacher, Avantgarde und neue Technik Alexeieff: 'Nuit sur le mont chauve'. In: *Film-Kurier*, March 28, 1936.

Schulze-Boysen, Libertas, Mit Zeitraffer und Zeitlupe durch die Reichswoche für den deutschen Kulturfilm: Die deutsche Mickey-Mouse am Horizont. In: *National-Zeitung*, October 4, 1941.

Shale, Richard, Dr., *Disney's Greatest Film: Walt and Victory Through Air Power.* The Walt Disney Family Museum, 13, 5, 2011.

St., Walt Disneys Märchenfilm "Schneewittchen und die sieben Zwerge." In: *Allgemeine Kölnische Zeitung*, February 26, 1950.

Steglich, Martin, Major, Der militärische Lehrfilm. In: *Film-Kurier*, September 5, 1944.

Stordels "Purzel" stellt sich vor. Ein Märchen-Zeichentrickfilm in Walt Disneys Fußstapfen? In: *Der Deutsche Film*, February 1939, p. 231.

Strom, Gunnar, Desider Gross and Gasparcolor, European Producers: Norwegian Products and Animated Commercials from the 1930's. In: *Animation Journal*, Spring 1998, pp. 28–41.

Der Traum eines Kritikers: Tobias-Knopp-Film in Hannover. In: *Kölner Rundschau*, March 5, 1950.

Trick-Schmalfilme für Kinder. In: *Der Film*, September 19, 1942.

Trick und Natur im Farbenfilm. In: *Film-Kurier*, December 9, 1935 (Gasparcolor).

Villa Wespe am Griebnitzsee. In: *Berliner Illustrierte Zeitung*, 13, 1941.

Walt Disney, Tiere und Musik. In: *FILM Revue*, Volume 2, No. 9, Baden-Baden, 1948, pp. 200–201.

Walt Disney Zauber des Zeichen-Films. In: *Film-Illustrierte*, Volume 2, No. 24, Düsseldorf, June 15, 1949, p. 2.

Wedel, Michael, *Filmgeschichte als Krisengeschichte. Schnitte und Spuren durch den deutschen Film*, Bielefeld, 2011.

Willim, Bernd, Europas Zeichentrick-Elite formiert sich. In: *Professional Production*, No. 8, 1992.

Wir sind die Neandertaler der Zukunft! Rolf Giesen interviewed by Marion Meier. In: *Die Welt*, September 6, 2013.

Wolfes, Kurt, Wirkliche Unwirklichkeit. In: *Lichtbild-Bühne*, January 1, 1937.

Wundervolle Märchenwelt. Ufa-Pavillon. In: *Film-Kurier*, September 21, 1940 [Vom Bäumlein, das andere Blätter hat gewollt].

Wundervolle Märchenwelt. In: *Deutsche Filmzeitung*, October 13, 1940.

Zander, Peter, Biene Maja summt in 3-D-Klassiker mit neuem Look im Kino. In: *Berliner Morgenpost*, September 10, 2014.

Der Zeichenfilm in der Ufa-Lehrschau. In: *Film-Kurier*, September 18, 1942.

Der Zeichenfilm ist ein modernes Medium. Gespräch mit Wolfgang Urchs. Urchs interviewed by Christel Strobel, Hans Strobel. In: *Kinder- und Jugendfilm Korrespondenz*, Issue 75-3, 1998.

Der Zeichen- und Trickfilm. Neue Ausdrucksmöglichkeiten für die künstlerische Kinematographie. In: *Kinematograph*, March 14, 1935.

Ein Zeichentrickfilm - eine Million Bilder. Zur Uraufführung des amerikanischen Films "GULLIVERS REISEN." In: *Mein Film*, Volume XVIII, Issue 45, Vienna, December 17, 1948.

Zschaler, Mathias, Zum Tod von Wolf Gerlach: Der Mainzelmann. In: *SPIEGEL Online Kultur*, November 13, 2012.

Zwerg Purzel stellt sich vor. In: *Der Film*, December 10, 1938.

Zwerg Purzel heiße ich. Der Hauptdarsteller eines deutschen bunten Märchen-Trickfilms stellt sich vor. In: *Filmwelt*, December 23, 1938.

20.000 Zeichnungen – ein Film. Interessante Versuche mit bunten deutschen Märchentrick-filmen. In: *Hamburger Fremdenblatt*, December 24, 1938.

Internet

Monographische Arbeiten zum Animationsfilm: Eine Bibliogaphie. Compiled by Franziska Bruckner, Erwin Feyersinger, Anton Fuxjäger, Ludger Kaczmarek, Maike Sarah Reinerth, Dominik Schrey and Hans J. Wulff. Medienwissenschaft/Hamburg.
Chronologie zum Animationsfilm in Deutschland. Editors: Rolf Giesen and Volker Petzold. www.diaf.de.

TV and DVD

Agde, Günter, *H. Fischerkoesen. Die besten Kinospots der 50er Jahre - Werbewelten im Zeichentrick.* Westermann Kommunikation VHS, 1996. Length: 153 minutes.
Als die Werbung flimmern lernte. Teil I: Die Wirtschaftswunderjahre. Cologne: Tacker Film, VHS, 1999, ca. 65 minutes.
Diehl, Ferdinand, *Ich habe mein Leben lang mit Puppen gespielt.* TV: ARD, April 11, 1988, 15:30–16:15.
Dresler, Wolfgang, *Trickfilm-Fieber.* DVD. Cologne: Tacker Film.
Dresler, Wolfgang, *Parolen & Polemik. Die Geschichte der deutschen Wahlwerbefilme.* DVD. Cologne: Tacker Film. Length: 112 minutes.
Gockell, Gerd, *Muratti & Sarotti. Geschichte des deutschen Trickfilms 1920–1960.* Berlin: absolut Medien, 1999.
Hans Fischerkoesen Der Deutsche Disney. TV: ARD WDR, February 20, 1995.
Das HB-Männchen mit seinen besten Spots. DVD. Cologne: Tacker Film. Length: 99 minutes.
Kellner, Joachim (ed.), *Hans Fischerkoesen. Werbewelten im Zeichentrick. Die besten Kinospots der 50er Jahre.* Deutsches Werbemuseum, 1996. DVD including booklet.
Kurt Stordel. Deutscher Trickfilmpionier. Märchenerzähler mit Zeichenstift und Kamera. TV: ARD, June 17, 1985, 13:25–13:55.
Loiperdinger, Martin (ed.), *Julius Pinschewer: Klassiker des Wernefilms.* DVD. Berlin: absolut Medien, 2010.
Marschall, Susanne, Bieberstein, Rada and Schneider, Kurt, *Lotte Reiniger – Tanz der Schatten.* TV: ARTE, June 9, 2013. Length: 60 minutes. Available as DVD.
Onkel Otto Die Kurzfilme – von damals bis heute. DVD 2005. Length: 78 minutes.
Raganelli, Katja, *Lotte Reiniger – Die Pionierin des Scherenschnittfilms.* Length: 60 minutes, 1997.
Schlosshan, Ricarda, *Krieg der Zeichner.* Interviewees: Jerry Beck, Rolf Giesen, J. P. Storm. TV: ZDF History, June 14, 2015. Length: 30 minutes.
Schummer, Rudolf J., *Filme im Schatten – Der Trickfilm im Dritten Reich.* TV: ZDF, August 26, 1975. Distributed by Institut für Film und Bild in Wissenschaft und Unterricht (FWU), Grünwald.
Stoll, Ulrich, *Hitlers Traum von Micky Maus – Zeichentrick unterm Hakenkreuz.* Interviewee: J. P. Storm. Cologne: De Campo Film commissioned by TV: WDR and ARTE, April 18, 1999. Length: 60 minutes.
Walter Ruttmann 1887–1941. Versuch einer Befreiung. TV documentary, Bayerischer Rundfunk, Teleclub, May 5, 1977. Length: 45 minutes. Manuscript in the files of Deutsche Kinemathek Berlin.
Wegenast, Ulrich (ed.), *Die Geschichte des deutschen Animationsfilms: Animation in der Nazizeit.* DVD. Berlin: absolut medien, 2011.
Wegenast, Ulrich (ed.), *Die Geschichte des deutschen Animationsfilms: Von tanzenden Zigaretten und Elchen. Der deutsche Animationsfilm in Werbung und Musikvideo.* DVD. Berlin: absolut medien, 2011. Length: 129 minutes.
Wilden, Heinz D., *Der deutsche Disney. Der Zeichner und seine Figuren.* TV. Cologne: WDR, 1995. Length: 45 minutes [Devoted to the work of Hans Fischerkoesen].

Name Index

Title Index